1,000,000 Books
are available to read at

www.ForgottenBooks.com

Read online
Download PDF
Purchase in print

ISBN 978-1-334-21626-8
PIBN 10739706

This book is a reproduction of an important historical work. Forgotten Books uses state-of-the-art technology to digitally reconstruct the work, preserving the original format whilst repairing imperfections present in the aged copy. In rare cases, an imperfection in the original, such as a blemish or missing page, may be replicated in our edition. We do, however, repair the vast majority of imperfections successfully; any imperfections that remain are intentionally left to preserve the state of such historical works.

Forgotten Books is a registered trademark of FB &c Ltd.
Copyright © 2018 FB &c Ltd.
FB &c Ltd, Dalton House, 60 Windsor Avenue, London, SW19 2RR.
Company number 08720141. Registered in England and Wales.

For support please visit www.forgottenbooks.com

1 MONTH OF FREE READING

at
www.ForgottenBooks.com

By purchasing this book you are eligible for one month membership to ForgottenBooks.com, giving you unlimited access to our entire collection of over 1,000,000 titles via our web site and mobile apps.

To claim your free month visit: www.forgottenbooks.com/free739706

* Offer is valid for 45 days from date of purchase. Terms and conditions apply.

English
Français
Deutsche
Italiano
Español
Português

www.forgottenbooks.com

Mythology Photography **Fiction** Fishing Christianity **Art** Cooking Essays Buddhism Freemasonry Medicine **Biology** Music **Ancient Egypt** Evolution Carpentry Physics Dance Geology **Mathematics** Fitness Shakespeare **Folklore** Yoga Marketing **Confidence** Immortality Biographies Poetry **Psychology** Witchcraft Electronics Chemistry History **Law** Accounting **Philosophy** Anthropology Alchemy Drama Quantum Mechanics Atheism Sexual Health **Ancient History Entrepreneurship** Languages Sport Paleontology Needlework Islam **Metaphysics** Investment Archaeology Parenting Statistics Criminology **Motivational**

AN HISTORICAL ATLAS OF CANADA

EDITED
WITH INTRODUCTION, NOTES, AND CHRONOLOGICAL TABLES
BY
LAWRENCE J. BURPEE

MAPS BY
JOHN BARTHOLOMEW AND SON, LTD.
EDINBURGH GEOGRAPHICAL INSTITUTE

TORONTO
THOMAS NELSON AND SONS, LIMITED
LONDON, EDINBURGH, PARIS, AND NEW YORK
1927

ACKNOWLEDGMENTS

WITHOUT the zealous co-operation and sound scholarship of quite a number of authorities, this Atlas could not have been published; the Editor and the Publishers gratefully acknowledge their indebtedness.

In particular we should like to thank Mr. F. C. C. Lynch, Director of the Natural Resources Intelligence Service, Ottawa. To Mr. Lynch and his talented staff we are obliged for the data of a large number of the maps, and for invaluable help in other ways.

Dr. A. G. Doughty, Deputy Minister of the Public Archives of Canada, kindly furnished copies of documents, and generously permitted the reproduction of his map of the Siege of Quebec.

Dr. E. Sapir of the University of Chicago revised the map of Indian Tribes and Linguistic Groups; Brigadier-General E. A. Cruikshank, of Ottawa, courteously allowed the use of his map of the Battle of Queenston Heights; and Mr. James White, of Ottawa, was most helpful with criticism and suggestions.

To Dr. Geo. H. Locke, Chief Librarian of the Toronto Public Library, and to Mr. Fred. Landon of the Public Libraries, London, Ontario, we are obliged for permission to copy several Ontario maps.

To Messrs. John Bartholomew and Son for their unfailing patience and skill in translating even the roughest sketches into the maps that are here presented.

Professor George M. Wrong of the University of Toronto, and Professor Trotter of Queen's, very kindly read the proofs of the text, and made valuable suggestions and corrections.

CONTENTS

(The number in italics under "Note page" refers to the "Notes on the Maps" at the end.)

INTRODUCTION vii

LIST OF MAPS AND NOTES—

	Map page	Note page
I.—INTRODUCTORY — PHYSICAL CONDITIONS AND NATIVE RACES .	.	1
1. Physical Map of North America .	1	1
2. Temperature, January	2	1
3. Temperature, July	2	1
4. Rainfall, Annual	2	1
5. Natural Vegetation	2	2
6. Canada—Forests	3	2
7. Indian Tribes and Linguistic Groups .	3	2
II.—DISCOVERIES AND EXPLORATIONS	.	2
8. Discoveries of the Vikings . . .	4	3
9. Toscanelli's Map	4	3
10. Discoveries of Columbus . . .	4	3
11. Part of Sebastian Cabot's World Map	4	3
12. Exploration of the St. Lawrence by Cartier, 1534-42	5	4
13. Map of Hudson's Voyages in the Arctic, 1610	5	4
14. Baffin's Map of his Voyages to the North, 1615-16	5	4
15. Lescarbot's Map of the St. Lawrence, 1609	6	4
16. Sanson's Map of America, 1650 .	6	4
17. Exploration of Bay of Fundy, 1604-7	7	5
18. Exploration of Hudson Bay . .	7	5
19. Routes of Champlain and Brûlé, Dollier and Galinée, 1615-70 .	8	5
20. Routes of Marquette, Jolliet, and La Salle, 1673-87	8	6
21. Routes of Hearne, Mackenzie, Franklin, and Back	8	7
22. Arctic Exploration	9	7
23. Pacific Coast Exploration . . .	9	8
24. Exploration of Rocky Mountain Region	9	8
III.—WAR MAPS AND PLANS . .	.	8
25. The Seven Years' War in America, with inset, Mohawk-Champlain Region	10-11	8
The Revolutionary War and Canada	.	9
26. French Explorers in the West, 1659-1743	12	7
27. Siege of Louisbourg, 1758 . . .	12	9

	Map page	Note page
28. Siege of Quebec, 1759	12	10
29. The Attack on Ticonderoga, July 8, 1758	13	12
30. Jesuit Missions in Huronia . . .	13	6
31. Seat of War, 1812-14	13	12
32. The Niagara Peninsula, 1812-14 .	14	13
33. Battle of Queenston Heights, October 13, 1812	14	13
34. Battle of Lundy's Lane, July 25, 1814	14	13
35. Battle of Crysler's Farm, November 11, 1813	14	14
36. Battle of Chateauguay, October 26, 1813	15	14
37. Attack on York (Toronto), April 27, 1813	15	14
38. Battle of Moraviantown (Thames), October 5, 1813	15	14
39. Operations on the Detroit River, 1812-13	15	15
Capture of Detroit	.	15
Rebellions of 1837-38 (see Maps Nos. 62 and 63)	.	15
Fenian Raids (see Map No. 32) .	.	16
40. Red River Expedition, 1870 . .	16	16
41. North Saskatchewan Rebellion, 1885	16	17
IV.—POLITICAL DEVELOPMENT .	.	18
42. North American Colonies, 1643 .	17	18
43. North American Colonies, 1655 .	17	18
44. North American Colonies, 1673 .	17	18
45. North American Colonies, 1697 .	17	19
46. North America—Treaty of Utrecht, 1713	18	19
47. North America—Treaty of Paris, 1763	18	19
48. British North America, by Royal Proclamation, 1763 . . .	18	20
49. North America—Quebec Act, 1774 .	19	20
50. North America—Treaty of Versailles, 1783	19	20
51. British North America, 1791 . .	19	20
52. British North America, 1818 . .	20	20
53. British North America, 1825 . .	20	21
54. British North America, 1849 . .	20	21
55. British North America, 1866 . .	20	21
56. Dominion of Canada, 1873 . .	21	21
57. Dominion of Canada, 1882 . .	21	22

CONTENTS

	Map page	Note page
LIST OF MAPS AND NOTES (*contd.*)—		
58. Dominion of Canada, 1898	21	22
59. Dominion of Canada, 1905	21	22
60. Dominion of Canada, 1927	22	22
V.—INDUSTRIAL DEVELOPMENT		23
61. Early Settlements in the Maritime Provinces	22	23
62. Early Settlements in Lower Canada	23	23
63. Early Settlements in Upper Canada (to 1840), and Ontario	23	24
64. Waterways of Canada		24
Trading Posts and Canoe Routes	24	24
65. Early Communications — Eastern Canada	25	25
66. The Great Lakes — Shipping and Canals	25	26
67. Railways of Canada: Eras of Construction, 1837–1927. Population 1871	26–27	26
68. Railway Systems, 1927. Population 1921	26–27	27

	Map page	Note page
VI.—BOUNDARY DISPUTES AND SETTLEMENTS		29
80. Oregon Boundary, 1846	32	29
81. Eastern Canada–United States Boundary	32	29
82. Canada and Alaska Boundary	32	30
83. Canada–Labrador Boundary	32	30
84. Lake of the Woods Boundary	32	31
VII.—POPULATION—DISTRIBUTION AND RACIAL ORIGIN		31
69. Racial Origins—French	28	31
70. Racial Origins—English	28	31
71. Racial Origins—Scottish	28	31
72. Racial Origins—Irish	28	31
73. Racial Origins—German and Austrian	29	31
74. Racial Origins—Dutch	29	31
75. Racial Origins—Russian and Ukranian	29	31
76. Racial Origins—Scandinavian	29	31
77. Canadian Migration	30	32
78. Hydro-Electric Development	30	28
79. Minerals developed, 1927	31	28

	Page
STATISTICS OF POPULATION	33
CHRONOLOGICAL HISTORY OF CANADA	35
CHRONOLOGY OF INTERCOMMUNICATION	41
CHRONOLOGY OF CANADIAN TOWNS	42
CHANGES IN PLACE-NAMES OF CANADIAN HISTORY	43
A WORKING BIBLIOGRAPHY OF BOOKS RELATING TO CANADIAN HISTORY	45

INTRODUCTION

BROADLY speaking the purpose of this Atlas is to tell the history of Canada visually, to unfold it by means of a series of maps. For each map an explanatory note is provided, but the vital thing is not the note but the map. Read the note and then study the map. As an occupation it is both profitable and fascinating. Maps may seem at first to be rather dead things, but in reality they are very much alive. Each has a story to tell—a story of human achievement, of discovery, of exploration and adventure by land and sea, of conflict between man and man or man and nature, of missionary enterprise, of the gradual development of political, social, and commercial institutions. The story is there. Read it and make it your own. Map reading has the immense advantage that when one has grasped the story each map has to tell, it becomes firmly planted in the memory. One not only knows that certain things happened, but can see how they came about.

It is of course important to understand the relationship of one map to another. It will be seen that, while the series as a whole tells the story of our country from its earliest beginnings, certain maps fall into fairly well-defined groups. One group relates the history of exploration, the early voyages to the Atlantic coast of America and the later voyages to the Pacific coast, the gradual penetration of the continent through the two great gateways—Hudson Bay in the north and the Gulf of St. Lawrence in the south—the exploration of the Great Lakes and the Mississippi, the discovery of the vast western plains, the penetration of the Rockies and the triumphant realization of the age-long dream of an overland route to the Western Sea, and finally the exploration of the far north, the Arctic coast, and the Arctic islands.

Another group of maps is devoted to wars and rebellions—the Seven Years' War, with the sieges of Louisbourg and Quebec and the battle of Ticonderoga; the War of 1812-14 with its principal engagements; and the Rebellions of 1870 and 1885. The earlier Rebellion of 1837-38 and the Fenian Raids may be studied with the aid of Maps Nos. 32, 62, and 63.

The heroic efforts of the Jesuit Fathers to bring Christianity to the Indians are illustrated in the Huronia map. The missions were not of course confined to Huronia, but the same spirit that animated the work on Georgian Bay inspired all the missions in the days of New France. And one may add with every confidence that, while the missionaries of all denominations in Western Canada have not had to face martyrdom, they too would have shown the same dauntless spirit if fate had demanded it of them.

As the story of Huronia is associated with the exploration of what is now Ontario by Champlain and Brûlé, Chaumonot, Brébeuf, and others, so one may with profit study together the maps of western exploration, of the fur trade with its curious mixture of commerce and romance, and of the Indian tribes. Similarly it is worth while in studying, through the special maps, the history of the Riel Rebellions, to link them up with the Indian tribes map, and the fur trade map with its emphasis upon the importance of waterways and portages. Also this latter map has a distinct bearing upon the later maps illustrating the development of transportation in Canada both by water and land.

In the same way one may study with profit, through the maps, the course of settlement in different parts of Canada; the origins of our people and how they are distributed; the intricate problems of international and interprovincial boundaries; and the political, social, and economic growth of the country. Incidentally we shall find it necessary to consider, by means of the group of physical maps, the reactions upon our human relationships of such conditions as climate, vegetation and rainfall, mineral resources and inexhaustible waterpowers.

These are but suggestions of the innumerable possibilities of profitable and intensely interesting study that are within reach if one will devote a little time and thought to these maps, and the accompanying notes and tables.

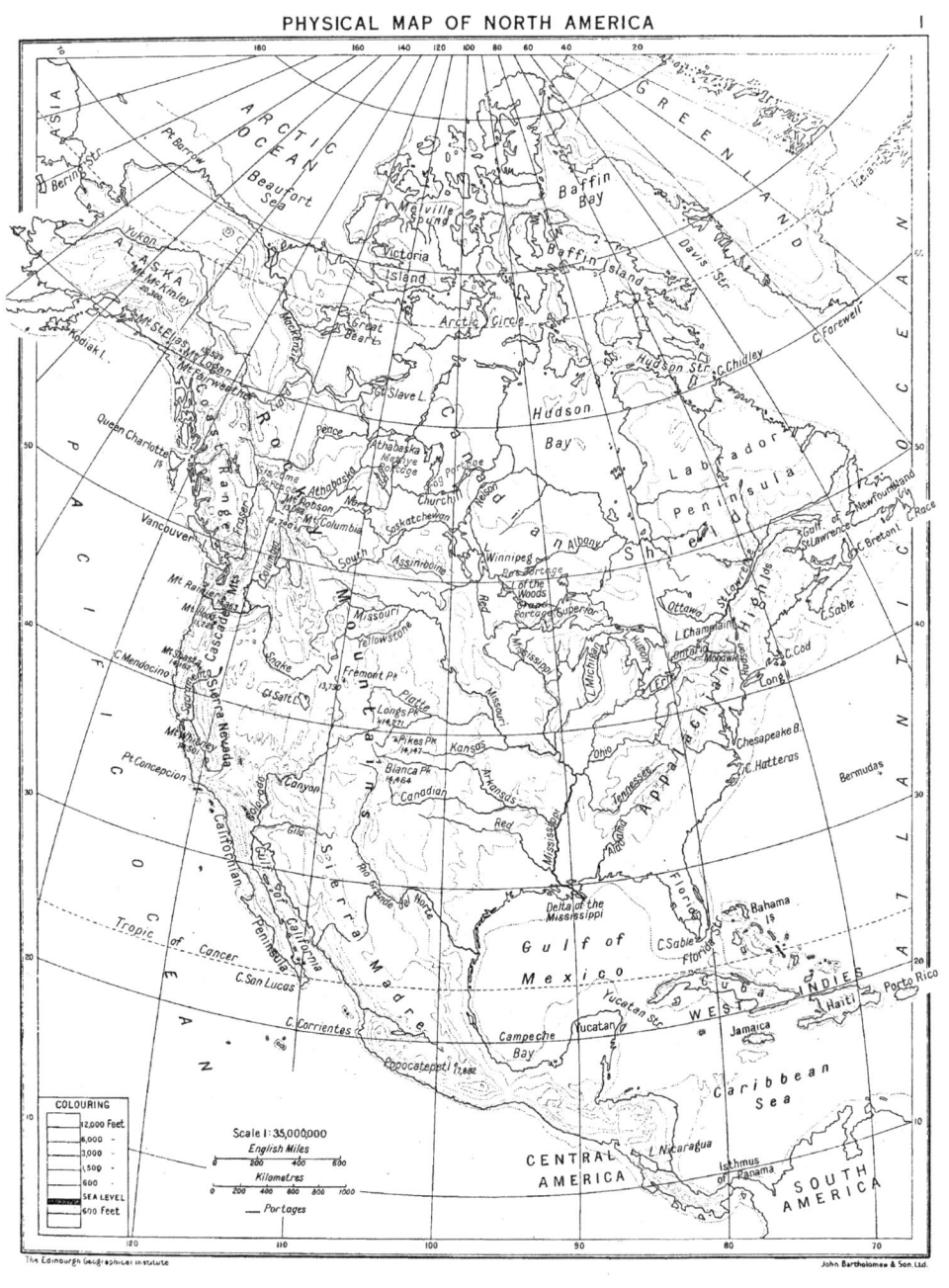

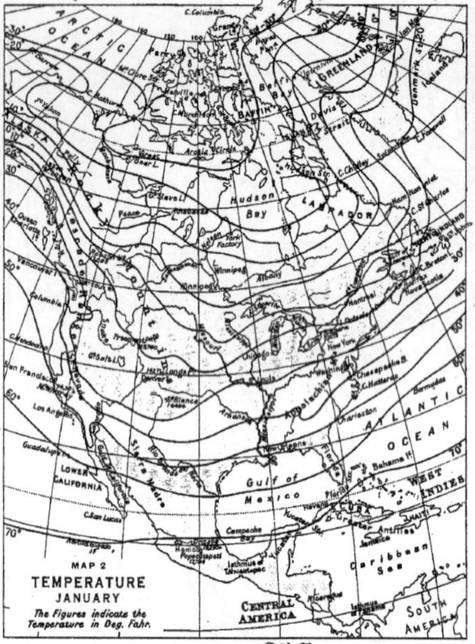

MAP 2
TEMPERATURE
JANUARY
The Figures indicate the
Temperature in Deg. Fahr.

MAP 3
TEMPERATURE
JULY
The Figures indicate the
Temperature in Deg. Fahr.

MAP 4
RAINFALL
ANNUAL
The Figures indicate the
Rainfall in Inches

MAP 5
NATURAL
VEGETATION

1 Tundra Ice-Cap
2 Temperate Forest
3 Tropical Forest
4 Grass Lands
5 Semi-Desert
6 Desert

The Edinburgh Geographical Institute
John Bartholomew & Son, Ltd.

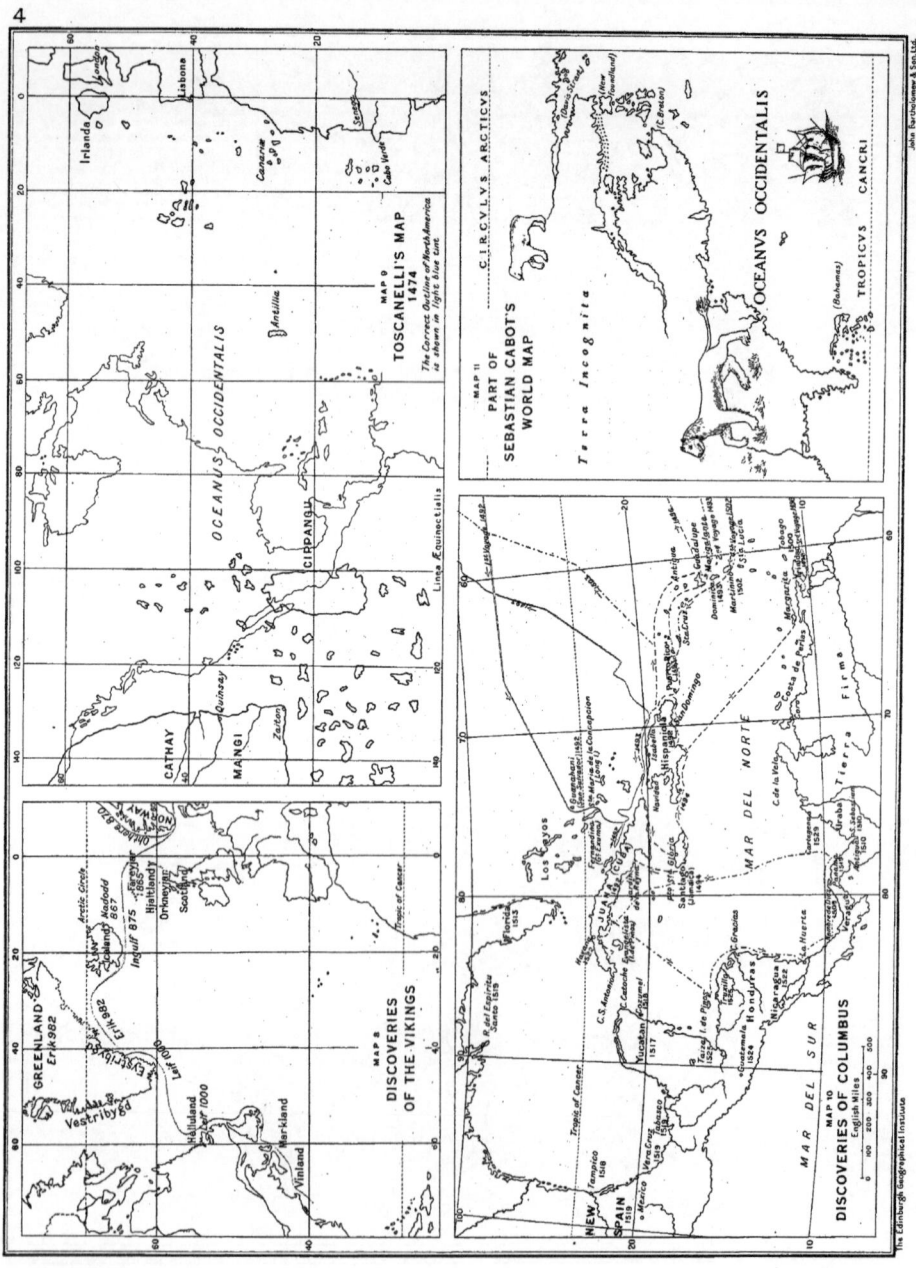

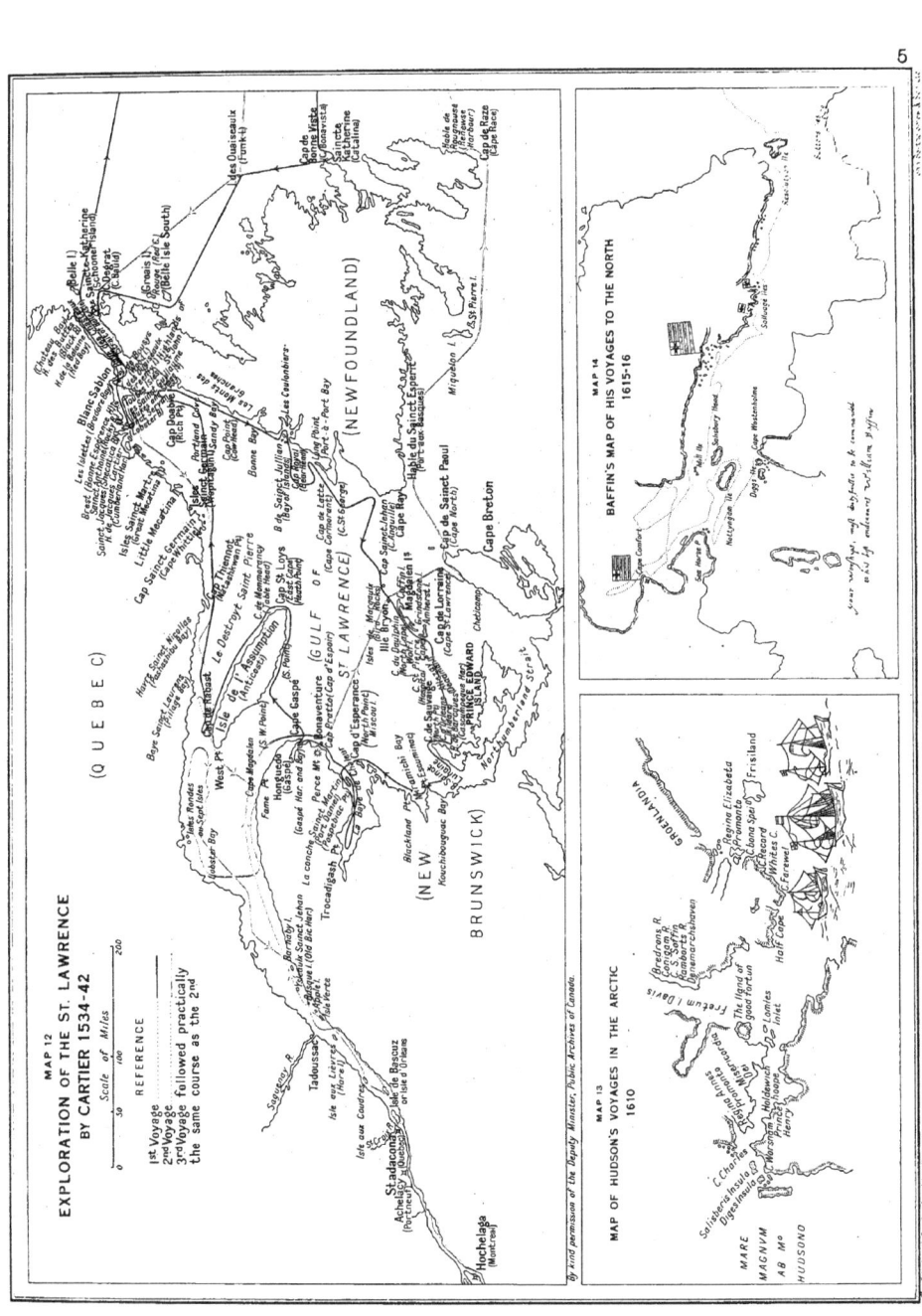

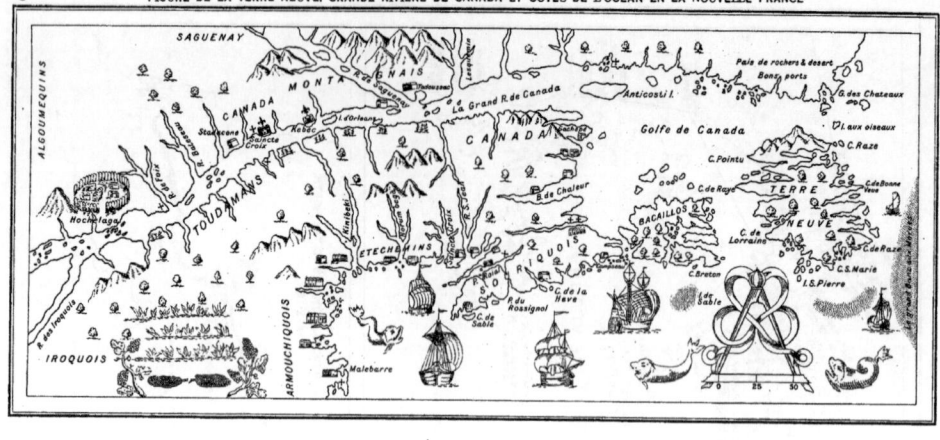

MAP 15
LESCARBOT'S MAP, 1609
FIGURE DE LA TERRE NEUVE, GRANDE RIVIERE DE CANADA ET COTES DE L'OCEAN EN LA NOUVELLE FRANCE

MAP 16
SANSON'S MAP, 1650

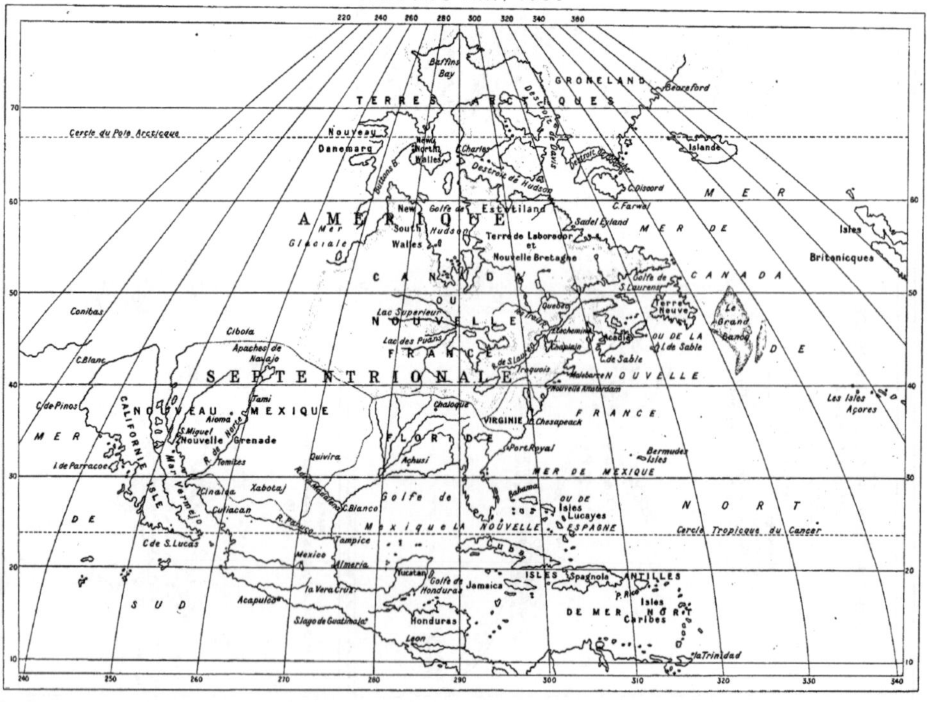

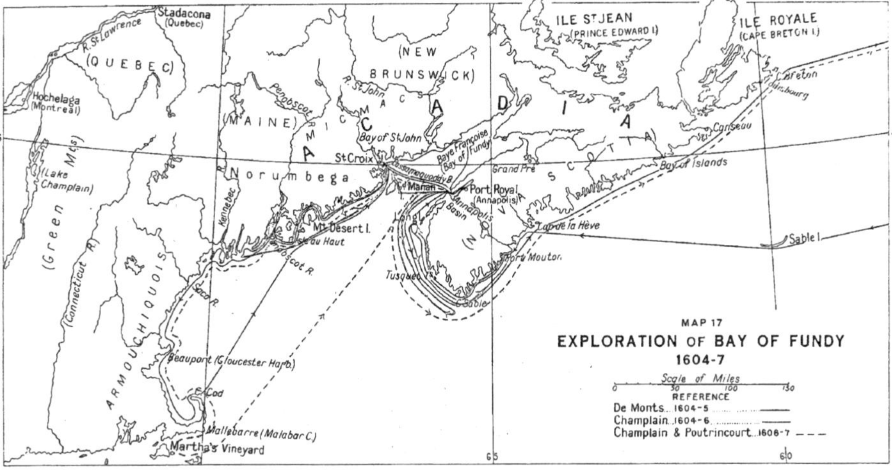

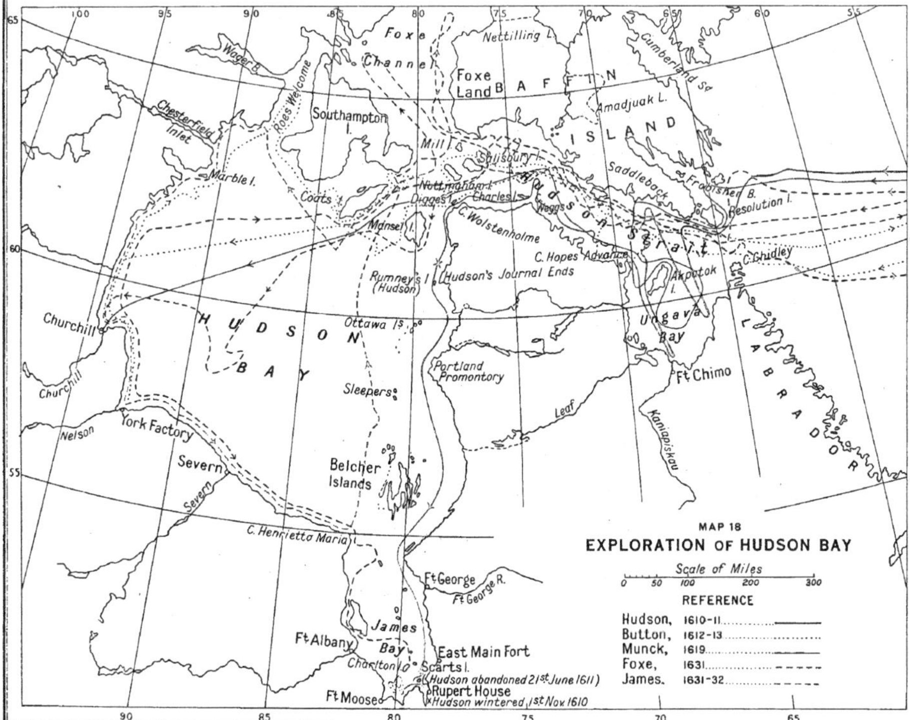

MAP 17
EXPLORATION OF BAY OF FUNDY
1604-7

Scale of Miles

REFERENCE
De Monts 1604-5
Champlain 1604-6
Champlain & Poutrincourt 1606-7

MAP 18
EXPLORATION OF HUDSON BAY

Scale of Miles

REFERENCE
Hudson, 1610-11
Button, 1612-13
Munck, 1619
Foxe, 1631
James, 1631-32

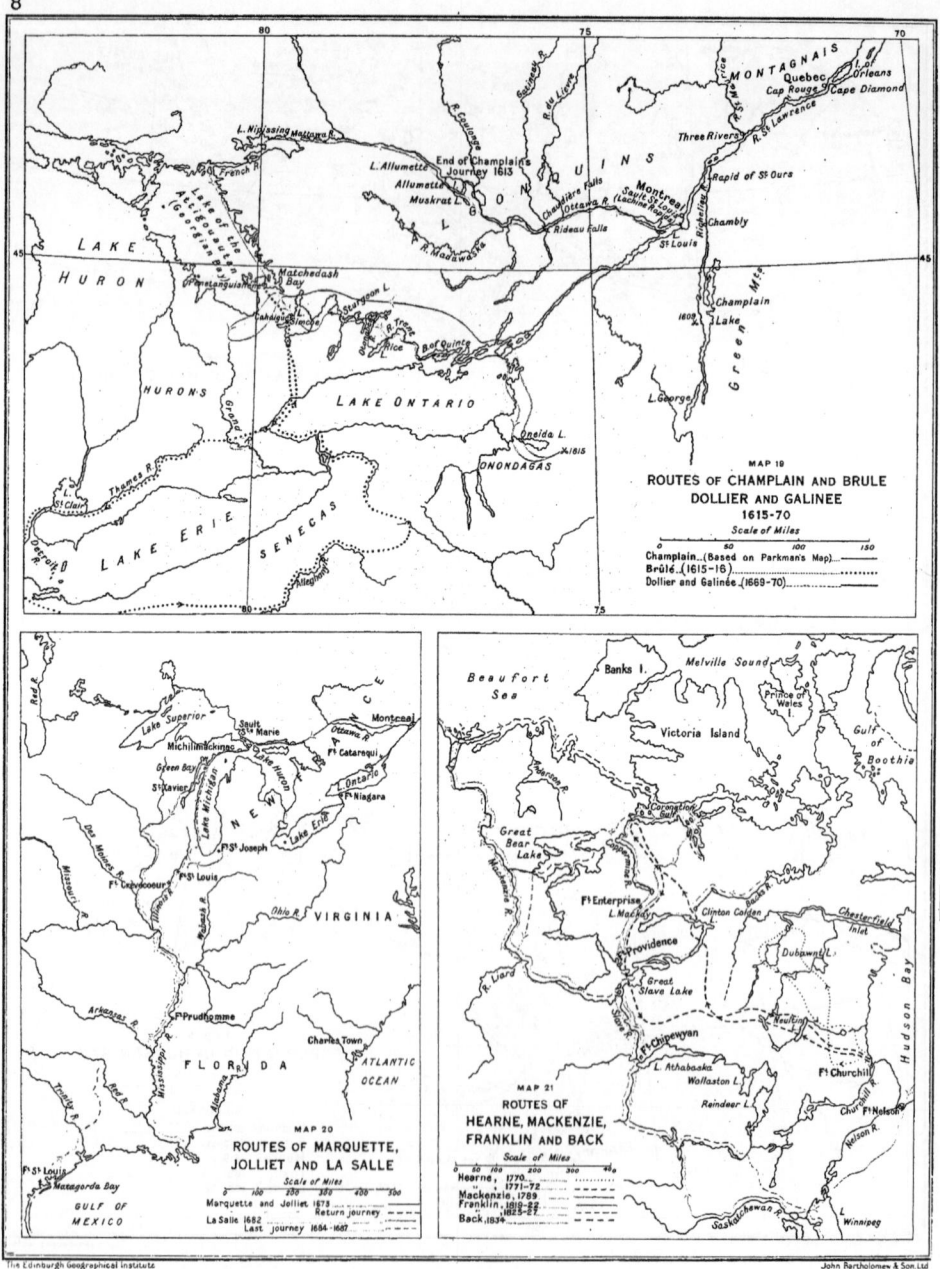

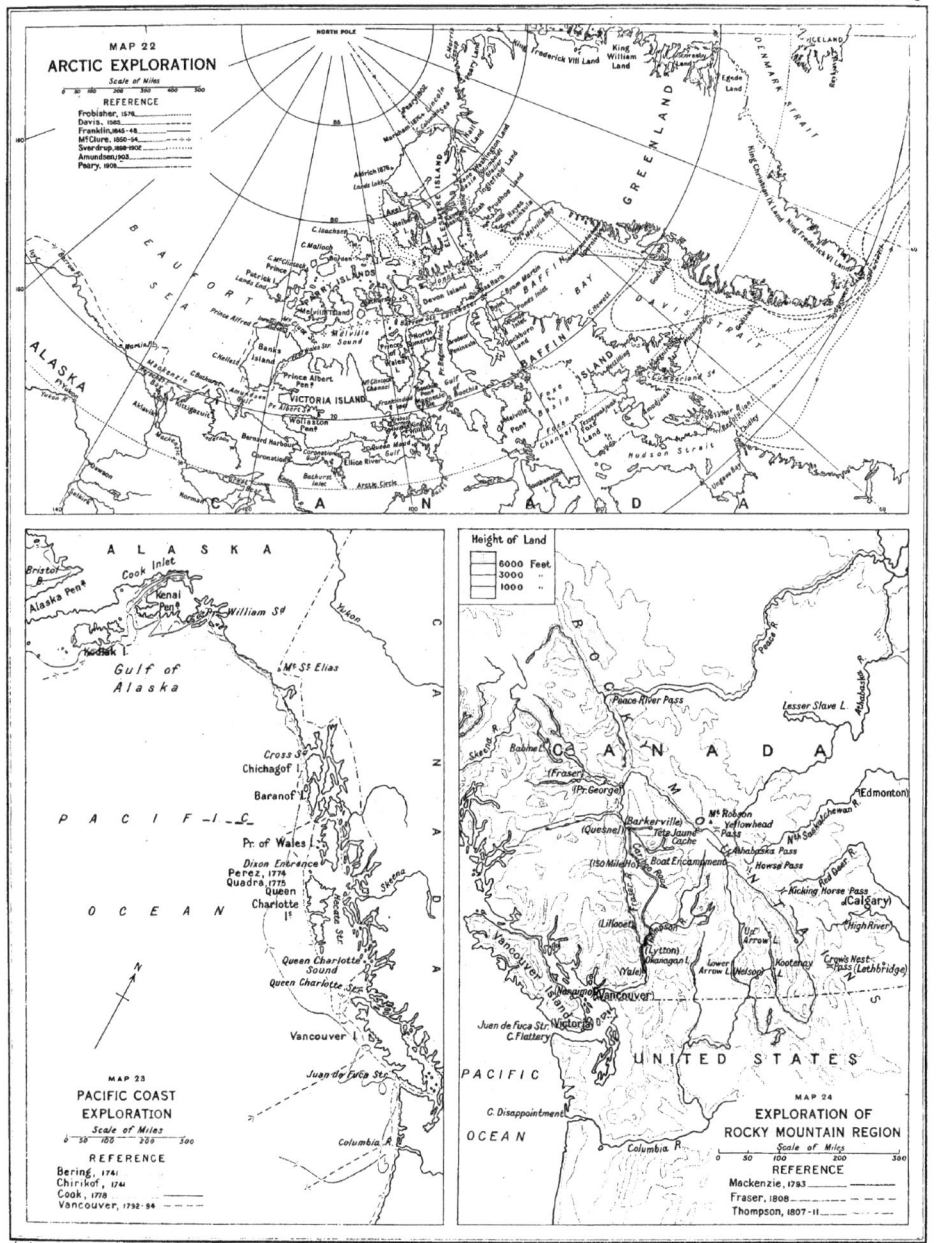

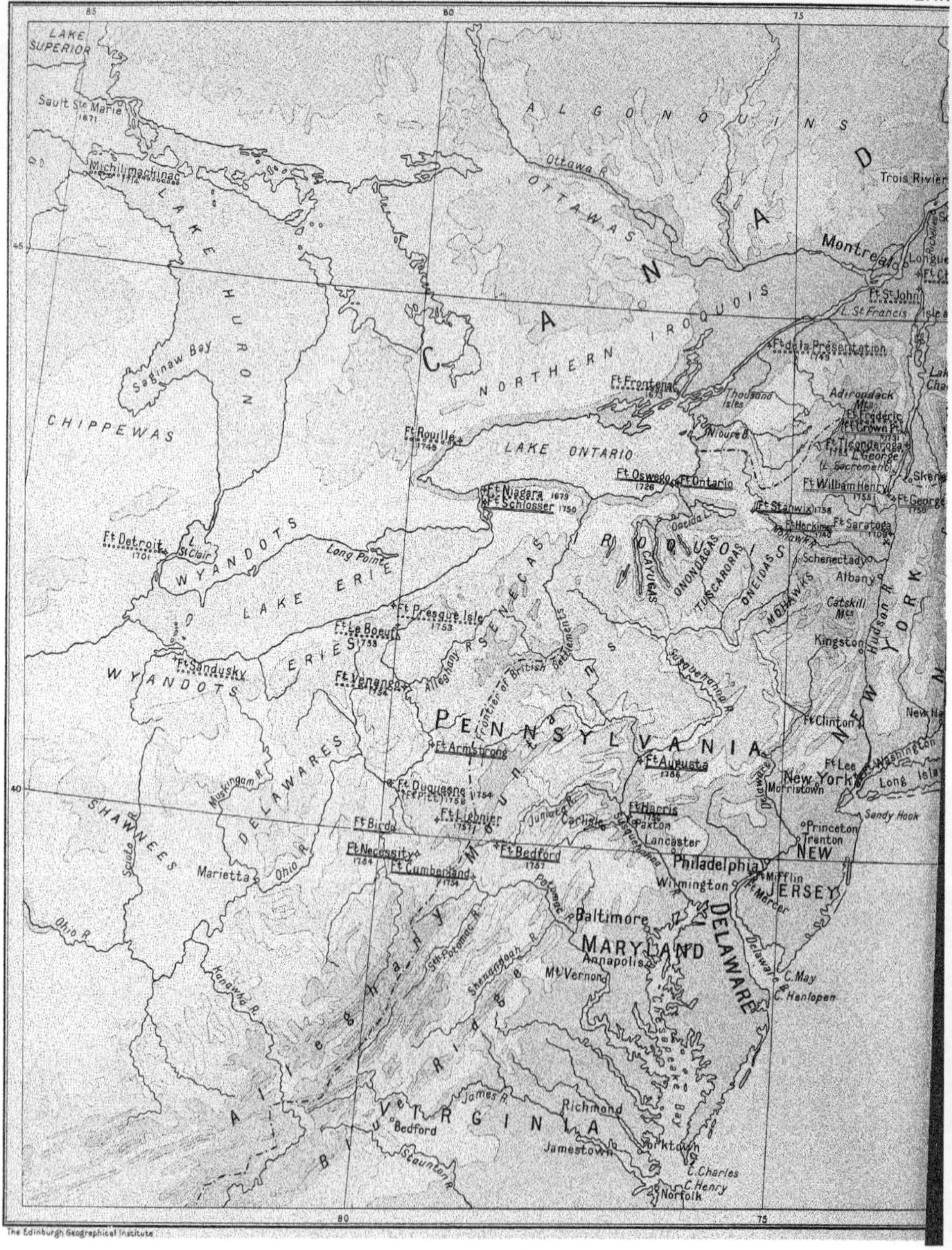

The Edinburgh Geographical Institute

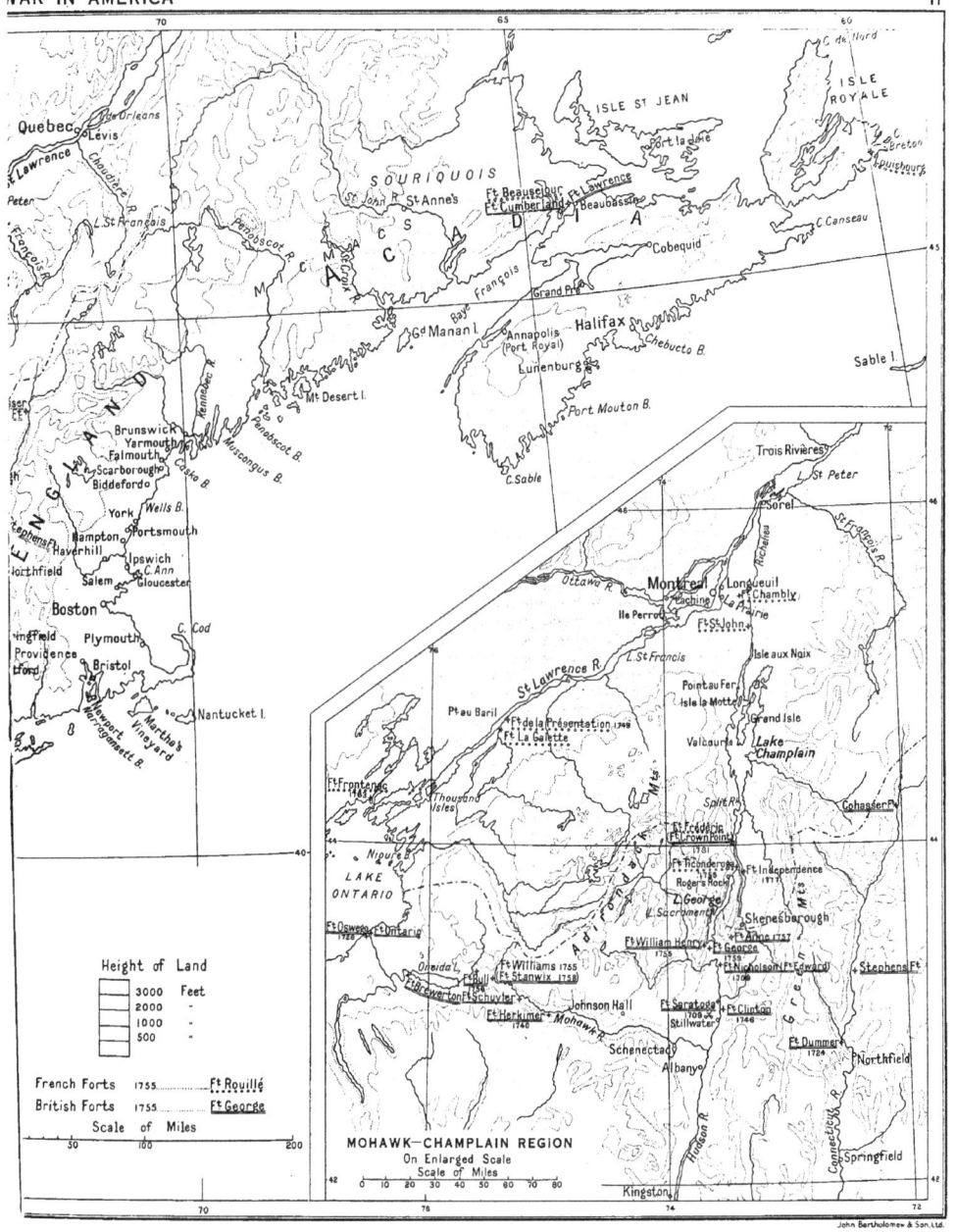

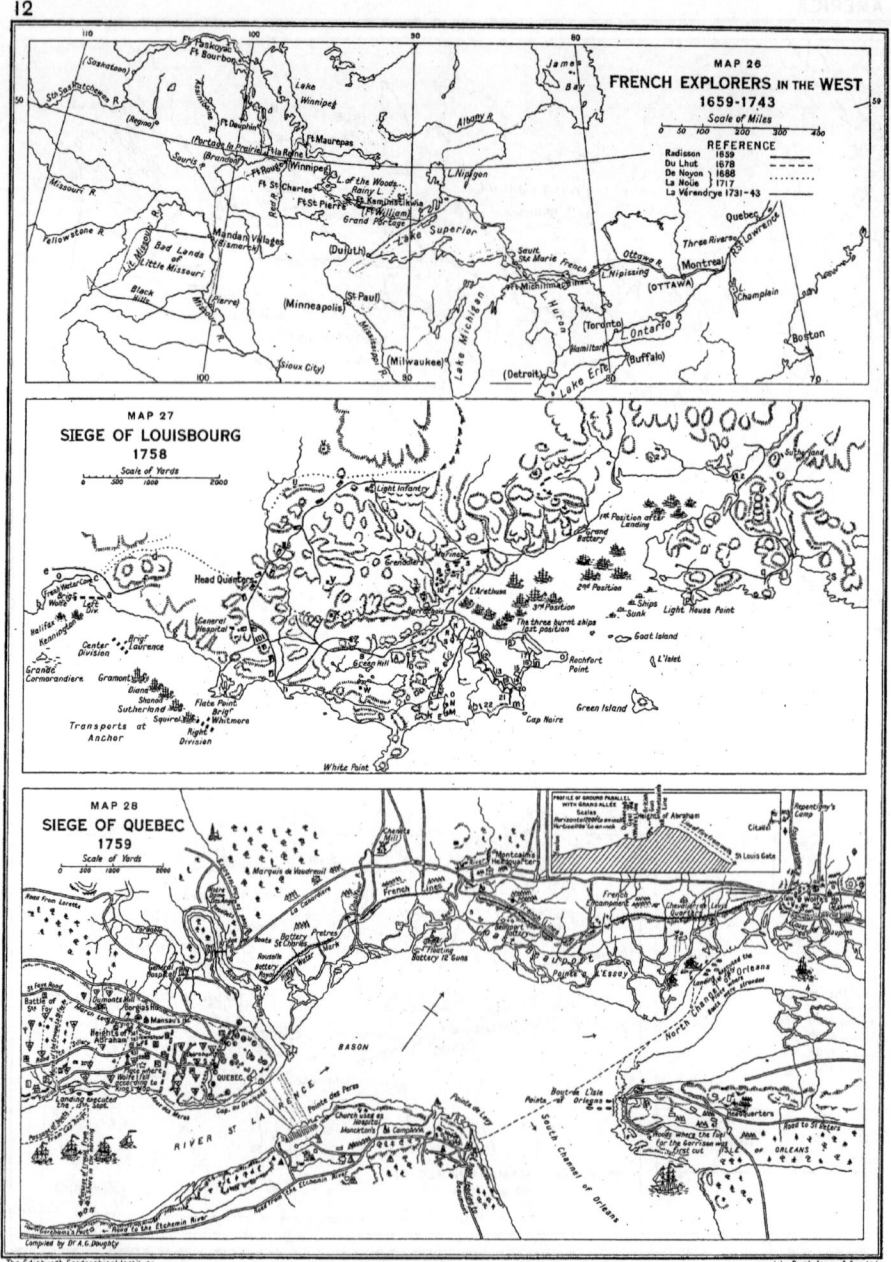

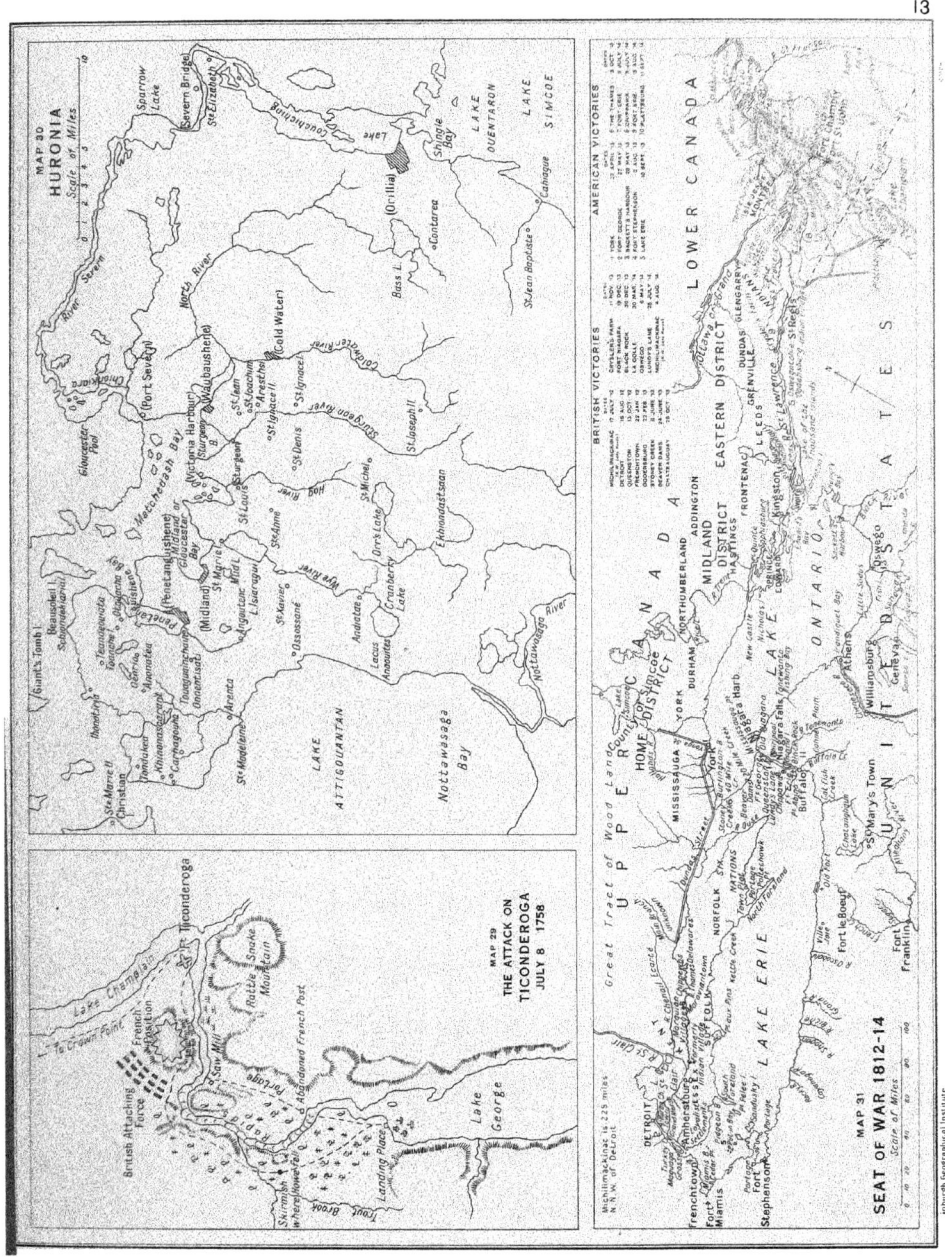

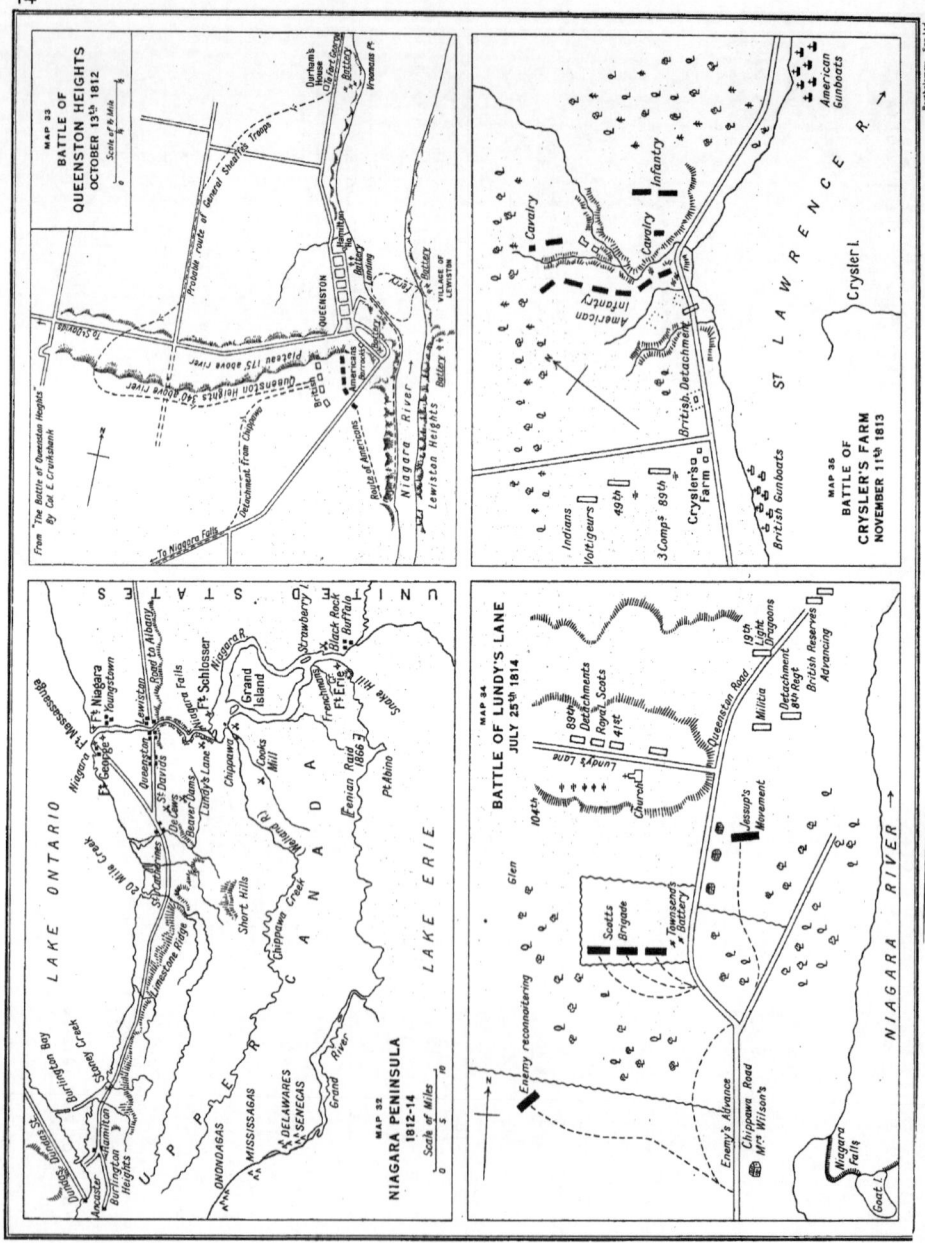

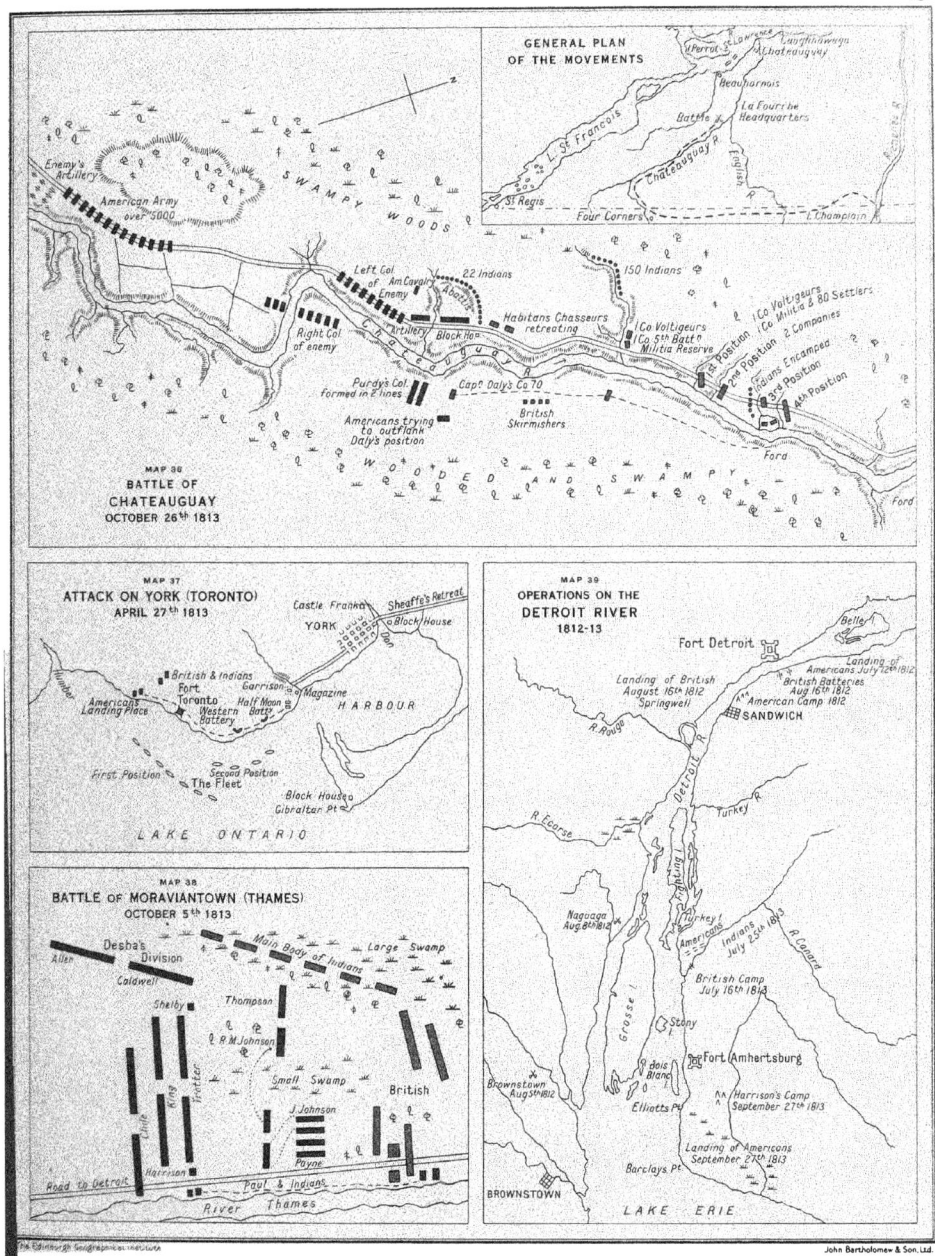

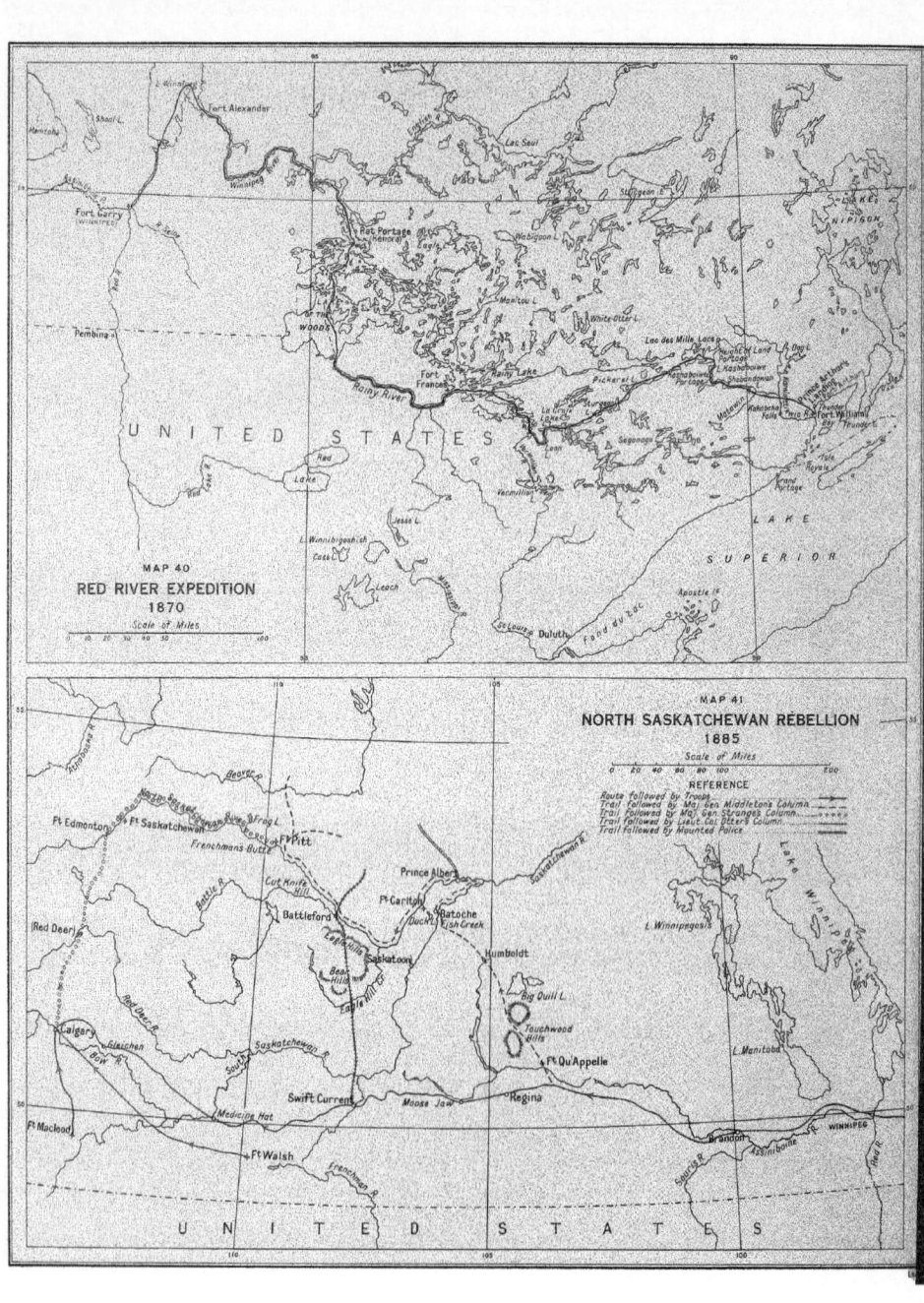

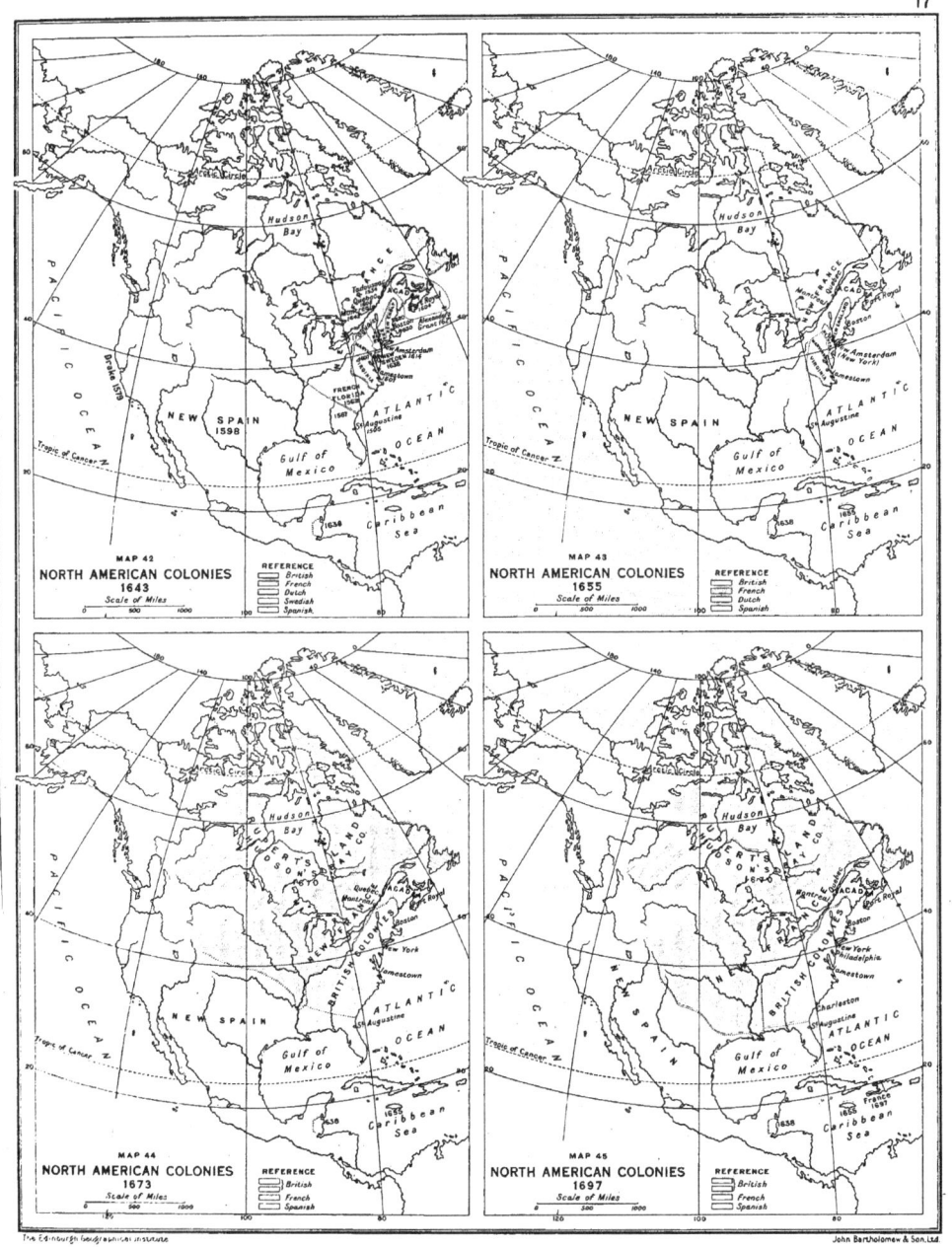

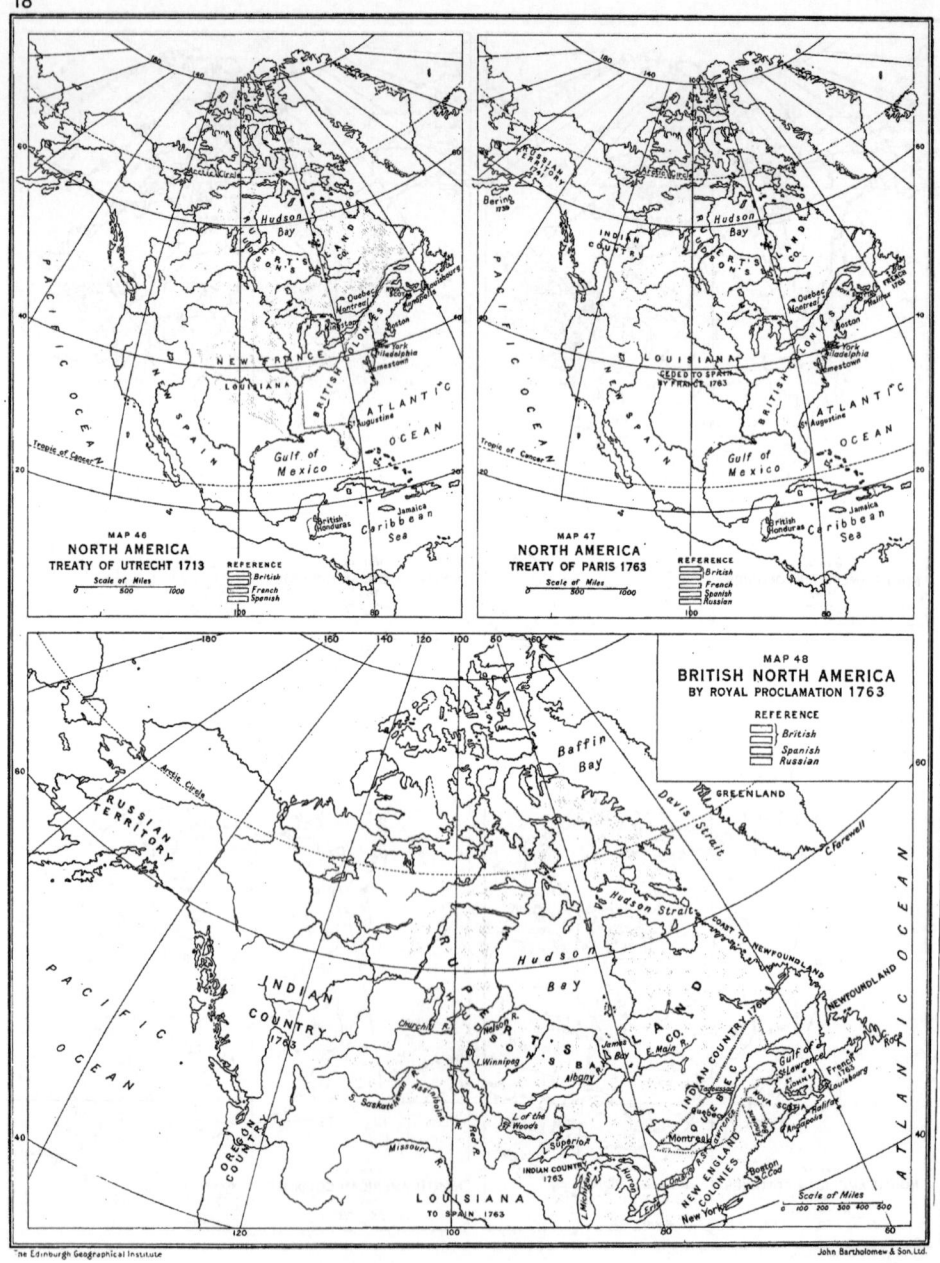

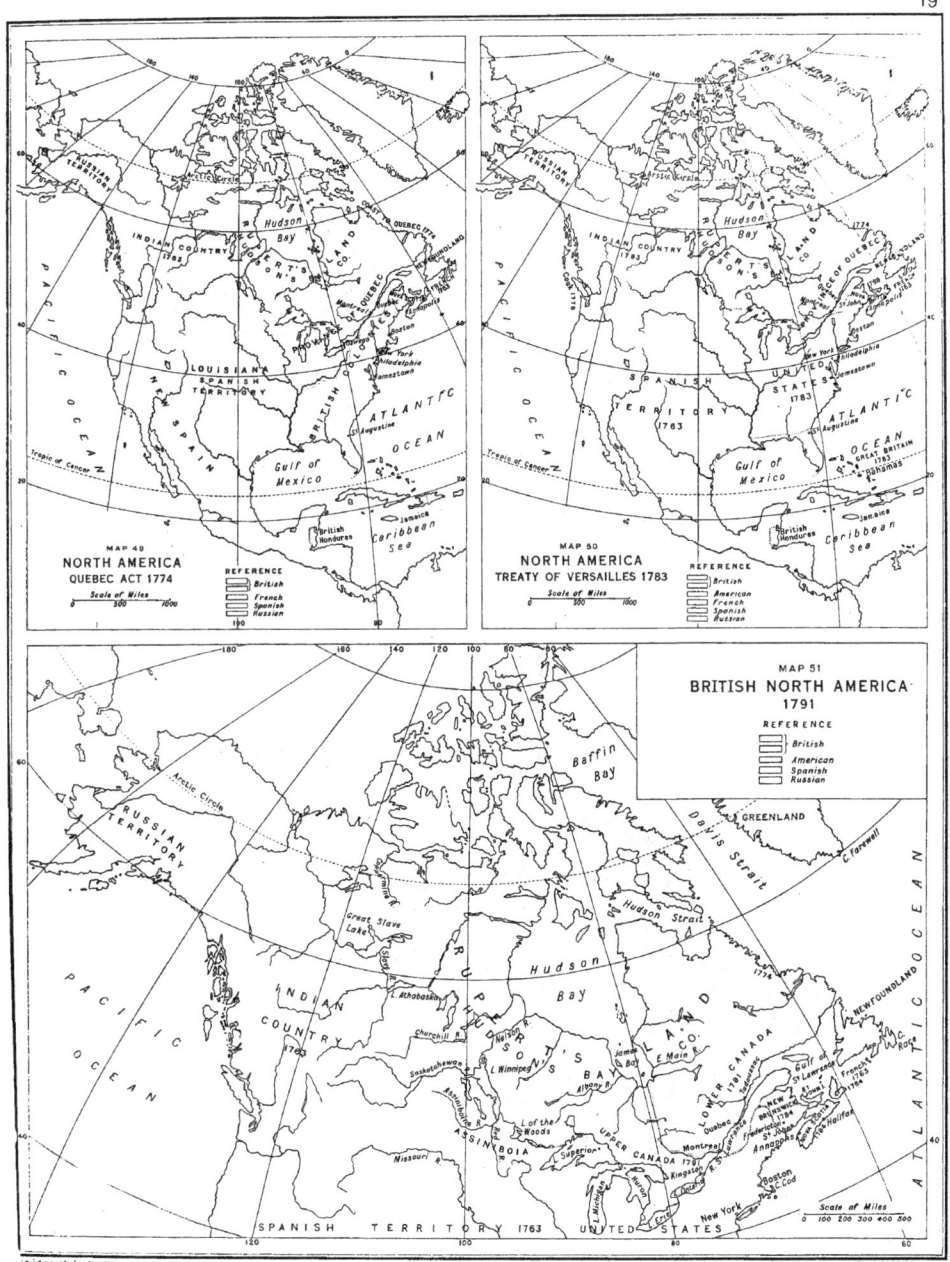

20

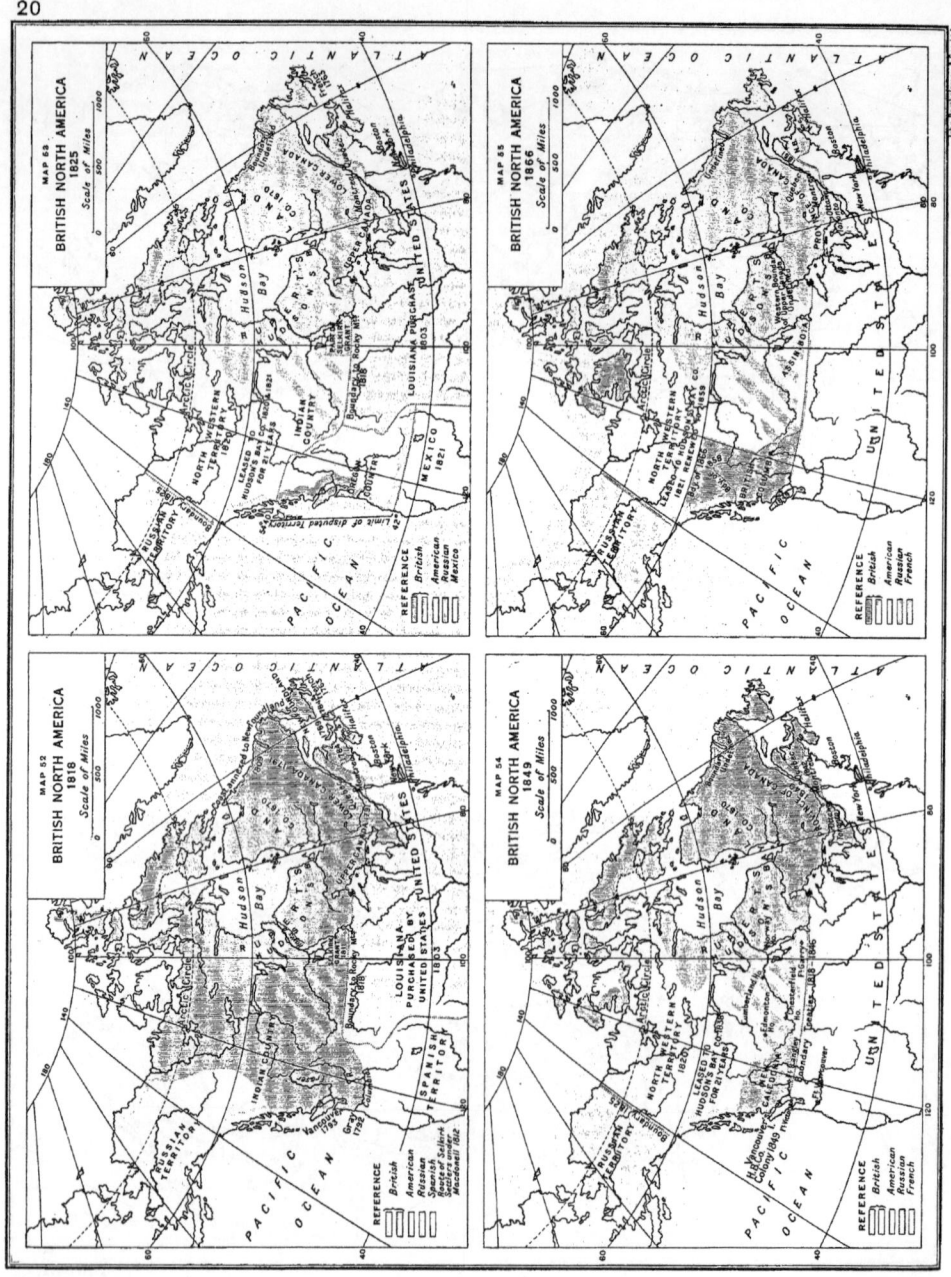

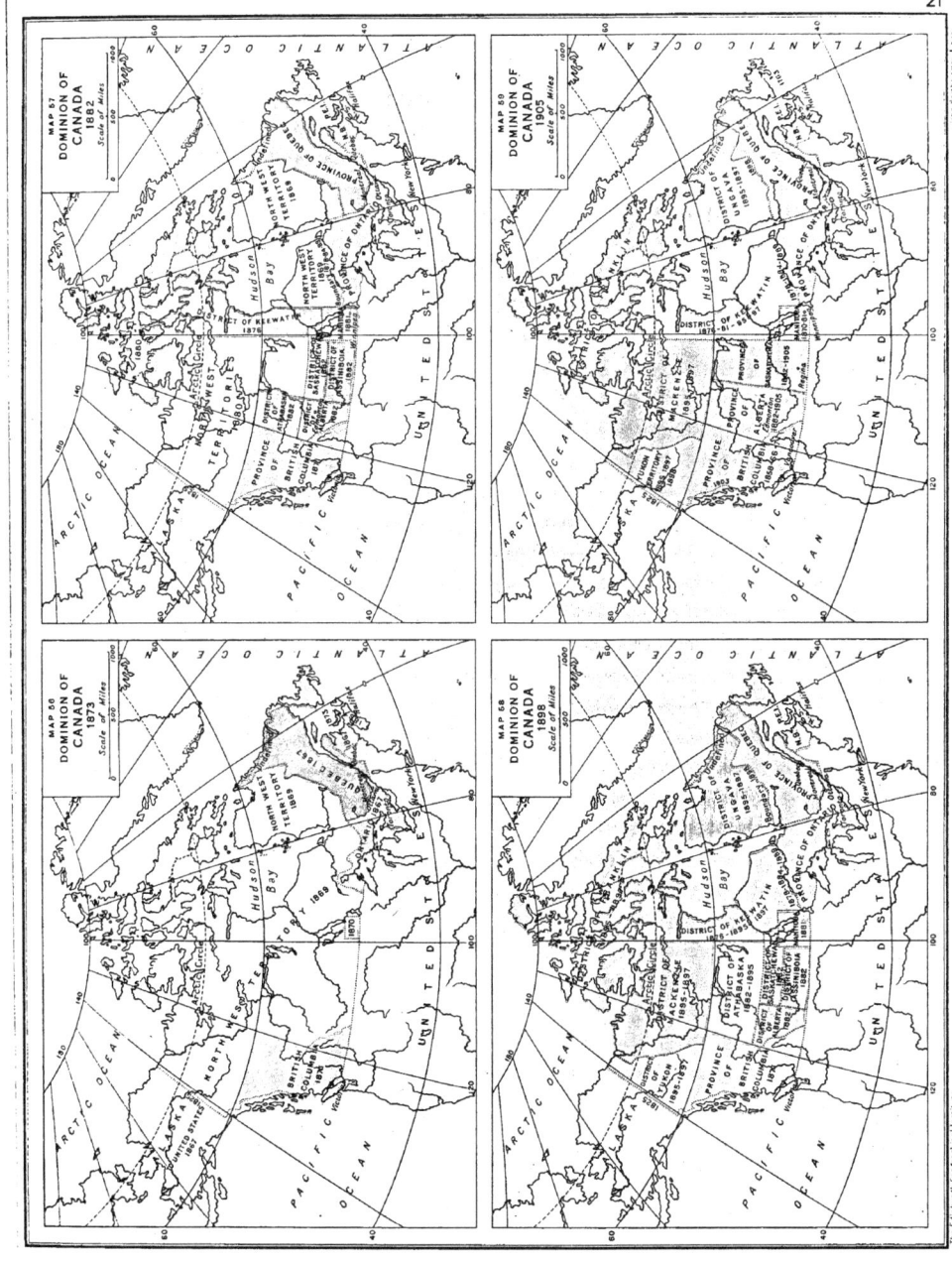

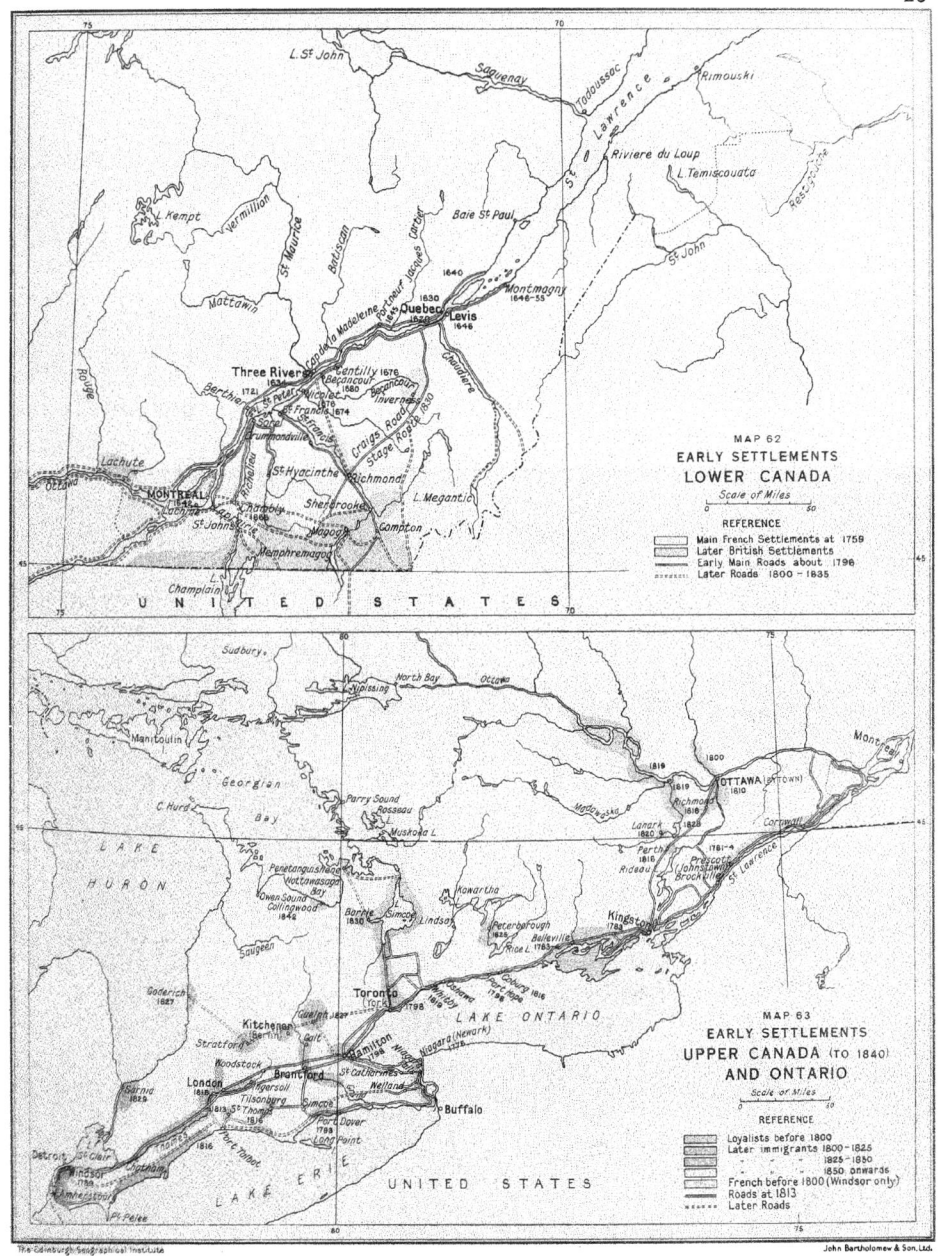

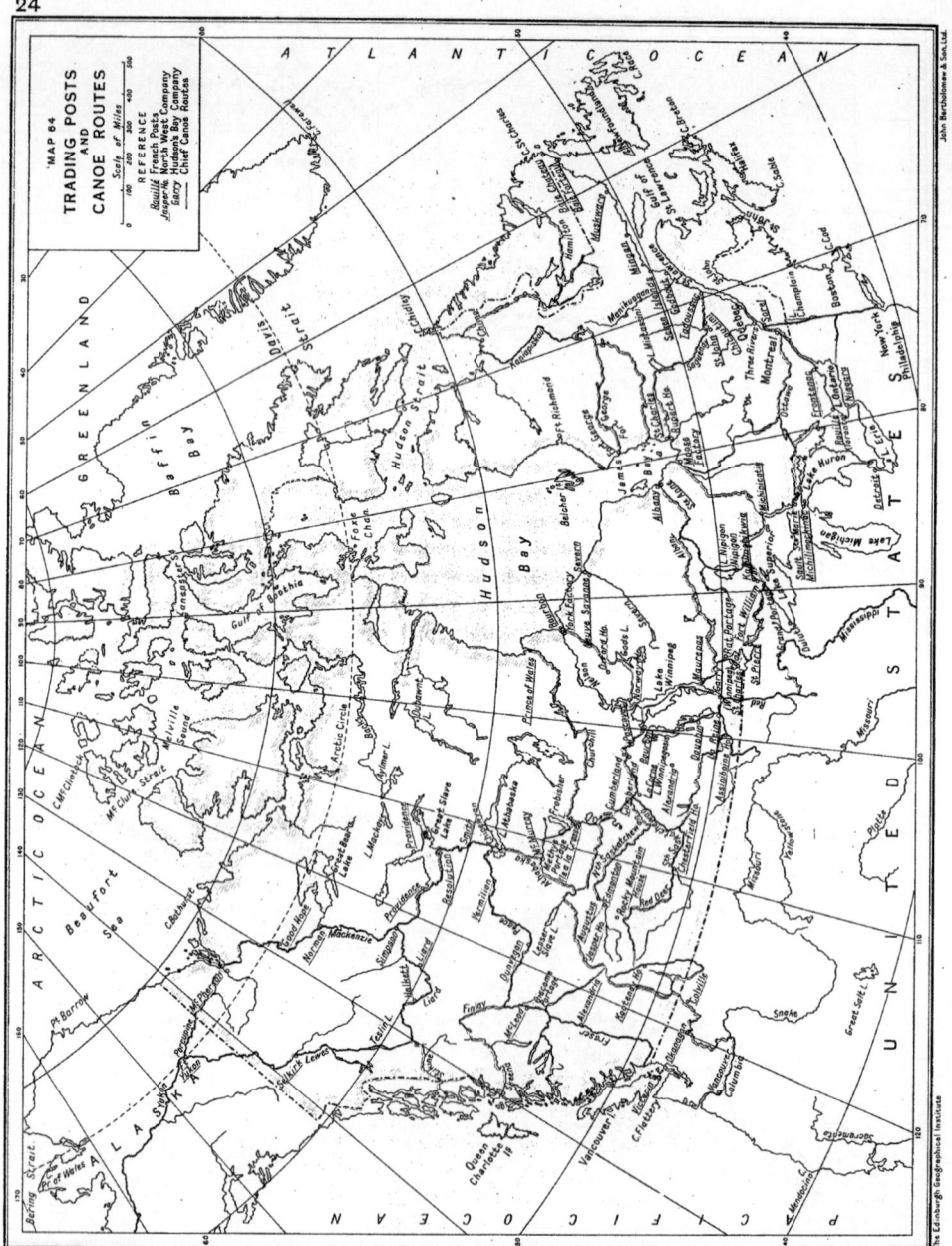

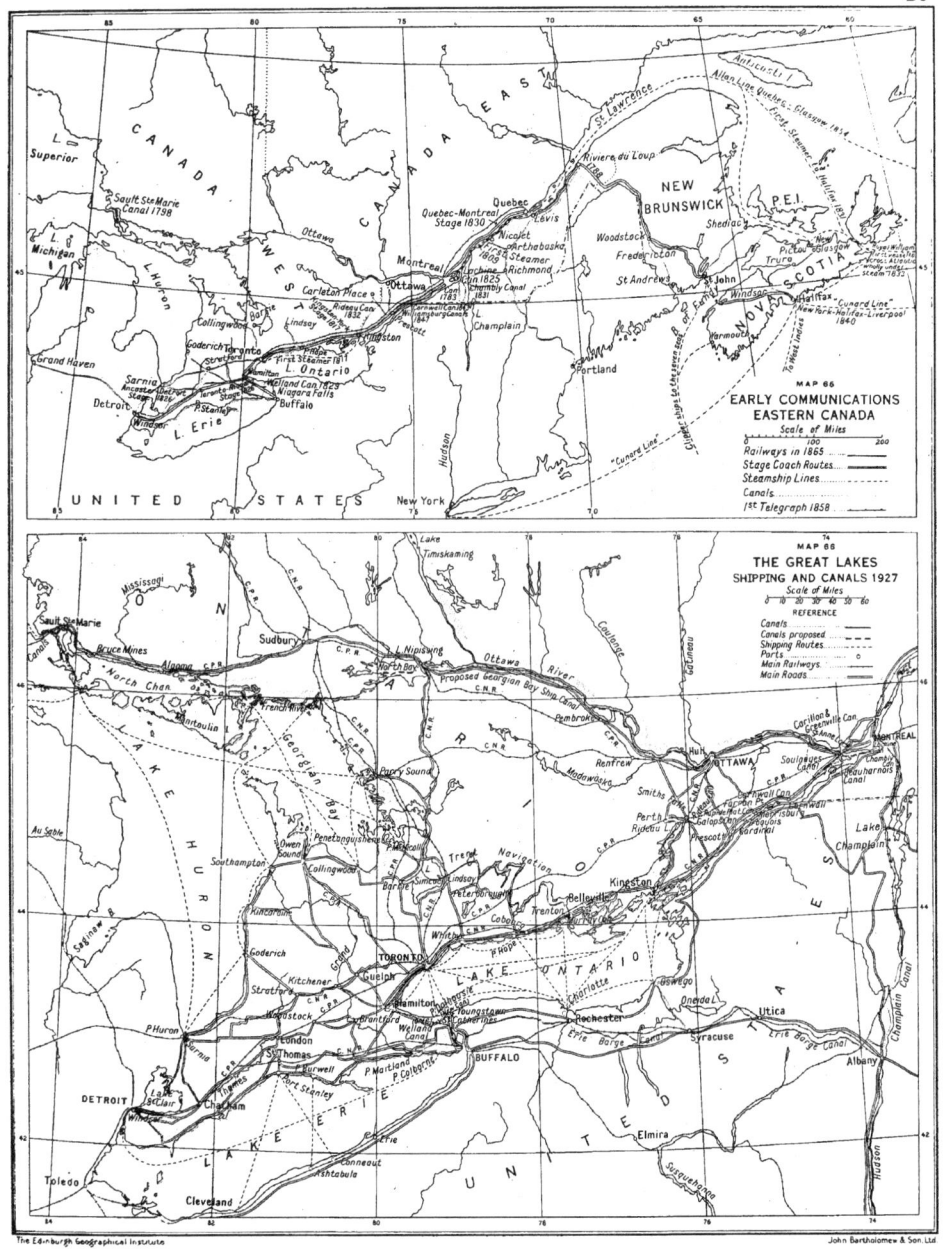

POPULATION 1871
General distribution of population is shown thus

POPULATION 1921
Relative density is shown by red dots. Each dot represents 10,000 persons

John Bartholomew & Son, Ltd.

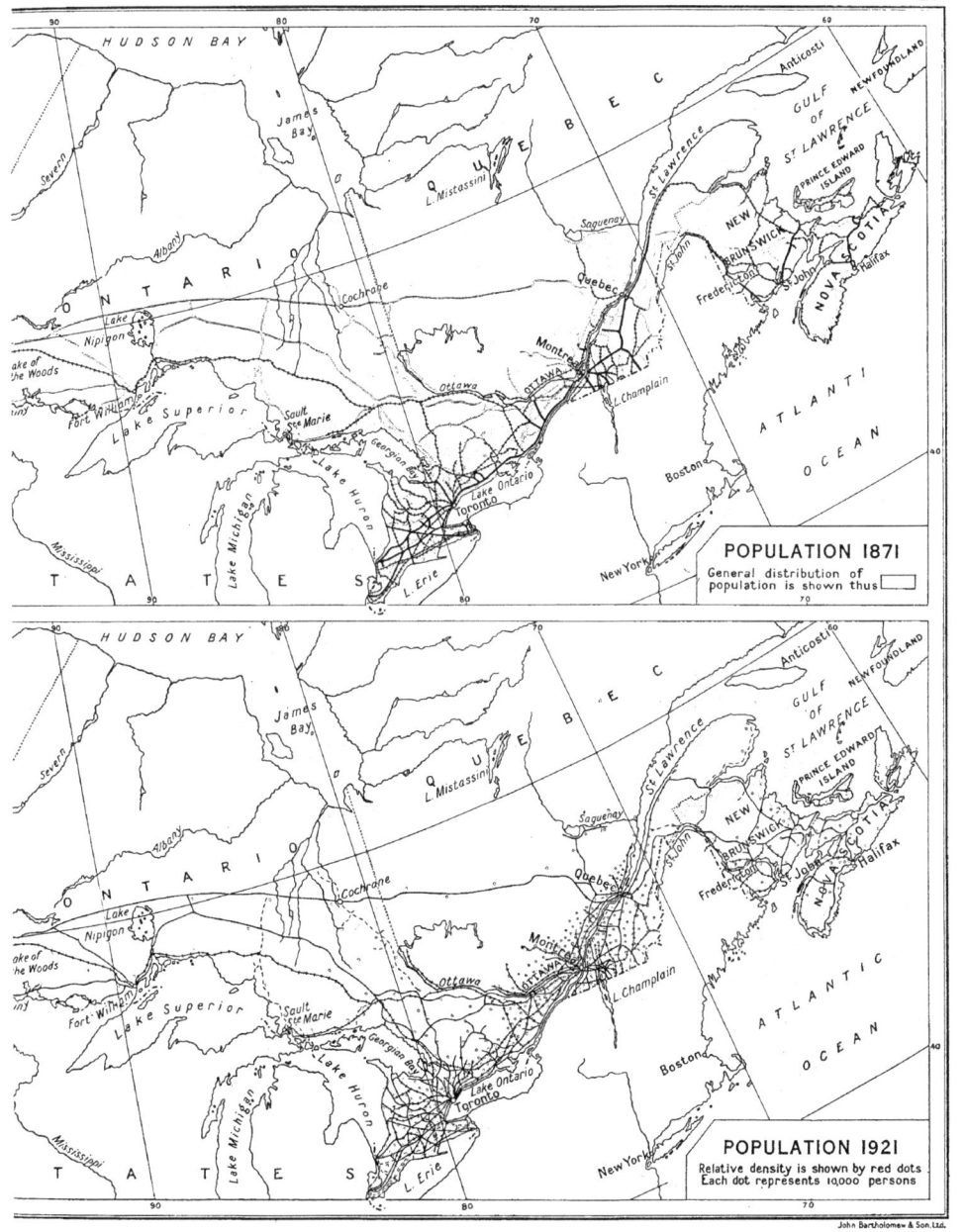

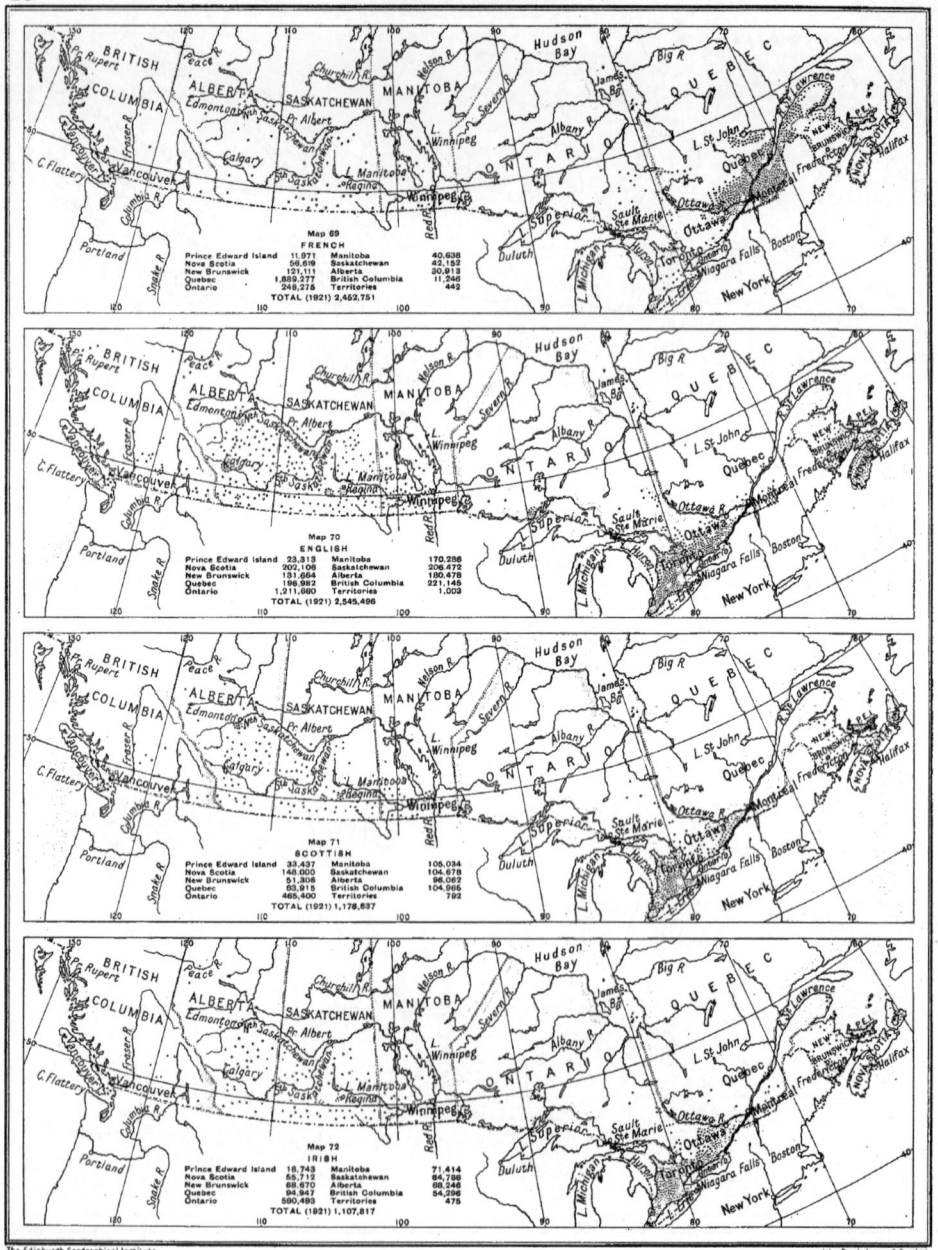

RACIAL ORIGINS

Map 69
FRENCH

Prince Edward Island	11,971	Manitoba	40,638
Nova Scotia	56,619	Saskatchewan	42,152
New Brunswick	121,111	Alberta	30,913
Quebec	1,889,277	British Columbia	11,246
Ontario	248,275	Territories	442

TOTAL (1921) 2,452,751

Map 70
ENGLISH

Prince Edward Island	23,313	Manitoba	170,286
Nova Scotia	202,106	Saskatchewan	206,472
New Brunswick	131,664	Alberta	180,478
Quebec	196,982	British Columbia	221,145
Ontario	1,211,660	Territories	1,003

TOTAL (1921) 2,545,496

Map 71
SCOTTISH

Prince Edward Island	33,437	Manitoba	105,034
Nova Scotia	148,000	Saskatchewan	104,678
New Brunswick	51,308	Alberta	98,062
Quebec	53,915	British Columbia	104,965
Ontario	465,400	Territories	792

TOTAL (1921) 1,176,637

Map 72
IRISH

Prince Edward Island	18,743	Manitoba	71,414
Nova Scotia	55,710	Saskatchewan	84,786
New Brunswick	68,670	Alberta	68,246
Quebec	94,947	British Columbia	54,296
Ontario	590,493	Territories	475

TOTAL (1921) 1,107,817

The Edinburgh Geographical Institute   John Bartholomew & Son, Ltd.

RACIAL ORIGINS

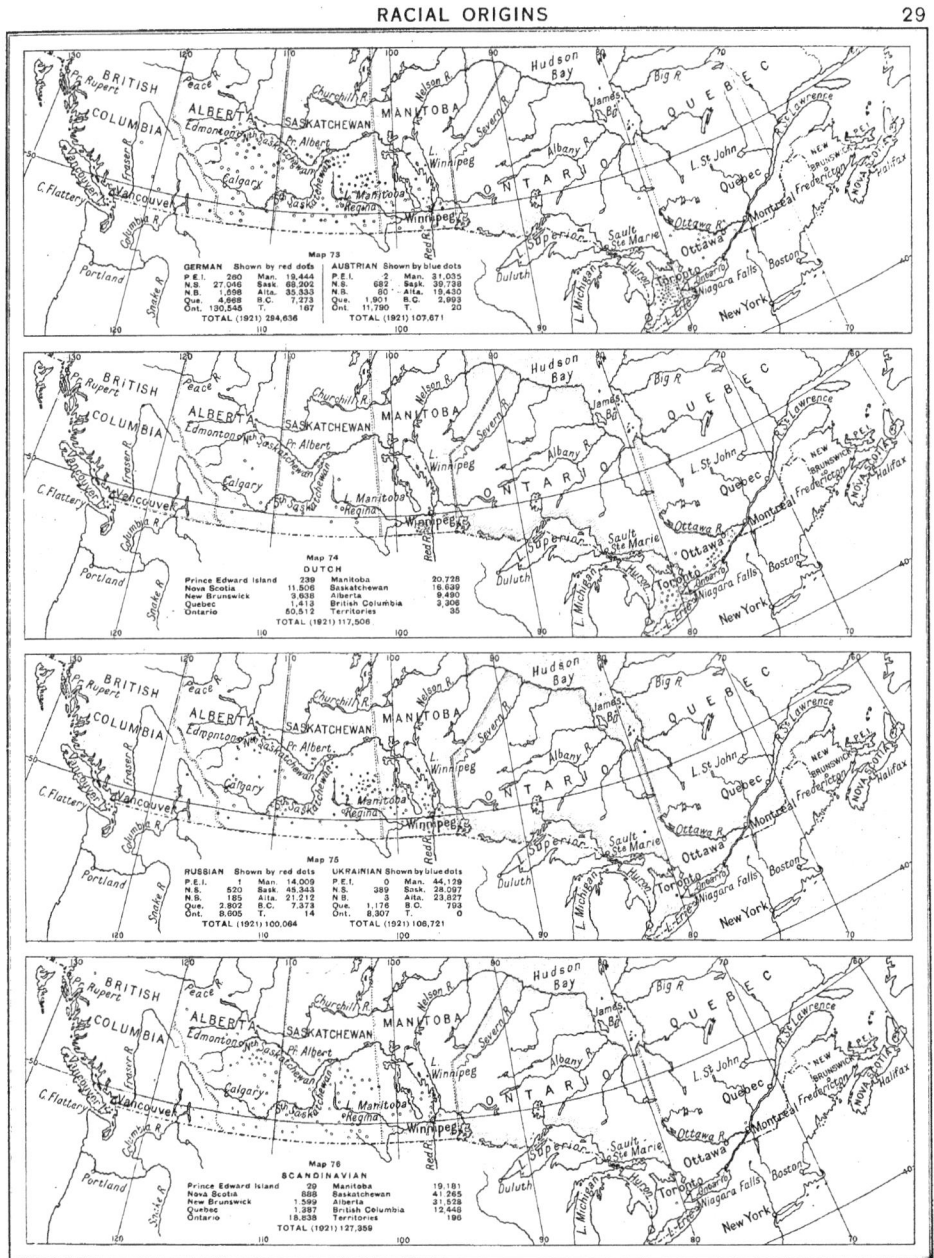

Map 73

GERMAN	Shown by red dots		AUSTRIAN	Shown by blue dots	
P.E.I.	280	Man. 19,444	P.E.I.	2	Man. 31,035
N.S.	27,046	Sask. 68,202	N.S.	682	Sask. 39,738
N.B.	1,598	Alta. 35,333	N.B.	80	Alta. 19,430
Que.	4,668	B.C. 7,273	Que.	1,901	B.C. 2,993
Ont.	130,545	T. 167	Ont.	11,790	T. 20
	TOTAL (1921) 294,636			TOTAL (1921) 107,671	

Map 74
DUTCH

Prince Edward Island	239	Manitoba	20,728
Nova Scotia	11,506	Saskatchewan	16,639
New Brunswick	3,638	Alberta	9,490
Quebec	1,413	British Columbia	3,306
Ontario	50,512	Territories	35
	TOTAL (1921) 117,506		

Map 75

RUSSIAN	Shown by red dots		UKRAINIAN	Shown by blue dots	
P.E.I.	1	Man. 14,009	P.E.I.	0	Man. 44,129
N.S.	520	Sask. 45,343	N.S.	389	Sask. 28,097
N.B.	185	Alta. 21,212	N.B.	3	Alta. 23,827
Que.	2,802	B.C. 7,373	Que.	1,176	B.C. 793
Ont.	8,605	T. 14	Ont.	8,307	T. 0
	TOTAL (1921) 100,064			TOTAL (1921) 106,721	

Map 76
SCANDINAVIAN

Prince Edward Island	29	Manitoba	19,181
Nova Scotia	686	Saskatchewan	41,265
New Brunswick	1,599	Alberta	31,528
Quebec	1,397	British Columbia	12,448
Ontario	18,838	Territories	186
	TOTAL (1921) 127,359		

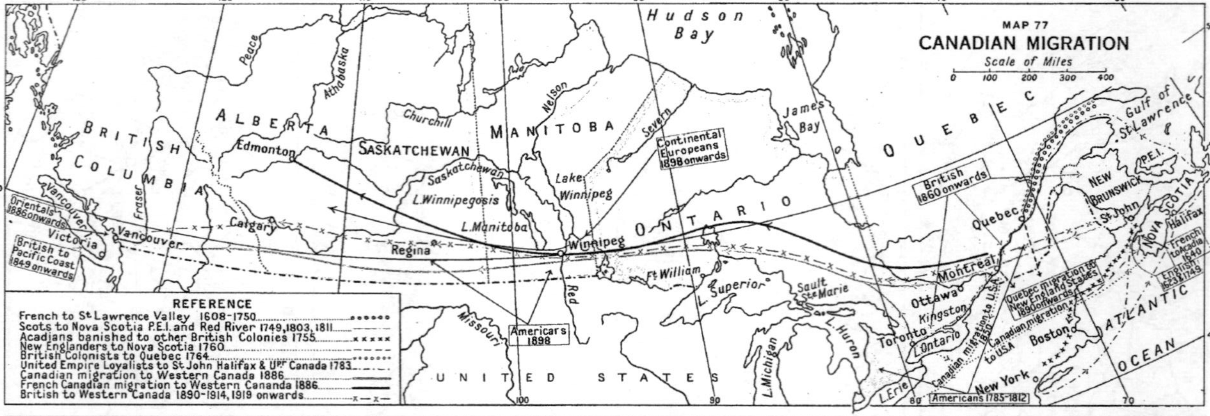

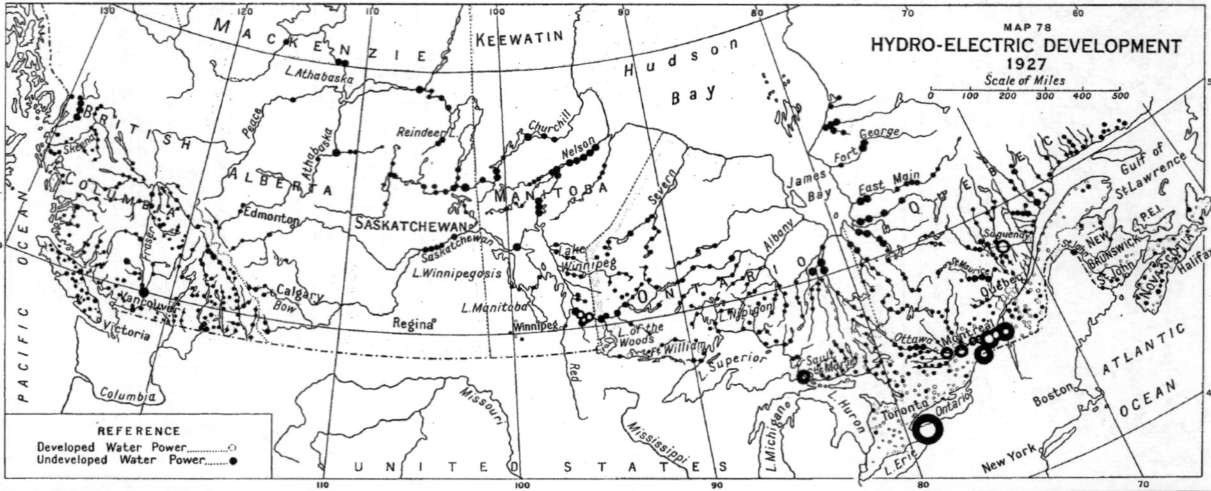

The Edinburgh Geographical Institute

John Bartholomew & Son, Ltd.

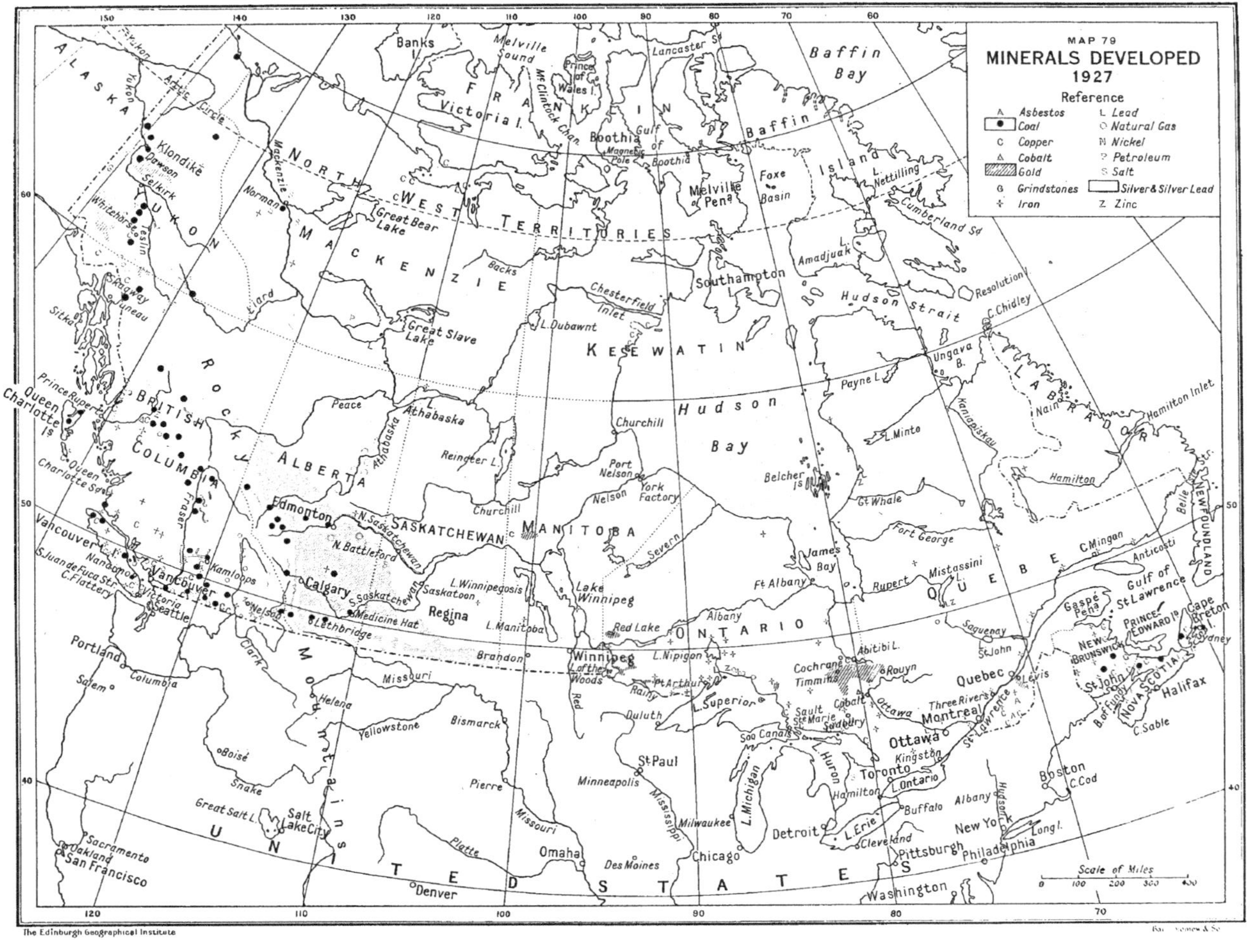

The Edinburgh Geographical Institute

MAP 80
OREGON BOUNDARY 1846
Scale of Miles
0 50 100 200 300
The Oregon Territory.
Claim of United States All Territory west Rocky Mountains from 42° north parallel to 54°40'
British Claim all Territory west of Rocky Mountains south to 42° parallel.
Treaty of 1818: Boundary to be along 49° parallel from Lake of the Woods to Rocky Mountains.
Treaty of 1846: Boundary as at present west from Rocky Mountains.
Ft Simpson
54°40'
Alexandria
Fraser R.
Rocky Mountains
Red Deer R.
Bow R.
Vancouver I.
Ft Langley
Victoria
Columbia R.
Missouri R.
Astoria
Walla Walla
Ft Vancouver
Snake R.
Boise
Spanish Treaty Line of 1819
Great Salt Lake

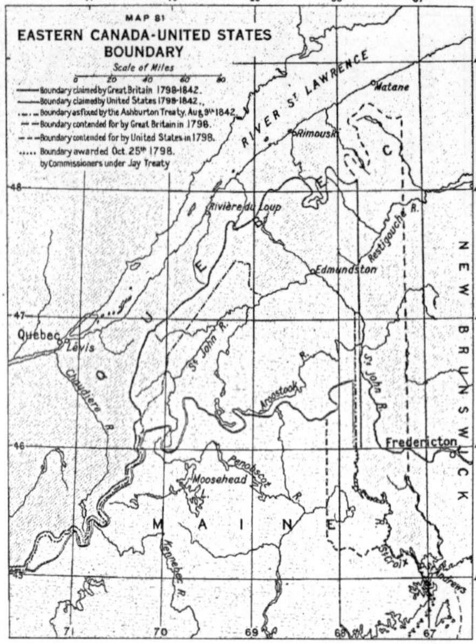
MAP 81
EASTERN CANADA-UNITED STATES BOUNDARY
Scale of Miles
0 20 40 60 80
Boundary claimed by Great Britain 1798-1842.
Boundary claimed by United States 1798-1842.
Boundary as fixed by the Ashburton Treaty, Aug 9th 1842.
Boundary contended for by Great Britain in 1798.
Boundary contended for by United States in 1798.
Boundary awarded Oct. 25th 1798. by Commissioners under Jay Treaty
RIVER ST LAWRENCE
Matane
Rimouski
Rivière du Loup
Restigouche R.
Edmundston
NEW BRUNSWICK
QUEBEC
Quebec
Levis
Chaudière R.
St John R.
Aroostook R.
Fredericton
Penobscot R.
Moosehead
MAINE
Kennebec R.
St Croix
St Andrews

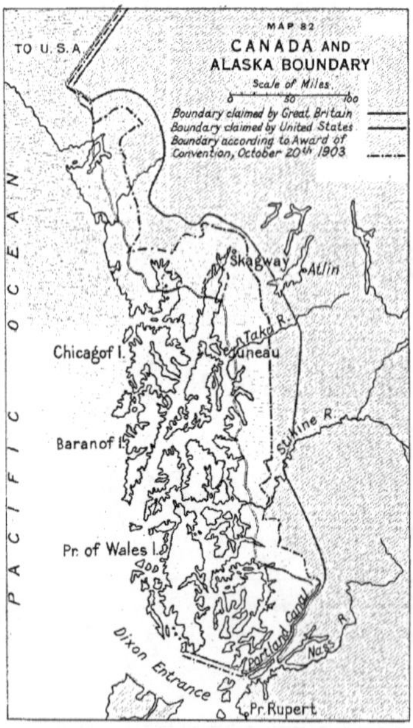
MAP 82
CANADA AND ALASKA BOUNDARY
Scale of Miles
0 50 100
Boundary claimed by Great Britain
Boundary claimed by United States
Boundary according to Award of Convention, October 20th 1903
TO U.S.A.
PACIFIC OCEAN
Skagway
Atlin
Taku R.
Chicagof I.
Juneau
Stikine R.
Baranof I.
Pr. of Wales I.
Portland Canal
Nass R.
Dixon Entrance
Pr. Rupert

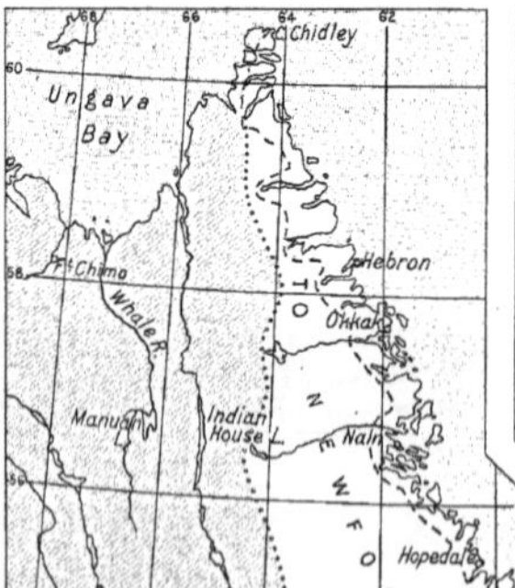
MAP 83
CANADA-LABRADOR BOUNDARY
Scale of Miles
0 20 40 60 80 100 120 140 160 180
Boundary defined March 1876
Approximate Boundary claimed by Canada
Approximate Boundary as decided by Privy Council's Report 1927
Chidley
Ungava Bay
Ft Chimo
Whale R.
Hebron
Okkak
NEWFOUNDLAND
Manuan
Indian House L.
Nain
Hopedale
Dyke L.
Mishikamau
Rigolet
Hamilton Inl.
Lake Melville
Cartwright
Dssokmanuan Lake
Hamilton R.
Battle
Strait of Belle Isle

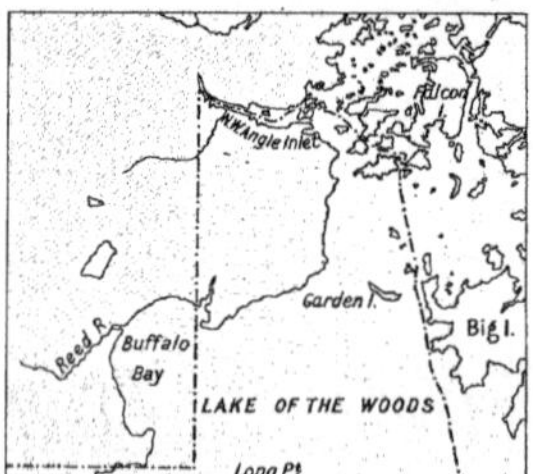
MAP 84
LAKE OF THE WOODS BOUNDARY
Scale of Miles
0 5 10
NW Angle Inlet
Garden I.
Big I.
Reed R.
Buffalo Bay
LAKE OF THE WOODS
Long Pt
Muskeg Bay
Oak Pt

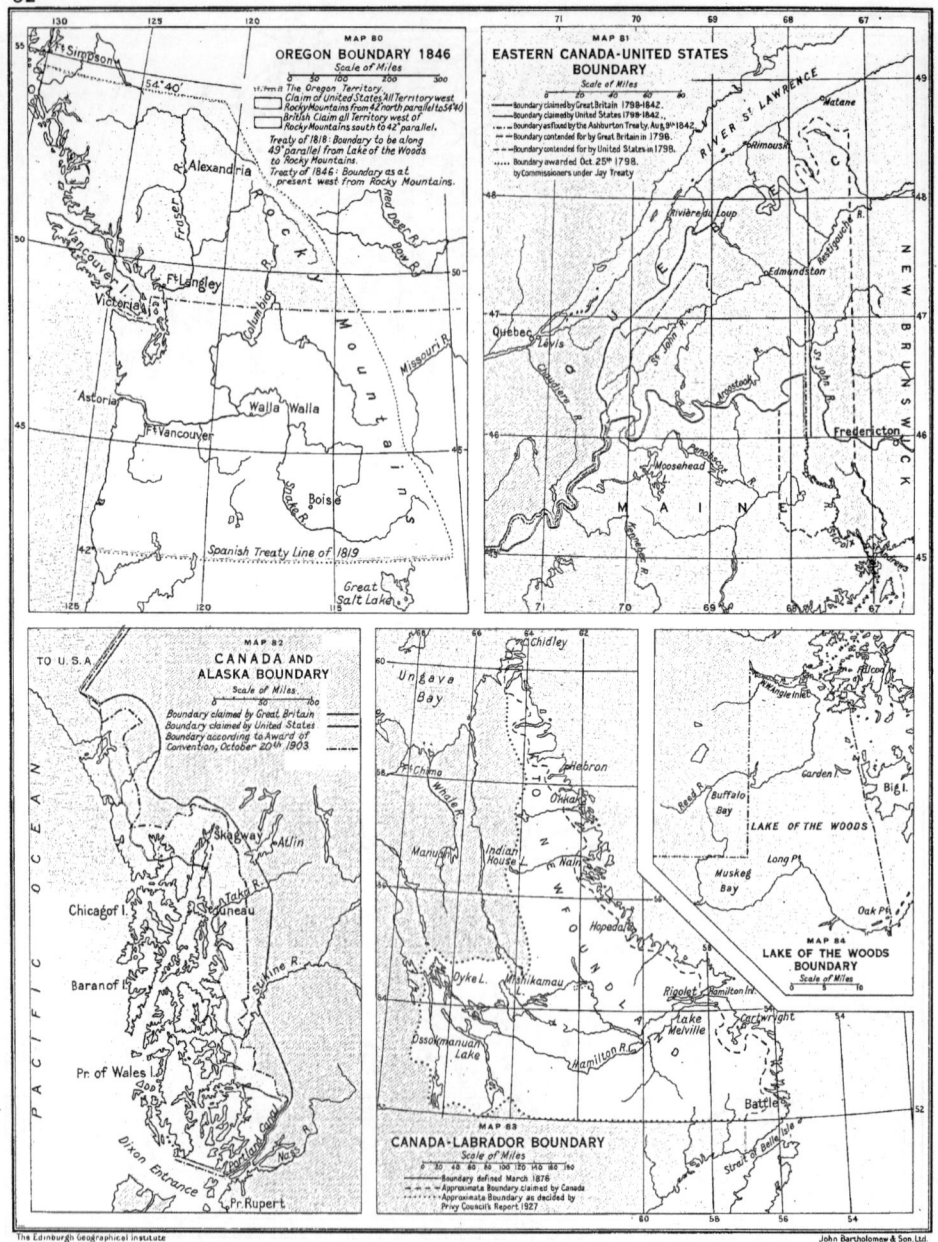

NOTES ON THE MAPS

I.—INTRODUCTORY—PHYSICAL CONDITIONS AND NATIVE RACES

MAP No. 1 shows the physical characteristics of North America, and particularly of Canada, mountain ranges and highest peaks, rivers and lakes, the elevation of the land being brought out by means of contrasting colours. A few of the famous portages, that played such an important part in the history of western exploration and the fur trade, are shown in red, to emphasize the interrelationship of waterways—Lake Superior to the Lake of the Woods and Lake Winnipeg, the Saskatchewan River to the Churchill, the Churchill to the Athabaska, the Peace to the Fraser.

Maps Nos. 2 and 3 show mean or average midwinter and midsummer temperatures, the summer lines being much more erratic than those of winter. A study of these lines will bring out many curious facts. For instance, the mean winter temperature of the southern part of Greenland is no more severe than that of Ontario ; and the mean summer temperature of the Yukon and southern Colorado are practically the same.

Map No. 4 similarly brings out the fact that the annual rainfall on the coast of British Columbia is greater than in Ontario or Quebec, and much greater than in Alberta, Saskatchewan, or Manitoba.

Map No. 5 reveals the enormous extent of the cleared and uncleared forest lands of Canada, and the relatively small area of natural grassland or prairie that to-day is producing such an immense quantity of grain. If the northern coast of the Dominion is barren, it counts within its area none of the desert or semi-desert that is so marked a feature of the south-western part of the continent.

Map No. 6 brings out in more detail the relative areas of prairie and forest land in Canada, and the density of the forest, from the mixed woodland and prairie along the North Saskatchewan to the heavily-wooded coastal areas of British Columbia.

Map No. 7 tells in a broad way the story of the Native Races that inhabited this land.

CLIMATE OF CANADA

MAPS NOS. 2-4

As Canada covers the northern half of the continent, with its borders on three oceans, and embraces a great variety of territory in latitude, altitude, distance from the sea, and topographical features, it follows that climatic conditions are also varied. The most southerly point of the Dominion is Pelee Island, in the same latitude as Rome, Italy, while the possibilities of agriculture extend down the valley of the Mackenzie almost to the Arctic Circle. Obviously there is room here for a wide range of climatic conditions, with all that these mean to plant and animal life.

In British Columbia, Vancouver Island and the coastal region have a very great rainfall, generally exceeding 100 inches annually. The temperature closely resembles that of England. On the other hand the interior plateaus between the Coast Range and the Rockies possess a relatively dry climate. The summers are warmer and the winters colder than along the coast.

Of Alberta it has been said by Sir Frederick Stupart that "it is doubtful whether there is any other territory on the surface of the globe with a winter climate as variable as that of this province." This results from the Chinook wind, which, blowing from the coast over the mountains, is almost capable of turning winter into summer in a few hours.

The climate of Saskatchewan and Manitoba is very similar, with a mean range of about 70° between the warmest and coldest months, and an actual recorded range of temperature at Winnipeg of 153°.

In Ontario the southern part of the province enjoys a climate tempered by lake influence ; similar conditions prevail in the north part of the province around James Bay ; while other parts of the province "are exposed to the severe cold waves from the far north-west which in winter sweep with unchecked severity over the country north of Lakes Superior and Huron." The climate of the peninsula of Ontario is much warmer than that of the northern part of the province.

Similar variations occur in the province of Quebec, but not to the same degree. In the Montreal district spring advances much more rapidly than in the lower valley of the St. Lawrence. In fact the eastern part of the province is cooler in summer and decidedly colder in winter than the south-western part. The entire northern region of the province is of course subject to long and severe winters.

NOTES ON THE MAPS

The Maritime Provinces have a climate which compares in many respects with that of southern Ontario. The spring, however, opens later, and the summers are cooler than in the peninsula of Ontario. Fine weather is enjoyed in the autumn months. The winters in Nova Scotia are not quite so cold as in southern Ontario, but in New Brunswick they are colder. Precipitation is heavy, and the snowfall in northern New Brunswick usually exceeds 100 inches.

Bibliography: Sir Frederick Stupart, *The Climate of Canada* (Handbook of Canada, for the British Association, 1924).

VEGETATION OF CANADA

Maps Nos. 5 and 6

From the point of view of vegetation North America has been described as a great triangle with its apex in Southern Mexico, and its base extending east and west from Newfoundland to Alaska.

The sub-Arctic and Arctic regions north of this line are practically treeless except in favoured localities, consist largely of muskeg and rock interspersed with areas of grass and shrub which afford abundant food for immense herds of caribou and musk-ox.

Stretching almost across Canada, and forming the upper belt of this continental triangle, is what is called the Canadian zone. Roughly speaking, this embraces most of the habitable area of the Dominion, or the southern half of the country. The Eastern Provinces and British Columbia are forested regions, while the immense interior plain, constituting the provinces of Manitoba, Saskatchewan, and Alberta, once considered a desert, is comparatively treeless, but blessed with so productive a soil that it is not inaptly described as the granary of the British Empire.

Bibliography: Francis E. Lloyd, *The Vegetation of Canada* (Handbook of Canada, for the British Association, 1924).

INDIAN TRIBES AND LINGUISTIC GROUPS

Map No. 7

It is impossible to understand properly the history of the settlement of North America, and particularly of that part of it known to-day as Canada, without a fairly accurate knowledge of the Indian tribes. The map shows their general distribution, so far as can be ascertained, about the time of the coming of the white man. That, it is hardly necessary to explain, is a variable date, much earlier in the eastern than in the western part of the country. Tribes speaking the same or a similar language are grouped under the same family name—*e.g.* the Chippewa, Ottawa, Blackfoot and Cree tribes all belong to the Algonkian stock; the Assiniboine are Siouan; and the Kutchin and Nahane are Athapaskan. It will be noted that the Indians with whom the early explorers first came in contact along the shores of the St. Lawrence were of Iroquoian stock; and that the unfortunate native inhabitants of Huronia were of the same family as the enemy who so nearly succeeded in exterminating them.

It is a circumstance not without historical interest that the most aggressive and troublesome of the tribes, Iroquois and Sioux, never occupied more than a comparatively small area in what is now Canada, while the Algonkian sprawled over a large part of the country. The native stock of the Pacific coast is divided up into a large number of groups and tribes, some of which are more widely removed in language than the Englishman and the Greek.

The nomenclature followed is that of the *Handbook of Canadian Indians*, published by the Geographic Board of Canada in 1913, which is based upon, but differs in minor particulars from, the *Handbook of American Indians*, published by the Bureau of American Ethnology in 1907 and 1910. The editor of the Canadian Handbook republished everything in the American Handbook relating to the Indians of Canada, amplifying and correcting the articles whenever necessary. He also compiled maps relating to the Indians of Canada, and added special articles respecting Canadian Indians.

II.—DISCOVERIES AND EXPLORATIONS

Maps Nos. 8–24, 26, and 30, tell the story of the exploration of British North America, the story of the unfolding of the map of Canada from sea to sea. It carries one back to the romantic voyages of the Vikings, and embraces the attempts to find a passage to Asia through the great barrier that we now know as America, which resulted in the gradual discovery of the Atlantic coast of this continent; the penetration into the interior by way of the Gulf of St. Lawrence and Hudson Bay; the exploration of the interior, and of the Pacific and Arctic coasts. To understand the story of the discovery of Canada is to understand the foundation of Canadian history.

DISCOVERIES OF THE VIKINGS

MAP No. 8

Our knowledge of the voyages of the Northmen to America is based mainly upon the monumental work of Charles Christian Rafn, *Antiquitates Americanæ*, 1837. The same Scandinavian race that colonized Iceland in 874, and Greenland in 985, apparently discovered portions of the mainland of North America.

Leif Eriksson, son of Eric the Red, discoverer of Greenland, voyaged south from Greenland in the year 1000. He landed first on a barren coast which he named Helluland, and which is believed to have been Labrador. His next landfall was on the shores of a wooded country which he named Markland, and which may have been Newfoundland or Nova Scotia. Two days later he landed on a more hospitable coast, which he named Vinland, and where he spent the winter. He ascended a river, and some of his men found grapes, hence the name.

For years a controversy has raged around the identity of Vinland, but as the evidence is extremely meagre it is improbable, unless some convincing runic inscription should be discovered, that we shall ever know anything more than that it lay somewhere on the north Atlantic coast of America.

Four years later Karlsefne attempted to found a colony in Vinland, but without success. One of his companions, Thorvald, was killed by the natives and buried there.

Bibliography: Stephen Leacock, *Dawn of Canadian History*; A. M. Reeves, *Finding of Vineland the Good*; Nansen, *In Northern Mists*.

TOSCANELLI'S MAP

MAP No. 9

Toscanelli was a friend of Columbus, who, it is believed, actually used, or was influenced by, this map.

The mistake of identifying the Caribbean Islands with the East Indies is too often viewed with contemptuous amusement by the modern reader. We must remember the state of geographic knowledge and conjecture in the days of Columbus, both of which are accurately reflected in this map. Granted the conditions, and the fact that the Indies were the long-sought object of his search, it was natural and inevitable for Columbus to believe what he did.

Cippangu on the map is of course Japan, and Cathay is China. Knowledge of these remote countries had come to Europe through the story of Marco Polo and other early travellers.

The map brings home to us the ignorance of mankind up to historically recent years concerning the earth's size and surface. This is further illustrated in the following diagram:

3000 B.C.	2000 B.C.	1000 B.C.	76 B.C.	A.D. 1000	A.D. 1569	A.D. 1925
Babylonian Empire	Egyptian Empire	Assyrian Empire	Julius Cæsar	Vikings in north Atlantic	Mercator — first reasonably correct world map.	

Bibliography: Uzielli, *Life and Times of Toscanelli*. His letters to Columbus are in an appendix to Edwards and Foster, *Life and Voyages of Americus Vespuccius*.

DISCOVERIES OF COLUMBUS

MAP No. 10

Christopher Columbus (1447–1506) was born in Genoa. He made several voyages, on one of which he is believed to have reached Iceland, and, encouraged by the Florentine astronomer Toscanelli, conceived the idea of reaching the Indies by sailing westward. After several years of discouragement, his plans were finally approved by Ferdinand and Isabella of Spain, and he sailed out into the unknown and untravelled west in 1492.

On 12th October he landed on an island which he named San Salvador, and which is believed to be what is known to-day as Watling's Island, in the Bahamas. From there he sailed to Cuba and Hayti and planted a small colony.

The following year he set forth on his second voyage, sighted Dominica, and after a desperate illness returned to Spain. On his third voyage, begun in 1498, he discovered the mainland of South America.

Misfortunes, however, followed thick and fast. The Royal Governor who had been sent out to govern these new possessions of Spain quarrelled with Columbus and sent him home in irons. He was released, and in 1502 sailed on his last great voyage, in which he explored the south shore of the Gulf of Mexico. He died at Valladolid.

His course on these several voyages may be traced on Map No. 10; but if we would see the New World with the eyes of Columbus we must forget the modern map and all that we now know of the continent of America, and, with Toscanelli's map (No. 9) before us, imagine ourselves on one of the gallant little ships of 1492.

Bibliography: Washington Irving, *Life of Columbus*; Justin Winsor, *Christopher Columbus*; Helps, *Life of Columbus*; Crompton, *Life of Columbus*.

PART OF SEBASTIAN CABOT'S WORLD MAP

MAP No. 11

John Cabot was a Genoese pilot who settled at Bristol about 1490. He succeeded in interesting Henry VII. in his plans for western discovery, and in 1497 set sail from Bristol in a small ship called the *Mathew*.

On this voyage Cabot landed on the shores of America, but the exact location of his landfall has been disputed by scholars for many years. The direct evidence of the voyage is contained in three letters—one from Lorenzo Pasqualigo, a Venetian merchant in Bristol, to his brothers in Venice: and the other two from Soncino, the ambassador of the Duke of Milan in England, to his prince.

On this evidence, and the testimony of more or less contemporary charts, it has been variously argued that John Cabot's landfall in 1497 was on the coast of Labrador, on the shores of Newfoundland, or on Cape Breton Island. The consensus of scholarly opinion is to-day in favour of the last.

The following year Cabot again sailed to the west, intending, in the words of Soncino, to reach Cipango, "where all the spices and jewels of the world grow." He steered toward the north-west, and is believed to have reached Hudson Strait, if not farther north. Turning south, he explored the coast of the continent to some undetermined point, possibly to the mouth of Chesapeake Bay, and from there sailed back to England.

The part taken by his son Sebastian in these and other discoveries has been a matter of controversy. Sometimes credited with the major part of the discoveries otherwise attributed to his father, there has been a tendency in recent years to deny him any share in the exploration of America. With evidence so meagre and conflicting the only safe conclusion is that Sebastian's part in his father's discoveries must be regarded as indeterminate.

The map is a portion of Sebastian Cabot's World Map of 1544.

Bibliography: Beazley, *John and Sebastian Cabot;* Weare, *Cabot's Discovery of America;* Biddle, *Memoir of Sebastian Cabot;* Leacock, *Dawn of Canadian History;* Biggar, *Voyages of the Cabots and Cortereal.*

EXPLORATION OF THE ST. LAWRENCE BY CARTIER, 1534-42

Map No. 12

JACQUES CARTIER (1491-1557) sailed from St. Malo in 1534, entered the Gulf of St. Lawrence by way of the Strait of Belle Isle, landed on the north shore of the Gulf, on Prince Edward Island, on Chaleur Bay, and on the Gaspé shore, and coasting around the eastern end of Anticosti, returned to France.

In 1535 he again sailed for the St. Lawrence, and ascending the river past the mouth of the Saguenay landed on the Island of Orleans, which he named Isle Bacchus. He brought his little vessels, the *Grande Hermine, Petite Hermine,* and *Emerillon,* into the St. Charles River, upon whose banks stood the Indian village of Stadacona (Quebec).

In the *Emerillon* Cartier proceeded up the river to Lake St. Peter, and leaving his ship there, continued on in boats to the Indian town of Hochelaga (Montreal). During his stay here he climbed Mount Royal, and saw the waters of the Ottawa.

He returned and wintered on the St. Charles, where his men had meanwhile built a fort opposite the Indian town. On the return voyage he sailed, for the first time, through Cabot Strait, between Newfoundland and Cape Breton.

In 1541 he made a third voyage to Canada, ascended the river as far as the Lachine Rapids, and wintered at Cap Rouge above Stadacona, where he was attacked by the Indians.

In the spring he sailed back to France, meeting on the way a fleet under Roberval, who was bringing out a company of colonists. Roberval wintered at Cap Rouge, where he built a strong fort, and the following year explored the Saguenay. The colony, however, did not prosper, and it appears that Cartier was sent out by the king to bring it home.

This map is based upon Biggar's map in his *Voyages of Jacques Cartier.*

Bibliography: Leacock, *The Mariner of St. Malo;* Pope, *Jacques Cartier;* Baxter, *Memoir of Jacques Cartier.*

MAP OF HUDSON'S VOYAGES IN THE ARCTIC, 1610

Map No. 13

HENRY HUDSON made four notable voyages. On the first, in 1607, he explored the coast of Spitsbergen; on the second, in 1608, part of Nova Zembla; on the third, in 1609, the Hudson River; and on the last, 1610-11, Hudson Bay.

His course in 1610 lay through the Strait and down the east coast of the Bay. He wintered at the head of James Bay, and sailed north in the spring of 1611 with an insufficient supply of provisions. His hungry and discontented crew finally mutinied and cast him adrift somewhere in the Bay with eight companions in a small boat. They were never heard of again.

The map is reproduced from Hessel Gerritz's *Detectio Freti,* 1612, and was based upon Hudson's own lost map. Compare it with that of Baffin, No. 14, and with Map No. 18.

Bibliography: Asher, *Henry Hudson the Navigator;* Read, *Historical Enquiry concerning Henry Hudson;* Burpee, *Search for the Western Sea.*

BAFFIN'S MAP OF HIS VOYAGES TO THE NORTH, 1615-16

Map No. 14

WILLIAM BAFFIN (c. 1584-1622), English navigator, made several voyages to the north-east and north-west—in 1612 to Greenland; in 1613-14 to Spitsbergen; in 1615 to Hudson Strait, which he examined and charted; and in 1616 to Smith's Sound and Baffin's Bay, which he explored and charted.

This map is interesting as an illustration of what was known of Arctic Canada in the early years of the seventeenth century. Compare with Maps Nos. 13, 18, and 22.

Bibliography: Markham, *Voyages of William Baffin.*

LESCARBOT'S MAP OF THE ST. LAWRENCE, 1609

Map No. 15

MARC LESCARBOT, born at Vervins, France, about 1570, accompanied Poutrincourt to Port Royal in 1606, and spent twelve months in the New World.

A man of education, quick wit, and lively imagination, he kept his eyes and ears open during his visit to America, and after his return to France wrote a history of New France, published at Paris in 1609, which is not only full of information but makes extraordinarily good reading. In 1907 the Champlain Society of Toronto published a new edition, with an English translation and notes by W. L. Grant and an introduction by H. P. Biggar.

The map here reproduced was prepared by Lescarbot, or from information supplied by him, and gives one an excellent idea of the state of geographical knowledge as to New France in the early years of the seventeenth century.

Bibliography: Parkman, *Pioneers of France in the New World.*

SANSON'S MAP OF AMERICA, 1650

Map No. 16

NICOLAS SANSON (1600-67), Geographer to the King of France, was one of the most eminent map-makers of his day. This map of 1650 gives a very fair idea of geographical knowledge in the middle of the seventeenth century. It will be noted that the eastern coast of North America, from Labrador to Central America, which had not only been pretty thoroughly explored but also more or less settled, is on the whole remarkably accurate. On the other hand the lower part of Greenland is separated by two imaginary straits, due apparently to a misunderstanding of Frobisher's narrative. A similar mistake, which also appears on many other early maps, is made in connection with James Bay, which is represented as two bays divided by a wide peninsula.

NOTES ON THE MAPS

The map is still more interesting as a commentary on the history of exploration in New France. The St. Lawrence is quite accurately represented, as well as Lake Erie and Lake Huron ; also Lake Nipissing, but not the Ottawa River, which formed part of the early route of exploration from Quebec and Montreal to the west. On the other hand the St. Lawrence runs through Lake Erie, and Lake Ontario appears to have been confused with the series of small waterways known as the Trent navigation which connects Lake Ontario with Georgian Bay. In the west only part of Lake Superior and Lake Michigan are shown, the latter then known as Lac des Puans ; and the country beyond Lake Superior is not even guessed at. At that time, as the map will show, nothing was known of the Pacific coast of the continent north of Mexico. Even the Gulf of California is shown as a strait ; and in the far north there is a very curious confusion of Hudson Bay with the long-sought North-West Passage, which is delineated as leading to the west out of Hudson Bay.

Bibliography : Parkman, *Old Régime in Canada.*

EXPLORATION OF THE BAY OF FUNDY, 1604-7

MAP No. 17

PIERRE DE MONTS, Seigneur de Guast (1574?-1611), was head of the company organized by Champlain for the purpose of planting colonies in New France. After visiting the St. Lawrence with Pontgravé in 1603, he turned his attention to Acadia. He sailed for the Bay of Fundy with Champlain in 1604, and was instrumental in establishing settlements on St. Croix Island in Passamaquoddy Bay and at Port Royal on Annapolis Basin.

The somewhat intricate voyage tracks shown on the map are not easy to follow, so the following time-table is given in order to clarify the movements of the various expeditions :

In May 1604, De Monts, with Champlain, Poutrincourt, and Pontgravé, skirted the Acadian coast from Cap de la Heve to Port Mouton. Champlain, in a small barque, was sent on ahead and explored the coast as far as Long Island, returning to Port Mouton. The ships sailed then to Annapolis Basin, explored the Bay of Fundy, including the harbour of St. John, and reached St. Croix Island, where buildings were erected. On September 2, Champlain was again sent forward and explored the coast as shown in the map, returning to St. Croix for the winter. Meanwhile Pontgravé and Poutrincourt had sailed for France to replenish their stores, returning in June 1605.

In that month De Monts and Champlain coasted to the south-west as far as Cape Cod, returning to St. Croix in August. The colony was then removed to a more suitable site in Annapolis Basin (Port Royal), and De Monts returned to France, leaving Pontgravé in command with Champlain as his lieutenant. No further exploration took place that year.

In March 1606 Pontgravé and Champlain set out twice, but owing to bad weather and various accidents got no farther than Grand Manan, and were forced to return. In April, Pontgravé and Champlain embarked the company for France, but at Cape Sable got news that De Monts had arrived so they returned to Port Royal. They found him on the *Jonas,* accompanied by Poutrincourt and Lescarbot.

On September 5, 1606, Poutrincourt and Champlain sailed over the same course as in 1605, but reached Martha's Vineyard before they turned back to Port Royal, which they made in November. This winter was the occasion of the Order of Good Cheer. In August 1607 came news from France which compelled the abandonment of the colony.

Bibliography : Parkman, *Pioneers of France in the New World ;* Colby, *The Founder of New France.*

EXPLORATION OF HUDSON BAY

MAP No. 18

IT has been argued that John Cabot, in his voyage of 1498, not only explored Hudson Strait, but also sailed around the Bay. Portuguese navigators also, perhaps with more probability, are held to have entered the Bay between 1558 and 1570. Both Martin Frobisher and John Davis have been credited with the discovery of the Strait—the former in 1578 and the latter in 1587. It seems more certain that George Weymouth, in 1602, sailed some way through the Strait.

In any event, the first unquestioned voyage into Hudson Bay was that of Hudson in 1610. Two years later Sir Thomas Button sailed for the Bay, in the same little *Discovery* that had carried Weymouth and then Hudson. He took with him a letter from King James to the Emperor of Japan, so confident were those who sent him that he would discover the North-West Passage. Crossing the Bay, he explored the west coast down to the mouth of the Nelson, where he wintered. In the spring he sailed north again, almost to Wager Bay, and then returned to England.

In 1615 Bylot and Baffin sailed for the Bay, in the *Discovery,* and explored Fox Channel. Four years later Jens Munck, a Danish navigator, sailed into the Bay and discovered the mouth of the Churchill, where he wintered. In 1631 two expeditions left England, commanded respectively by Luke Foxe and Thomas James. They both sailed down the west coast of Hudson Bay. Foxe turned back from Cape Henrietta Maria, but James continued his exploration down the west shore of James Bay, and wintered on Charlton Island.

Hudson Bay had now been almost completely explored, and it became improbable that the North-West Passage was to be found in this direction. The subsequent discovery of Fury and Hecla Strait by Parry finally disposed of the idea as a practicable scheme.

Bibliography : Burpee, *Search for the Western Sea ;* Laut, *Adventurers of England on Hudson Bay.*

ROUTES OF CHAMPLAIN AND BRÛLÉ, DOLLIER AND GALINÉE, 1615-70

MAP No. 19

IN 1613 Samuel Champlain ascended the Ottawa River as far as Allumette Island. In his narrative he describes such well-known points on the river as the Lake of Two Mountains, the mouth of the Rideau River, the Chaudière Falls and Chats Falls. He had been induced to explore the Ottawa by a young impostor named De Vignau, who told him that by this route he had reached the Northern Sea. De Vignau's deception was exposed by the Algonquin chief Tessoüat at Allumette Island.

Two years later Champlain again ascended the Ottawa accompanied by Etienne Brûlé. Paddling up-stream, they came to the mouth of the Mattawa, and turning westward reached Lake Nipissing. They descended French River to Georgian Bay, and coasting down to the south came to certain villages of the Huron Indians, where Father Le Caron had shortly before established a mission.

Champlain had promised to help the Hurons in their war with the Iroquois. In the autumn of 1615 he set out from the Huron villages with a party of warriors. Their route was by way of Lake Simcoe and what is to-day known as the Trent Navigation to the Bay of Quinte. Crossing the foot of Lake Ontario, they entered the Iroquois country and attacked the enemy. The result was indecisive, and the Hurons decided to retreat to their own land.

Meanwhile Brûlé had been sent by another route to secure the support of a friendly tribe, the Carantonans, who lived on the Susquehanna. The only evidence as to where he went is that supplied by Champlain's map of 1632. From this it may be assumed that Brûlé turned south from Lake Simcoe to Lake Ontario by way of the Humber River, thence from Burlington Bay to the Grand River, then over to the Thames, and down the latter to Lake St. Clair and the Detroit River, then to the Ohio River and up that stream to the portage to the Susquehanna. After his adventurous sojourn among the Senecas, he apparently returned by way of the Niagara, Lake Ontario, the Humber and Lake Simcoe to the Huron villages. He evidently saw Niagara Falls, as they are shown on Champlain's map, and it is generally recognized that much of the information on the map must have been furnished by Brûlé.

La Roche Daillon visited the Neutral Nation, north of Lake Erie, in 1626-27, and Brébeuf and Chaumonot in 1639-40 and 1640-41, but there is no evidence that any of the three actually saw Lake Erie. The first recorded discovery of that lake was by Dollier de Casson's party in 1669-70. As will be seen by a reference to the map, their course was up the south side of Lake Ontario to Burlington Bay, thence to Grand River, down it to Lake Erie, where they wintered. In 1670 they travelled west to the Detroit River, through that river, Lake St. Clair and St. Clair River to Lake Huron, around the east side of that lake and south of Manitoulin Island to St. Mary's River, and up that river to Sault Ste. Marie.

Bibliography: Colby, *The Founder of New France*; Dionne, *Samuel Champlain*; Butterfield, *History of Brûlé's Discoveries*.

JESUIT MISSIONS IN HURONIA

MAP No. 30

IN the summer of 1626 the Jesuit missionaries Brébeuf and Noüe, and the Recollet Daillon, left Quebec with a party of Hurons, and by way of the Ottawa River, Lake Nipissing, and French River, arrived at the Huron village of Otoüacha, near the present town of Penetanguishene, on Georgian Bay. Huronia, the country of the Hurons, occupied part of the present county of Simcoe, between Lake Simcoe and Nottawasaga Bay. The Indian town of Toanché, a mile or so inland, was Brébeuf's headquarters for the next three years. In 1627 Noüe returned to Quebec, and Daillon the following year, leaving Brébeuf to labour alone as a missionary. In the summer of 1629 he too was summoned back to Quebec.

Five years later Brébeuf returned to Huronia, accompanied by Fathers Daniel and Davost. For three years they made the village of Ihonatiria their headquarters, and under extremely discouraging conditions worked unceasingly for the conversion of the Hurons. In 1637 they moved their quarters to the village of Ossossané, having been reinforced in the meantime by Fathers Jogues, Garnier, Le Mercier, Pijart, and Chastelain; and the following year again moved to Teanaostaiaë. That year they were joined by Lalemant, who for the next eight years was to be superior of the mission, Le Moyne and du Peron. A strong fort was built which was named Ste. Marie, and the missionaries made progress in their good work.

In the summer of 1642 the Iroquois attacked an Indian town in Huronia and massacred the inhabitants. Five years later the Iroquois returned in greater numbers, attacked the mission station of St. Joseph, killed Father Daniel, and carried off 700 Huron prisoners. In 1649, emboldened by success, they once more attacked Huronia. Twelve hundred strong, the warriors marched against the mission. Having destroyed the village of St. Ignace, they next attacked St. Louis, where they captured Brébeuf and Gabriel Lalemant and burnt them to death. They then retreated without attacking Ste. Marie, where Father Ragueneau, who had succeeded Jerome Lalemant as superior, was in charge.

Ragueneau, realizing that there was no safety on the mainland from Iroquois attack, moved the mission to Isle St. Joseph, now Christian Island, where he built a strong fort. Misfortunes followed the missionaries and their converts in the shape of famine and disease, and finally in 1650 Ragueneau reluctantly decided to abandon Huronia, and lead the remnant of his flock to Quebec. The descendants of the tribe may still be found at Lorette, on the St. Charles, north of Quebec.

This mission of Huronia, the position and extent of which are clearly indicated on the map, was not by any means the only field of the Jesuit missionaries, but it was the most compact, and in some respects the most ambitious. The Jesuits also laboured for many years among the Iroquois and among various Algonquin tribes in the Maritime Provinces and the north country.

The names shown in brackets on the map are modern, introduced to show the relative position of the Huron missions to present-day towns and villages. The others represent Jesuit missions or Huron towns.

Bibliography: Parkman, *Jesuits in North America*; Campbell, *Pioneer Priests of North America*; Marquis, *The Jesuit Missions*; Harris, *Pioneers of the Cross in Canada*. An interesting article on Missions in Canada will be found under that title in White, *Handbook of Indians of Canada*.

ROUTES OF MARQUETTE, JOLLIET, AND LA SALLE, 1673-87

MAP No. 20

JACQUES MARQUETTE (1637-75) and Louis Jolliet (1645-1700), who had both travelled extensively in the country of the Great Lakes, were sent in 1673 on a journey of exploration to the south-west. They descended the Mississippi, which they reached by way of Lake Michigan, Green Bay, the Fox and Wisconsin Rivers, as far as the mouth of the Arkansas, and returned to Lake Michigan by way of the Illinois River. Jolliet was unfortunate enough to lose the records of his journey at the foot of the Lachine Rapids, almost within sight of Montreal. As a result of their expedition they satisfied themselves that the Mississippi flowed neither into the Atlantic nor the Gulf of California, as had been variously supposed, but into the Gulf of Mexico.

René Robert Cavelier Sieur de La Salle (1643-87) set out in 1669 with Dollier de Casson and Galinée toward the west. Leaving them at the western end of Lake Ontario, he explored the Ohio. His later explorations have been the subject of controversy, but it is certain that in 1681-82 he, first of white men, descended the Mississippi to its mouth. Upon his return he sailed for France, and in 1684 set out with four ships to establish a colony at the mouth of the Mississippi. The ill-fated expedition culminated in the murder of the explorer by his own men.

Bibliography: Parkman, *La Salle*; Griffin, *Discovery of the Mississippi*.

FRENCH EXPLORERS IN THE WEST, 1659-1743

MAP No. 26

THE true discoverer of the Canadian Northwest and of a considerable part of the American Northwest was Pierre Gaultier de Varennes, Sieur de La Vérendrye (1685-1749). With his sons he explored the country from Lake Superior to the Assiniboine, and from the Saskatchewan perhaps to the upper waters of the Yellowstone. These men were in the best possible sense patriotic adventurers. With rare and unselfish devotion, under peculiarly trying circumstances, hampered at every step by the jealous intrigues of those who should have given them loyal support, they gave their lives and their fortunes to the cause of western discovery.

Earlier explorers paved the way for the achievements of the La Vérendryes. Etienne Brûlé is thought to have got to the eastern end of Lake Superior about 1620. Jean Nicolet (1598-1642) in 1634-35 reached Green Bay and ascended Fox River to the Wisconsin portage.

Pierre Esprit Radisson (1620-1710) and Médard Chouart in 1658-60 followed Nicolet's route to the Wisconsin, ascended that stream to the Mississippi, and explored much of the country about the upper waters of that great river. In 1661-62 they again returned to the west, explored the south shore of Lake Superior, wintered among the Sioux, and in the spring made a tremendous journey in which they are believed to have reached the shores of James Bay.

Daniel Greyselon Du Lhut (1636-1710) explored the country about the western shores of Lake Superior in 1678-81, and built a trading post at the mouth of the Kaministikwia. Jacques de Noyon, born 1668, started inland from this port in 1688, ascended the Kaministikwia to Lac des Mille Lacs, made his way to Rainy Lake, and by way of Rainy River reached the Lake of the Woods. Zacharie Robutel de La Noüe in 1717 followed De Noyon's route as far as Rainy Lake.

La Vérendrye was the first to use the afterwards famous Grand Portage route from Lake Superior. He or his sons were probably the first white men to look upon the waters of Lake Winnipeg, Lake Winnipegosis, Lake Manitoba, Winnipeg River, Red River, the Assiniboine, and the Saskatchewan. He built trading posts on Rainy Lake, the Lake of the Woods, Winnipeg River, Red River, the Assiniboine, Lake Manitoba, and the Saskatchewan; visited and described the Mandan Indians on the Missouri; and two of his sons finally reached an outlying spur of the Rocky Mountains in the Yellowstone country. La Vérendrye's dream had been to find a practicable route overland to the Pacific, but all his efforts were clogged by lack of support or opposition in the east. With reasonable backing he might have succeeded, but that was never forthcoming. Finally he was recalled by the Governor, and Jacques Repentigny Legardeur de Saint-Pierre sent out to complete his work. Saint-Pierre achieved nothing himself, but his lieutenant, De Niverville, in 1751, pushed his way up the Saskatchewan and built a post somewhere on the south branch, possibly in what is to-day the Province of Alberta.

Bibliography: Burpee, *Search for the Western Sea*, and *Pathfinders of the Great Plains*; Laut, *Pathfinders of the West*; Parkman, *Frontenac*; Colby, *Canadian Types of the Old Régime*.

ROUTES OF HEARNE, MACKENZIE, FRANKLIN, AND BACK

MAP No. 21

SAMUEL HEARNE (1745-92), an employee of the Hudson's Bay Company, after two abortive attempts, left Prince of Wales Fort in December 1770 on an overland journey to the mouth of the Coppermine. His route outward was by way of Nueltin Lake, crossing Kazan and Dubawnt Rivers, Clinton-Golden Lake, and thence north-west across the Barren Lands to the Coppermine.

Returning, he travelled south on the east side of the Coppermine and west of Lake Mackay to Great Slave Lake, and then turned east through country much of which has never been explored since his day to the Dubawnt and Kazan, reaching Prince of Wales Fort in June 1772. Two years later he built Cumberland House on the Saskatchewan. In 1775 he became Governor of Prince of Wales Fort, and was in charge when it was captured by Admiral La Perouse in 1782.

Alexander Mackenzie (1755-1820), an officer of the North West Company, left Fort Chipewyan, on Lake Athabaska, June 1789, and by way of Slave River and Great Slave Lake reached the river which afterward bore his name, and which he descended to its mouth, returning to Chipewyan in September of the same year. He had expected that it would lead him to the Pacific, and was correspondingly disappointed when he found that it emptied into the Arctic. His farthest point north was Whale Island, in the mouth of the Mackenzie, where he noted the rise and fall of the tide.

Sir John Franklin (1786-1847) led an overland expedition in 1819-22 from York Factory by way of the Hayes route, the Saskatchewan, Lake Athabaska, Great Slave Lake, and the Yellowknife River to the Coppermine. He wintered at Fort Enterprise, and descending the Coppermine in the spring of 1821, explored the Arctic coast eastward to Kent Peninsula, and made his way back to Fort Enterprise, he and his men narrowly escaping death by starvation.

Three years later he returned to the far north, wintered on Great Bear Lake, where he built Fort Franklin, and in the spring of 1826 descended the Mackenzie to the delta. Here he turned west and explored the coast to Gwydyr Bay near Point Beechey, while Richardson turned east and completed the gap between the mouth of the Mackenzie and the mouth of the Coppermine. His last voyage will be dealt with in connection with the map of Arctic exploration.

George Back (1796-1878), who had accompanied Franklin on both his overland expeditions, went out in 1833 to ascertain the fate of Captain Ross, the Arctic explorer. In August he reached Great Slave Lake, and from its eastern end ascended a small stream to Cook Lake, thence to Walmsley Lake and Artillery Lake. He followed Lockhart River to Clinton-Colden Lake and Aylmer Lake, and portaged over to Sussex Lake, the source of what is now known as Backs River. The following year he descended this river to its mouth, and explored the coast to Point Ogle, the extreme northeastern point of Adelaide Peninsula.

Thomas Simpson and Peter Warren Dease in 1839, John Rae in 1846-47 and 1854, John Richardson in 1848, and James Anderson in 1855, carried on the work of discovery in the far north. Between 1821 and 1855 the northern coast of the continent was explored from Point Barrow in the west to Melville Peninsula in the east. At later dates the Barren Grounds between the Arctic coast and Great Slave Lake were partly explored by the Tyrrells, Warburton Pike, and Hanbury.

Bibliography: Burpee, *Search for the Western Sea*; Leacock, *Adventurers of the Far North*; White, *Atlas of Canada*.

ARCTIC EXPLORATION

MAP No. 22

IN previous notes brief particulars have been given of the various overland expeditions to the Arctic coast of

Canada, and east and west along that coast; and of the exploration of Hudson Bay. It now remains to describe with equal brevity the exploration of the Arctic Islands of Canada as set forth on Map No. 22.

Ross explored the Gulf of Boothia in 1829. In 1845 Franklin sailed from England to make discoveries in the north. His ships had to be abandoned, and he and his men perished in a desperate attempt to reach one of the remote northern posts of the Hudson's Bay Company. After having discovered the North-West Passage the *Erebus* and *Terror* were abandoned off the east point of Victoria Island. McClure sailed into the Arctic through Bering Straits in 1850, and explored Banks Island; Rae explored the southern part of Victoria Island in 1851; McClintock reached Prince Patrick Island in 1853; Parry had been on Melville Island in 1819; Inglefield in 1852, and Greely in 1882, had been on the east coast of Ellesmere Island, and in 1902 Sverdrup explored its west coast; between 1903 and 1906 Amundsen sailed west from Baffin Bay to Bering Strait, the first man to make the North-West passage. Peary in 1909 made his way over the ice to the Pole.

Bibliography: Greely, *True Tales of Arctic Heroism;* Markham, *Life of Sir John Franklin;* Smith, *Arctic Explorations from British and Foreign Shores.*

PACIFIC COAST EXPLORATION

Map No. 23

Captain James Cook (1728–79) in 1778 explored the Pacific coast from the mouth of the Columbia up to and through Bering Straits. In 1792 and 1793 George Vancouver (1758–98) surveyed the coast from California north to Alaska, including many of the channels and islands. Robert Gray (1755–1806) entered the mouth of the Columbia River in 1792. The Spanish navigators, Perez and Quadra, had sailed as far north as Queen Charlotte Islands in 1774 and 1775; and the Russians, Bering and Chirikof, had visited the coast or islands from Prince of Wales Island to Kodiak Island in 1741. Their efforts, like those of Cabot, Frobisher, Hudson, and other navigators on the Atlantic side, were largely directed to the discovery of a sea passage through the continent, although the Russians, Captain Gray, and some others who contributed to the cause of exploration, were mainly interested in the sea-otter trade. The net result of their discoveries was to disclose the outlines of the west coast of the continent. See also Note on Oregon Boundary, p. 29.

See Laut, *Vikings of the Pacific;* Besant, *Captain Cook;* Coats and Gosnell, *Sir James Douglas;* Denton, *Far West Coast.*

EXPLORATION OF ROCKY MOUNTAIN REGION

Map No. 24

Alexander Mackenzie, whose memorable journey to the mouth of the Mackenzie River has been briefly described in an earlier note, left Fort Chipewyan in October 1792, and wintered on Peace River east of the mountains. The following spring he followed the Peace through the mountains, ascended the Parsnip to its source, portaged over to the Fraser, up the Blackwater, and finally down the Bella Coola to the sea. On a rock in North Bentinck Arm he painted this inscription: *Alexander Mackenzie from Canada by land, the twenty-second of July, one thousand seven hundred and ninety-three.* Lat. 52° 20′ 48″ N. He arrived back at Fort Chipewyan in August 1793, and was subsequently knighted for his services to the cause of exploration.

David Thompson (1770–1857), who had served the Hudson's Bay Company from 1784 to 1797, left them and joined the North West Company in the latter year, and remained in their service until 1812. During that period he carried out most elaborate and accurate explorations and surveys throughout the region between Lake Superior and the Rockies. He first crossed the mountains by Howse Pass in 1807, and in the next four years surveyed the entire system of the Columbia from source to mouth, including the Kootenay.

Simon Fraser (1776–1862) joined the North West Company in 1792. In 1805 he was sent over the mountains to establish trading posts in what was then called New Caledonia, now British Columbia. In May 1808 he left Fort George with John Stuart and a party of men to descend the river that has since borne his name. After almost incredible difficulties he finally reached its mouth, and eventually made his way back to Fort George.

Bibliography: Leacock, *Adventurers of the Far North;* Laut, *Pioneers of the Pacific Coast.*

III.—WAR MAPS AND PLANS

While wars and battles are no longer regarded as the most vital features of a nation's history, they must still be studied as an important part of that history. Compared to the Great War, the earlier conflicts in which Canada was engaged seem comparatively trivial, but they all had a distinct, and sometimes a very serious, bearing upon the development of the country.

Maps Nos. 25, 27–29, and 31–41, picture the wars, rebellions, battles, and sieges that are found in the fabric of Canadian history from 1756 to 1865.

SEVEN YEARS' WAR IN AMERICA

Map No. 25

The Seven Years' War (1756–63), in its larger aspects a struggle between Frederick the Great and England on one side, and Austria, France, Russia, Poland, and Sweden on the other, had consequences in America that were momentous. It was itself in a sense part of a greater and more extended struggle. As William Wood has said: " The fight for Canada is the most justly famous episode of the Seven Years' War, which, in its turn, is the central phase of the Great Imperial War between France and England, that lasted from 1688 to 1815, and decided the oversea dominion of the world."

After years of desultory fighting and intrigue between the French in New France and the English in New England, the latter, unable to agree among themselves on any scheme of attack or defence, appealed to the home country for help. Braddock came out in 1755, and was soundly beaten by the French and their Indian allies on the Monongahela, on his way to attack Fort Duquesne at the Forks of the Ohio, where the city of Pittsburgh stands to-day.

Meanwhile in Acadia the English had captured Fort Beausejour, and carried out the expulsion of the Acadians. On Lake George the French, under Dieskau, were beaten by the New Englanders under Johnson. In 1756 Montcalm took command, captured Oswego, and retrieved the defeat of Dieskau by defeating Webb and capturing Fort William Henry.

Two years later the tide turned. Wolfe captured Louisbourg, and although Montcalm defeated Abercromby at Ticonderoga, Fort Frontenac fell to Bradstreet and Duquesne to Forbes. As Parkman says, " The centre of the French had held its own triumphantly at Ticonderoga, but their left had been forced back by the capture of Louisbourg, and their right by that of Fort Duquesne, while their entire right wing had been wellnigh cut off by the destruction of Fort Frontenac." The end came in 1759 with the capture of Ticonderoga, Crown Point and Niagara, Wolfe's brilliant victory on the Plains of Abraham, and the capitulation of Montreal in 1760.

The main map shows the general theatre of the Seven Years' War in America—New France from Quebec to Michilimackinac, Acadia, and the British Colonies from Fort William Henry to Norfolk, Virginia. The inset is designed to show in greater detail the debatable ground about Lake Champlain, where so much of the long conflict centred; and to make more clear the vital importance of the two great natural thoroughfares between New France and New England, by way of Lake Champlain and the Mohawk River respectively.

It is significant that the Indian name for Lake Champlain was *Caniad-eri-Guarunte*, meaning the mouth or door of the country. This detail illustrates the Indian's sense of strategy, which the map so strikingly confirms. One sees at a glance how inevitable it was that the early invading forces should have come either up the St. Lawrence, or up the Hudson–Champlain corridor. As trade and settlement moved west the Mohawk route became more useful, however, diminishing the importance of the two main lines of approach, St. Lawrence and Hudson.

Fort de la Présentation on upper St. Lawrence was also known as Fort Lévis.

Bibliography: Parkman, *Half Century of Conflict*, and *Montcalm and Wolfe*; Wood, *Fight for Canada*; Bradley, *Fight with France for North America*; Wood, *The Winning of Canada*; Fiske, *New France and New England*.

THE REVOLUTIONARY WAR AND CANADA

MAP No. 25

MAP No. 25 (Inset), illustrating the Seven Years' War, incidentally serves to throw light upon the Revolutionary War in so far as it affected Canada. One of the early incidents of that war was the invasion of Canada in 1775-76. Ticonderoga and Crown Point, each garrisoned by but a handful of men, were surprised and captured, and Montgomery led an expedition north into Canada. Chambly and St. Johns fell, and Montreal followed.

Meanwhile Arnold had led a small force by way of the Kennebec against Quebec. Montgomery joined him there from Montreal. The combined force amounted to 2,000 men. Carleton, in the citadel, had a nondescript following of 1,600 or 1,800. With these he had no difficulty in defending Quebec. On the last day of the year an attempt was made to storm the town. The invaders were crushingly defeated and Montgomery killed. Arnold retreated to Sorel and Montreal, and before the end of June 1776 had again crossed the boundary, and the invasion was at an end.

Throughout the remainder of the Revolutionary War, Canada was the base for military expeditions and raids against different parts of the Colonies to the south. Threats of another invasion were made from time to time, but never materialized.

An aftermath of this war was the exodus of the United Empire Loyalists to Canada.

Bibliography: Lucas, *History of Canada, 1673-1812*.

SIEGE OF LOUISBOURG, 1758

MAP No. 27

THE fortress of Louisbourg, it may be noted at the outset, was begun in 1709, and took many years to complete, at a cost of 30,000,000 livres. It was named after Louis XIV. The fortress was captured by the British under Pepperell and Warren in 1745, ceded back to France by the Treaty of Aix-la-Chapelle, and again captured by the British under Amherst, Wolfe, and Boscawen in 1758.

The British fleet appeared off Louisbourg on 2nd June of that year. Stormy weather prevented a landing until the 8th, when a detachment under Wolfe succeeded in getting ashore in spite of stiff opposition. The landing was at Flat Point, Gabarus Bay. Some days later Wolfe, with 1,200 men, made his way around the harbour, captured the battery on Lighthouse Point, opened fire on the island battery, and with the aid of guns along the shore silenced it.

A reference to the map will make it clear that the main defence of Louisbourg was the rampart that extended across the base of the tongue of land known as Rochefort Point. Towards these defences Amherst gradually extended his trenches. Meanwhile, to prevent Boscawen from getting into the harbour, the French commander, Drucour, had sunk six vessels at the entrance.

Day by day the lines of trenches were pushed ever nearer the walls. On the 22nd a shell fell through the roof of the citadel and set it on fire. The next night the barracks were consumed. Many of the houses in the town followed. Finally Drucour, realizing the desperateness of his position, agreed to capitulate. Five thousand six hundred officers, soldiers, and sailors became prisoners of war. Amherst had 11,000 men under his command.

The map is reproduced from a large and beautifully executed manuscript map, unsigned, in the Public Archives at Ottawa, with an extraordinary wealth of detail, much of which it has been of course impossible to reproduce on the present very much reduced scale.

The following notes are on the margin of the original map:

PLAN of the *SIEGE* of *LOUISBURG* in 1758, carry'd on by the British Army commanded by his Excellency Major-General Amherst, and the Fleet commanded by Admiral Boscawen. The Place capitulated the 26th July, a month after breaking Ground. N.B.—The works of the Besiegers are colour'd yellow, and those of the Besieged blue.

REFERENCES vid. Journal

Landing on the 8th of June—

(a) First landing-place being that of the lefte Division, commanded by Brigadier Wolfe. This Division attack'd the Enemies' left Flank, and after a short skirmish beat them off. (b) Landing-place of the other two Divisions, preferable to the first as there was no opposition. (c)

NOTES ON THE MAPS

The first forming of our Troops to go in pursuit of the Enemy. (d) Our Troops halted, having been for some time stopp'd by the Fire of our own shipping. The red Dots mark our Pursuit, and the blue the Enemies' Retreat.

ENEMIES' WORKS to oppose the Landing

The Intrenchments from (e) to (f) contain'd 1 24-pounder, 4 6-pounders, and 3 1-pounder swivels. This post, call'd Fresh Water cove or Ance de la grande cormorandière, was commanded by Monsr. St. Julien, colonel, with 1,200 Men. The Works from (g) to (h) contain'd 2 12-pounders, 2 6-pounders, 2 swivels, 1 8-inch and 1-inch Mortar. This post, call'd Flat point, was commanded by Monsr. Marin, Lieutenant-colonel, with 800 men. The works from (i) to (k) contain'd 2 24-pounders, 2 12-pounders, & 4 6-pounders. This post, call'd white point, was commanded by Lieut.-colonel Antoné with 700 Men. Cap Noir, or black-rock, contain'd at (l) 2 24-pounders and at (m) 2 12-pounders. Rochfort point contain'd at (n) 2 12-pounders, at (o) 12 36-pounders. These two posts were relieved daily from the Town. The Lighthouse point, to the eastward, contain'd at (p) 3 12-pounders, at (q) 4 6-pounders, at (r) 1 6-pounder, and at (s) 2 6-pounders. These Works were abandoned immediately after we landed.

ENCAMPMENT of the *BESIEGERS*

The Encampments are number'd with the proper Numbers of the Battalions, or letter'd with innitials, where they have no numbers. (t) A Redoubt guarded by Marines to cover the landing of the Boats at fresh water Cove. (u) Redoubts and Flèches to cover the rear of our camp. (v) Blockhouses to cover our left Flank and rear. (w) Right Redoubt. (x) Center Redoubt. (y) Left Redoubt. (z) advanced Redoubt. These Redoubts were made to hinder the Besieged from reconnoitring our Camp, and to cover the Communications to our advanced Works, and Roads made by the Besiegers for transporting their Cannon and Stores.

WORKS of the *BESIEGERS* for carrying on the Siege

(A) Lodgement on green hill begun the 26th of June. (B) Epaulment to cover the road to the said Lodgement from the Fire of the Arethusa Frigate. (C) Brigadier's post begun the 2nd of July. (D) The first Parallel begun on the 4th July and compleated with the Redoubts (E) on the 14th. (F) Parallel on the left begun the 16th at night near the Barrachois, and carryed to the hill (G), the 22nd at night. (H) Communication from the right to the left parallel begun the 19th at night. (I) Branch of the Approaches begun the 22nd at night. (K) Branch begun the 24th. (L) Branch begun the 25th at night. (M) Battery of 4 6-pounders against Cap noir open'd the 16th. (N) Battery of 5 24-pounders, finish'd the 25th, but never fired, the Enemy having capitulated. (O) Two Batteries, one of 8, the other of 6 24-poundares, open'd the 22nd. (P) Battery of 1 13-inch, 2 10-inch, and 4 8-inch Mortars, open'd likewise the 22nd. (Q) Battery of 4 24-pounders and 1 8-inch Howitzer open'd the 26th in the morning. (R) Battery of 4 24-pounders, open'd the 24th. (S) Kettle of Mortars consisting of 2 8-inch, 5 Royals, and 12 Cohorns, open'd the 22nd at night and advanced to the 23rd.

WORKS erected round the Harbour, from the Lighthouse to the Barrachois, by Brigadier-General Wolfe.

1. Lighthouse Battery against the Island Battery. Town and Rochfort Point of 4 24-pounders and 4 32-pounders first open'd the 6th of June with 5 24-pounders only. 2. Batteries against the Shipping, open'd occasionally as the Ships moved. 3. Grenadier Redoubt made the first of July. 4. A Flèche with 1 6-pounder for scouring the Ground round the Barrachois. 5. Battery of 2 13-inch Mortars open'd the 6th of July. 6. Battery of 4 32-pounders and 2 24-pounders open'd 15th July. 7. Redoubt Battery of 2 24-pounders. 8. Battery of 2 24-pounders; both this and the former play'd against the Dauphin's Bastion and Cavalier. 9. Kettle of 5 royal and 12 cohorn Mortars against the Arethusa Frigate. 10. Redoubt to secure the Flanks of the Batteries.

THE TOWN and *WORKS* of the Besieged

11. Dauphin's Bastion. 12. King's Bastion or Citadel. 13. Queen's Bastion. 14. Princess's Bastion. 15. Loopholed curtain. 16. Bastion Bruillard. 17. Maurepas gate and Bastion. 18. Battery la Grave. 19. Raveline unfinished. 20. Tenaille unfinish'd. 21. Intrenchment to secure the post of Cap noir. 22. Breastworks to cover small Parties, advanced to retard the Siege.

Bibliography: Parkman, *Montcalm and Wolfe* (chap. xix.); Wood, *Logs of the Conquest of Canada*, and *The Great Fortress*; McLennan, *Louisbourg*; Bourinot, *Cape Breton*; and on the siege of 1745, Parkman, *Half Century of Conflict* (chaps. xix. and xx.); and Archibald, *First Siege of Louisbourg*, in Transactions, Royal Society of Canada, 1887.

SIEGE OF QUEBEC, 1759

MAP NO. 28

THE city of Quebec, founded by Champlain in 1608, was subjected to siege on several occasions. In 1629 David Kirke appeared before the town with a small fleet and captured the fort. In 1690 Sir William Phipps, with a much larger fleet, made an unsuccessful attempt. Then there was the great siege of 1759, and in the following year, after the Battle of Ste. Foy, Murray defended the fortress against Lévis. Finally, in 1775-76, Montgomery and Arnold made an unsuccessful attempt to capture Quebec.

This map, prepared by Arthur G. Doughty, illustrates the siege of 1759, and the Battle of the Plains of Abraham. Wolfe sailed from Louisbourg with an army of about 9,000 men. The fleet, under Saunders, consisted of ships of the line, frigates, sloops, and transports. Before the end of June they were all anchored off the Island of Orleans, a few miles below Quebec.

Meanwhile Montcalm had posted his army of 16,000 men along the banks of the St. Lawrence between the St. Charles and the Montmorency. Wolfe seized the heights of Lévis, planted batteries and bombarded the city. About the end of July he made a direct attack on the French position, but was driven back with heavy loss. Quebec seemed to be impregnable. Week after week passed, plan after plan was considered and rejected.

Finally, Wolfe conceived the seemingly desperate idea of scaling the heights immediately above the city, at what is now known as Wolfe's Cove. The attempt was made on the night of 12th September, and was completely successful. Before morning an English army of 3,500 men was drawn up on the Plains of Abraham, and it was so placed that it was securely out of the line of fire of the guns of the citadel.

Montcalm, on discovering the situation, hastily ordered the regiments on the Beauport side to meet the attack. Here, as always, he was thwarted by the stupid jealousy of the Governor Vaudreuil, who held back several

NOTES ON THE MAPS

thousands of the troops, while Ramesay, who commanded the garrison, sent him only three field-pieces when he asked for twenty-five. The two armies were about equal in numbers, and also in artillery, as Wolfe had only managed to drag up two field-pieces.

Montcalm, after consulting his officers, decided on an immediate attack. The French came on rapidly, firing as they advanced. Wolfe ordered his men to reserve their fire until the enemy was within forty paces, when they poured in a deadly stream of bullets. The French were thrown into hopeless confusion, and began to retreat. Wolfe gave the order to charge and himself led the way. Twice he was hit, and a third shot lodged in his breast. As he lay dying some one cried, "They run!" "Who run?" he asked. "The enemy, sir. They give way everywhere!" He turned on his side and murmured, "Now, God be praised, I will die in peace."

Montcalm received a fatal wound as he retreated with his men toward the St. Louis Gate. As he entered the town, supported by two of his men, with blood streaming from his wound, the women cried, "O mon Dieu! le Marquis est tué!" "Ce n'est rien," he replied, "ne vous affligez pas pour moi, mes bonnes amies." Vaudreuil in a panic abandoned Quebec to its fate and retreated to Jacques Cartier. There he was met by Lévis, who persuaded him to lead his men back to Quebec. They found, however, that on the 17th Ramesay had surrendered the town to Townshend.

KEY TO NUMERICAL REFERENCES ON MAP NO. 28

The Battle of Ste. Foy, April 28, 1760

① Ten companies of French Grenadiers sent forward early on the morning of the 28th April to watch the movements of the British and to seize advantageous posts. Upon the advance of the British they retired. Six companies of the Grenadiers then went round to the Ste. Foy road, where they took possession of Dumont's house and mill.

② First forming of the British troops, two deep, with 120 volunteers on right, and a company of Rangers on left, slightly in advance of the main body. The regiments formed in the following order, beginning at the Ste. Foy road: Part of 28th; 15th Regt.; 35th Regt.; 43rd Regt.; 2nd Bat. Royal Americans; 47th Regt.; 3rd Bat. Royal Americans; part of 28th.

③ Second position of British troops after the action began. The 35th Regt. and the 2nd Bat. R.A. were dropped from the line to form the reserve. The ground in the open was very slippery.

④ First forming of the French line four deep. They got into position while the British were moving from ② to ③.

⑤ Second position of the French, in which they were favoured by the wood on their right and the snow.

⑥ French reserve which advanced with their line.

⑦ Position of the French round Dumont's Mill.

⑧ Works begun by the French on the evening of the 28th, ⓐ battery of 4 guns, ⓑ battery of 6 guns, ⓒ battery of 3 guns, ⓓ 2 mortars. All the batteries were opened between the 10th and 13th of May.

⑨ Blockhouses constructed by the British during the winter of 1759 to prevent surprise. They proved of great service.

⑩ Six mortars to prevent British ships from flanking French camp.

⑪ French provision magazine at Foulon.

⑫ Wolfe's redoubt, built by the British after the Battle of the Plains, which saved many lives during the retreat.

⑬ Barricade of snow barrels set up by the British to protect the works.

The Works on the Island of Orleans

1. Hospital and batteries completed on the 8th of July 1759. The army encamped here from the 3rd to the 8th.
2. The 28th encamped here on the 8th of July.
3. Headquarters on the island of Orleans.
4. Battery to protect North Channel.

The Heights of Abraham

[1] Samos Battery and House.
[2] Verger's Post.
[3] Place where troops were formed after gaining the heights.
[4] Place where Bougainville arrived at 11 o'clock on the morning of the 13th September.
[5] Place where Bougainville appeared at 12 o'clock in rear of British Army.
[6] Coppice in rear of British line.
[7] British line formed at 8 o'clock, consisting of 3,111 men.
[8] The swamp.
[9] French line formed about 9.30.
[10] Position of Wolfe at head of line.
[11] Position of Montcalm at head of line.
[12] Camp on evening of 13th.
[13] Place where Canadians made a stand after the battle on the 13th.
[14] British camp after the 13th.
[15] Place near where Montcalm was wounded on the 13th of September.
♦ Wolfe's Monument.

The Town of Quebec

① Chateau and Fort St. Louis.
② Cathedral.
③ Jesuits' College.
④ Ursuline Convent.
⑤ Hotel Dieu.
⑥ Intendant's Palace.
⑦ Notre Dame de la Victoire.
⑧ St. Louis' Gate.
⑨ St. John's Gate.
⑩ Military Prison.
⑪ Esplanade.
⑫ Palace Gate.

NOTES ON THE MAPS

Batteries in the Town

(A) Cape Diamond
(B) La Glacière
(C) St. Louis
(D) Ste. Ursule } Bastion.
(E) St. John
(F) La Potasse

Redoubts

(G) Redoubt of Cape Diamond.
(H) Redoubt Royal and Barracks.
(I) Dauphiness's Redoubt and Barracks.

Pointe de Levy

1. Batteries at Pointe des Peres to destroy the Lower Town. The shots, indicated by straight lines, fell short and caused great amusement to the French. The guns were replaced by sea mortars, and the shots indicated by curved lines reached the Upper and Lower Town, destroying the principal buildings.
2. Posts of Rangers established to prevent surprise by Indians in rear of camp.
3. Corps of 48th Highlanders to support camp.
4. Advanced post of Major Dalling's Corps.
5. Road to ferry.
6. Lines of Abbatis de Bois for the security of the camp.
7. Forty-third Regiment, in which the Author served.
8. Battery of two guns to protect the ships from the floating batteries.

The Works at Montmorency

1. Lines to protect the regiments run up in three hours by Townshend on July 9, 1759.
2. Batteries to oppose the French works on the opposite side of the river which annoyed the British camp.
3. The Light Infantry commanded by Colonel Howe on a high ground which was occupied by the Indians.
4. Townshend's quarters and barn. The barn was destroyed on leaving the camp in September.
5. Place where Captain Danks's Rangers were attacked by the Indians on the night of the 9th of July, and had so many killed and wounded as to be almost disabled for the rest of the campaign.
6. Repentigny's camp was three-quarters of a mile farther up the river. The exact place cannot be shown on this plan.

Bibliography: Doughty, *The Siege of Quebec and the Battle of the Plains of Abraham*; Parkman, *Montcalm and Wolfe*; Fiske, *New France and New England*; Bradley, *Fight with France for North America*; H. R. Casgrain, *Wolfe-Montcalm*; Wood, *The Passing of New France*, and *The Winning of Canada*; Willson, *Life and Letters of James Wolfe*; Wood, *The Fight for Canada*.

THE ATTACK ON TICONDEROGA, JULY 8, 1758

MAP No. 29

BUILT by Lotbinière in 1755-56 on a point at the southern end of Lake Champlain, Ticonderoga formed the most advanced post of the French toward the English colonies, both for attack and defence.

In June 1758 the British army, under Abercromby and Lord Howe, was gathered at the head of Lake George. Montcalm and his troops were encamped at Ticonderoga. A month later the British, 15,000 regulars and provincials, set out to attack Ticonderoga. They travelled up Lake George in a fleet of batteaux and whaleboats, landed at the northern end of the lake, and marched through the forest on the west side of the little stream that connects the two lakes. In a skirmish with an advanced body of French, the gallant Howe, the brains of the army, was killed, and the incompetent Abercromby was left in sole command. Wolfe described Howe as "the noblest Englishman that has appeared in my time, and the best soldier in the army.". His loss at this juncture was irreparable.

Montcalm had constructed a formidable defence in the shape of a massive breastwork of trees along the summit of a ridge that crossed the peninsula about half a mile in front of the fort. To musketry attack the position was practically impregnable. The breastwork could have been battered down by artillery, or, by sending part of the army north to the narrows of Lake Champlain, Abercromby might have cut Montcalm's line of communications and starved him into submission, but fortunately for the French he decided to carry the breastwork by assault. Regiment after regiment was hurled against the abattis, only to be mowed down as they struggled through the mass of sharpened branches that lay in front of it. Finally Abercromby abandoned the attempt and retreated in disorder, having lost nearly 2,000 men in killed and wounded, more than half as many as made up Montcalm's entire army. A very good account of the engagement will be found in Parkman's *Montcalm and Wolfe* (chap. xx.). See also Casgrain, *Wolfe-Montcalm*, (chap. v.); Fiske, *New France and New England* (chap. ix.); Wood, *The Passing of New France*.

Ticonderoga was finally captured by Amherst in 1759. See Parkman, *Montcalm and Wolfe* (chap. xxvi.).

SEAT OF WAR, 1812-14

MAP No. 31

THIS map shows the general field of operations along the frontier. As Colonel Wood has said, it was "a sprawling and sporadic war." Without considering such incidents as the capture of Washington, the Battle of New Orleans, and the various naval engagements on the high seas, which lay altogether outside the Canadian side of the war, its theatre stretched from Lake Champlain and Chateauguay in the east to Michilimackinac in the west. And it was equally sporadic in place and in time.

The bulk of the fighting took place in what is now Ontario, and was then Upper Canada, and Upper Canada then possessed altogether less than 100,000 people. Five times as many of the enemy were actually enlisted for service in this war. But the vast bulk of them were raw militia, while a very considerable percentage of the forces on the Canadian side were trained soldiers.

For that reason, and because the Canadians had the double inspiration of Brock's genius and the consciousness that they were fighting to defend their own homes,

NOTES ON THE MAPS

the United States forces were not merely disappointed in their confident expectation that, as Jefferson put it, "the acquisition of Canada . . . will be a mere matter of marching," but lost most of the land engagements. On the other hand, their superiority in equipment and training on the lakes gave them the victory in naval engagements.

The principal engagements of 1812 were the capture of Detroit and the battle of Queenston Heights; of 1813, the battles of Beaver Dams, Crysler's Farm, and Chateauguay, and the naval fight on Lake Erie; and of 1814, the battle of Lundy's Lane and the naval engagement of Plattsburg.

The figures in red on the map represent what are regarded as British victories; those in blue, American victories. Red: (1) Michilimackinac, July 17, 1812; (2) Detroit, August 16, 1812; (3) Queenston, October 13, 1812; (4) Frenchtown, January 22, 1813; (5) Ogdensburg, February 22, 1813; (6) Stoney Creek, June 6, 1813; (7) Beaver Dams, June 24, 1813; (8) Chateauguay, October 26, 1813; (9) Crysler's Farm, November 11, 1813; (10) Fort Niagara, December 19. 1813; (11) Black Rock, December 30, 1813; (12) La Colle, March 30, 1814; (13) Oswego, May 6, 1814; (14) Lundy's Lane, July 25, 1814; (15) Michilimackinac, August 4, 1814. Blue: (1) York, April 27, 1813; (2) Fort George, May 27, 1813; (3) Sackett's Harbour, May 29, 1813; (4) Fort Stephenson, August 2, 1813; (5) Lake Erie, September 10, 1813; (6) The Thames, October 5, 1813; (7) Fort Erie, July 3, 1814; (8) Chippawa, July 5, 1814; (9) Fort Erie, August 15, 1814; (10) Plattsburg, September 11, 1814. See William Wood, *The War with the United States*.

Bibliography: Lucas, *Canadian War of 1812*; Wood, *War with the United States*; Hannay, *History of the War of 1812*; Roosevelt, *Naval War of 1812*; Mahan, *Sea Power in its Relations to the War of 1812*.

THE NIAGARA PENINSULA, 1812-14

MAP No. 32

IN the war of 1812-14 most of the fighting was concentrated in the neck of land between Lake Erie and Lake Ontario, although the object of the Americans from first to last was to reach Montreal. If there had been no Brock at the outset, and any real leadership on the United States side, the Niagara frontier would probably have been an almost negligible factor in the situation. As it was, Brock, by capturing Detroit in August 1812, forced the issue. The United States naval victory on Lake Erie in September 1813 tended further to narrow the field of conflict. From the Battle of Queenston Heights to the hard-fought field of Lundy's Lane, nearly all the desperate fighting of the war was confined to this narrow peninsula. Between these two major engagements the tide of battle swayed back and forth —Fort George, Stoney Creek, Beaver Dams, Fort Niagara, Black Rock, Chippawa, and Fort Erie.

Bibliography: Lucas, *Canadian War of 1812*; Wood, *The War with the United States*.

BATTLE OF QUEENSTON HEIGHTS, OCTOBER 13, 1812

MAP No. 33

IN October 1812 the United States general. Van Rensselaer, had 4,000 troops on his side of the Niagara. Smyth, another American commander, had 2,800 more above the Falls. Brock's forces amounted to 1,700 men. Van Rensselaer had planned a combined attack against Fort George and Queenston Heights, but, when Smyth refused to co-operate, changed it to a feint against Fort George and an attack on Queenston Heights. Brock was kept in doubt until the last moment as to where the real attack would materialize. Van Rensselaer concentrated his force at Lewiston, and himself led the advance guard, which landed at Queenston early in the morning of 13th October. The rest of his 4,000 were to cross over as soon as practicable.

Van Rensselaer was badly wounded as they attempted to climb the steep bank, and the command devolved upon Captain Wool, who left 300 to guard the landing and led an equal number by a difficult path to the Heights. Meanwhile Brock at Fort George had got word of the attack, and rode furiously up the river. Climbing the Heights, he found eight gunners with a single eighteen-pounder attempting to check the enemy at the landing-place. While examining the situation, Wool and his men surprised him, and Brock had just time to order the gun to be spiked and retreat down the hill. He immediately collected 100 men, led them up the Heights, and recaptured the gun. But as he stood there he was shot dead by one of the enemy who had retreated to the woods a few yards away.

For hours the fight raged back and forth about this single gun on the Heights. It was captured and recaptured time and again. Sheaffe, who took command after the death of Brock, came up with reinforcements. Winfield Scott had 1,600 men on the Heights, but a good many of them were raw militia and became panic-stricken, so that when Sheaffe made his final charge they broke and fled. Scott surrendered with nearly 1,000 of his men, having lost 300 in killed and wounded.

Bibliography: Lucas, *Canadian War of 1812*; Wood, *The War with the United States*.

BATTLE OF LUNDY'S LANE, JULY 25, 1814

MAP No. 34

IN July 1814, Sir Gordon Drummond, the British commander-in-chief, had 4,400 men stationed at various points between York (Toronto) and Long Point on Lake Erie. Jacob Brown, the United States general, had about the same force concentrated in and about Buffalo. Brown crossed the Niagara and took Fort Erie. Advancing down the river, he met Riall, Drummond's second-in-command, near Chippawa River, with 2,000. Riall sent 600 men against double the number of American militia and broke them up. He then attacked the regulars with his entire force, the odds being nearly the same against him, and was forced to retreat. Brown continued his triumphant way down the river, hoping by a combination with Chauncey's squadron on Lake Ontario to crush Drummond. That plan fell through, and he concentrated his army at Chippawa, intending to march across the peninsula against Burlington.

On 25th July he came in touch with Pearson's advance guard of 1,000 men at Lundy's Lane. Riall was then busy clearing both banks of the lower Niagara, and Drummond was at Fort Niagara. Neither side knew the intentions of the other, but the two main forces, each in furtherance of its own plan, were converging on Lundy's Lane from opposite quarters. When Drummond arrived he placed his seven field-guns on the crest of the rise, and, as at Queenston, the stubbornly fought battle raged around these guns. Brown had 4,000, and Drummond 3,000, but in those actually engaged the odds fluctuated throughout the day, the British being at the outset in superior force. The battery repeatedly changed hands. The fierce conflict continued far into the night. About midnight the enemy retreated, leaving the British masters of the field of Lundy's Lane. The loss had been heavy on both sides, and among the wounded were Drummond and Riall, Brown and Winfield Scott.

Bibliography: Lucas, *Canadian War of 1812*; Wood, *The War with the United States*.

BATTLE OF CRYSLER'S FARM,
NOVEMBER 11, 1813

MAP No. 35

In the plan of campaign of 1813 the United States generals, Hampton and Wilkinson, each with about 7,000 men, were to make Montreal their common objective. Hampton was advancing from the south toward the Chateauguay River, and Wilkinson from the west down the St. Lawrence. They were to join forces at St. Regis, opposite Cornwall. Wilkinson sent 2,000 men across the river under Brown to clear the country down to Cornwall, and followed these with another 2,000 under Boyd. The British, with a greatly inferior force, disputed every inch of the way, manœuvring to delay the advance, while Morrison with another small force, partly on land and partly on the water, harassed the rear of the United States army.

Boyd turned to attack Morrison at Crysler's Farm, a few miles above Cornwall, on 11th November—1,800 Americans against 800 British. Morrison's force was drawn up on fairly open ground, with the river on one flank and woods on the other Boyd attempted to drive a wedge in between the British and the river, but without success, and after a stubborn fight the enemy withdrew. Their loss was 400 men against 200 British.

Boyd joined Wilkinson at Cornwall, and the United States army recrossed the river into their own territory, having achieved nothing.

Bibliography: Lucas, *Canadian War of 1812*; Wood, *The War with the United States*.

BATTLE OF CHATEAUGUAY, OCTOBER 26, 1813

MAP No. 36

As already mentioned in the note on Crysler's Farm, Hampton was advancing down the Chateauguay as part of a combined movement with Wilkinson toward Montreal. With 7,000 men, he naturally expected no serious opposition on the part of the few hundreds that could be mustered to oppose him. But it happened that those hundreds were well-disciplined French-Canadian troops under de Salaberry, a brilliant and experienced officer, while Hampton was a poor leader, and his army not much better than an undisciplined mob.

On October 26, 1813, de Salaberry occupied a position on the north bank of the river, where several small tributaries offered opportunities of effective defence. Macdonell, with another small force, supported him in the rear. The British total was under 1,600, of which only 460 were in the firing line. The odds in the actual fight were about four to one.

De Salaberry faced Hampton on a narrow front, with the river on his left and woods on his right. Hampton, knowing nothing of Macdonell's force, sent Purdy around on the night of the 25th with 1,500 men to cross a ford and attack de Salaberry in the rear. They lost their way in the dark, and in the morning found themselves between the two British forces.

De Salaberry, holding the main force of the enemy in check on his front, wheeled part of his men to the left and attacked Purdy's flank. Macdonell, hidden in the bush, had his buglers sound the advance from different quarters, creating the impression of a considerable force. Purdy's men broke in confusion. Hampton having failed in his frontal attack became discouraged, and the whole unwieldy United States army retired from the field. With Wilkinson's abortive effort on the Canadian side of the St. Lawrence, the ambitious campaign against Montreal came to an inglorious end.

Bibliography: Lucas, *Canadian War of 1812*; Wood, *The War with the United States*.

ATTACK ON YORK (TORONTO), APRIL 27, 1813

MAP No. 37

In 1813 York (now Toronto) was a village of less than 700 people. It was, however, the capital of Upper Canada and the centre of the political life of the Province. At this time the United States had the naval command of Lake Ontario and might at any time attack York, yet Prevost and Sheaffe had made practically no provision for its defence.

On 27th April Chauncey's squadron, with 1,700 United States troops under Dearborn, appeared before the harbour. The enemy landed on the west side of York and advanced toward the village, while at the same time their ships engaged the ill-equipped batteries. Sheaffe had altogether about 600 white men, with a few Indians, to defend the capital. With some of these he attempted to check Dearborn, but was forced to retreat. Abandoning the little town to its fate, he marched his regulars off toward Kingston, leaving the handful of militia to capitulate. During the advance of the Americans the powder magazine blew up, which killed or disabled over 200 of the enemy, including General Pike.

The enemy only held York for a few days and then sailed back to their own side of the lake, first burning the Parliament Buildings with the library and records and carrying off a quantity of public and private property. Sheaffe was relieved of his command in Upper Canada, and his place taken by General de Rottenburg.

Bibliography: Lucas, *Canadian War of 1812*.

BATTLE OF MORAVIANTOWN (THAMES),
OCTOBER 5, 1813

MAP No. 38

The naval battle of Lake Erie on September 10, 1813, in which the United States squadron under Perry had decisively defeated the British squadron under Barclay, had radically changed the military situation, as the enemy now had complete command of Lake Erie with all that that involved. Procter, who commanded the British forces on the Detroit frontier, had nothing to do but fall back. Harrison, the United States general, had at his disposal an overwhelmingly superior force, and was determined to wipe out the disgrace of Hull's surrender in 1812. Procter had plenty of time to withdraw his men and stores from the frontier, but, unable to make up his mind, he postponed action until the last minute, and in the end had to beat a precipitate retreat north to Lake St. Clair and up the River Thames, with the enemy almost on his heels. On 5th October he turned to meet Harrison at Moraviantown. Procter had less than 500 white troops, with a somewhat larger body of Indians under Tecumseh. Harrison's army numbered about 3,500.

As the map will show, Procter held a good position for defence, with the river on his left and a swamp on his right. Tecumseh had posted his braves under cover on the right, and had urged Procter to withdraw his forces gradually, leaving the Indians to attack Harrison's flank and rear. The plan was not carried out, perhaps was impracticable, as Harrison had foreseen and made provision for such a contingency. In any event the British regulars, discouraged by the vacillations of Procter, responded feebly to the attack. The Indians fought better until the brave and resourceful Tecumseh fell, when they too lost heart. Procter fled ignominiously, and Harrison remained victorious.

Bibliography : Lucas, *Canadian War of 1812*.

OPERATIONS ON THE DETROIT RIVER, 1812-13

MAP No. 39

THE Detroit frontier figured from time to time in the operations of the opposing forces throughout a considerable part of the war of 1812-14. At the very outset General Hull, after bombarding the village of Sandwich, crossed the river to the Canadian side and issued a bombastic proclamation to the Canadians. He sent raiding parties inland as far as Moraviantown, but Proctor having reached Amherstburg with reinforcements, Hull withdrew his entire force from the Canadian side of the river. The appearance of Brock on the Detroit frontier and the capture of Detroit are dealt with in another note.

At this period Detroit had about 800 inhabitants, and was protected by a fort. On the same side of the river, but lower down, were the villages of Brownstown and Frenchtown. On the Canadian side was the village of Amherstburg, with Fort Malden, stood opposite Brownstown, and the smaller village of Sandwich was about sixteen miles higher up the river.

The remoteness of the Detroit frontier from the British source of supply made it exceedingly difficult to hold. The water route by Lake Erie was essential, and with the loss of control there after the naval engagement between Perry and Barclay, there was nothing for it but retreat. The battle of Moraviantown followed, and with it the temporary loss of the western part of Upper Canada. The enemy retreated to the frontier, but held the Canadian side of the Detroit River, including Amherstburg, to the end of the war.

Bibliography : Lucas, *Canadian War of 1812*.

CAPTURE OF DETROIT

MAP No. 39

TAKING advantage of the unpreparedness of the United States at the beginning of the war, Brock rushed a small force of regulars and militia, 300 men, to the western frontier and attacked Detroit. Here he was joined by Tecumseh with 1,000 warriors. With the Provincial Marine he mustered 1,500 men. Hull, the United States general, had 2,500, but some of them were absent on detachment and most of them lacked discipline.

The attack was opened by the five-gun battery at Sandwich on August 15, 1812. After dark Tecumseh crossed the river with 600 Indians, to cut off the retreat of Hull's army. Brock followed with 700 men, half regulars and half militia, landing below Detroit early on the morning of the 16th. He had planned to await Hull's attack in the open, but learning that American reinforcements were approaching he at once led his force against Detroit. The fort with its 20-foot walls and thirty-three guns offered a formidable problem, but Hull fell into a panic and ran up the white flag.

The capture of Detroit involved the surrender of Hull's entire army, with large quantities of military stores and provisions, together with the brig *Adams*. The territory of Michigan became for the time being a British possession. The moral effect was even more important. Coming on top of Hull's invasion of Canada and his proclamation to the Canadian people, it put heart into the British cause, brought over those who were wavering, and discouraged the enemy.

Bibliography : Wood, *The War with the United States* ; Lucas, *The Canadian War of 1812*.

REBELLIONS OF 1837-38

MAPS Nos. 62 AND 63

THIS is not the place to enter into either the causes or the consequences of the Rebellions of 1837-38 in Upper and Lower Canada, beyond reminding the student that they were in each case the culmination of long-continued agitation for popular government, and that eventually all the important demands of the agitators were granted. The underlying purpose was in the main praiseworthy, although the means adopted were not. Mackenzie and Papineau, with their followers, resorted to rebellion, and achieved nothing.

Baldwin and La Fontaine (the latter had himself been one of Papineau's followers) by constitutional means gained all that their hot-headed associates had vainly sought. The authorities quite properly refused to grant reforms demanded at the point of the bayonet ; they found it impossible to withstand the pressure of public opinion voiced by the responsible leaders of the people. However, what we are concerned with here is rather the actual incidents of the rebellions, and it will be convenient to consider them separately. They will be understood more clearly by consulting Maps Nos. 62 and 63.

Lower Canada.—Following a riot in Montreal in November 1837, the *Patriotes*, as they were called, rose in arms along the Richelieu. The governor, Sir John Colborne, sent a detachment of troops under Lieut.-Colonel Wetherall to St. Charles, and another under Colonel Gore to St. Denis. A reference to the map will show these two small towns or villages on the Richelieu, not far apart, and approximately north-east of Montreal. Wetherall had about 300 men and a couple of field-pieces ; Gore, about the same number, with two guns and a howitzer.

At St. Denis the rebels had destroyed the bridges, and were helped by the fact that the roads were almost impassable. Gore attacked their position, but finally had to retreat, leaving his howitzer behind.

Wetherall, on the other hand, completely defeated the *Patriotes* at St. Charles. Out of a total of about 1,500 men, they lost between 200 and 300, besides a number taken prisoners. At St. Denis the rebel force had been about 2,000, and their loss 100. The casualties among the troops were inconsiderable.

Wetherall and Gore swept up and down the Richelieu, but met with no further resistance. A party of rebels and American sympathizers crossed the border from Swanton, but were quickly disposed of by the Missisquoi volunteers.

The country south of the St. Lawrence being now pacified, Colborne turned his attention to the district north of Montreal. He himself led a force of 2,000 men against St. Eustache, sending Major Townsend to St. Benoit. Although the rebels were outnumbered, they fought stubbornly at St. Eustache, making their last stand in the church. The loss was appalling. At St. Benoit they surrendered almost without a struggle. Thus ended the campaign of 1837.

Papineau and his lieutenants had already fled to the United States. Wolfred Nelson and several others were captured and exiled to Bermuda. The others were outlawed. Eventually all were pardoned.

The rebellion broke out again in 1838, but was for the most part confined to small raids. More serious engagements took place at Lacolle on the border of Odelltown, at Napierville, and at Beauharnois, but Colborne now had an ample body of troops, and crushed each attempt without difficulty.

Upper Canada.—That the rebellion in Upper Canada was never anything more than a tempest in a teapot was due entirely to the fact that the overwhelming majority of the people of that province preferred to secure reforms by constitutional means, and had no sympathy with the methods of William Lyon Mackenzie. Had it been otherwise the rebels must have won, because the governor, Sir Francis Bond Head, with amazing fatuousness, had sent the only regular regiments in Upper Canada out of the province on the very eve of the rebellion, and as a crowning folly had removed the guard from the stores of arms and ammunition in Toronto.

Mackenzie planned to assemble his followers at Montgomery's Tavern, three miles north of Toronto, march into the city where he expected to be joined by a large number of sympathizers, seize the arms which Head had obligingly left at his disposal, take the governor and his officials into custody, and set up a government of his own.

Disagreement and vacillation among the rebels put off the contemplated movement from day to day, until the news finally leaked out, and when Mackenzie and his followers marched towards the city on the night of December 5, 1837, the militia were ready for them, and the rebels ignominiously fled, leaving their leaders Mackenzie and Lount to fend for themselves.

They made their way back to Montgomery's Tavern, where they prepared to make a stand with a few hundred insurgents. There Colonel Fitzgibbon found them the following day, when he marched out with 1,000 militia, and quickly broke up their feeble efforts at resistance. Mackenzie fled to the United States.

In the London district Dr. Duncombe, one of Mackenzie's supporters, made an attempt to rouse the country, but with indifferent success. Colonel MacNab was sent against him—and Duncombe also fled to the south. So ended 1837.

Rebel enterprises in 1838 were confined to sporadic raids from the American side by sympathizers. Badly organized, and utterly lacking in military leadership, they led to nothing. The most spectacular was the adventure of Navy Island, which ended in the cutting adrift and burning of the rebel vessel the *Caroline* by a party of volunteers under Captain Drew. Raids were also made at Amherstburg, Pelee Island, and Windmill Point near Prescott, but in each case the militia defeated the insurgents and sent them back to their own side of the border.

Bibliography: Burpee, *Lower Canadian Rebellion*, and *Upper Canadian Rebellion* (in *Canada in the Great World War*, vol. i.).

FENIAN RAIDS

Map No. 32

THE Fenian Brotherhood, organized in Ireland and the United States about 1858, attempted in 1866 to express its hatred of England and all things English by invading Canada. The purpose apparently was to conquer the province and annex it to the United States. Elaborate plans were made for the raid, but it proved to be nothing but splutter. The Canadian militia was called out and enjoyed a few days' excitement.

The same year the New Brunswick border was threatened, but that too did nothing more than qualify the members of several New Brunswick regiments for Fenian Raid medals.

In May "General" O'Neil led a party of Fenians across the international border from Buffalo to Fort Erie and marched to Ridgeway, where there was an incipient skirmish, after which O'Neil retreated precipitately to his own side of the boundary.

The following year he led his followers into Quebec, but was once more repulsed.

With perseverance worthy of a better and more promising cause, O'Neil in 1871 moved west and tried yet again on the Red River. The United States, aroused at last to the impropriety of allowing its citizens to invade the territory of a peaceful and friendly neighbour, sent a detachment of troops from Fort Pembina, arrested the valiant O'Neil, and dispersed his followers. A reference to Map No. 32 will make sufficiently clear the scene of these several raids.

The whole series of raids is rather suggestive of comic opera; nevertheless they created much uneasiness and ill-feeling along the international boundary, and put Canada and the Maritime Provinces to a great deal of expense.

It was proposed when the Treaty of 1871 was being negotiated that the United States should compensate Canada for damage and expense caused by the raids. The former, while insisting on settlement of the Alabama claims, declined even to consider her responsibility for the Fenian Raids.

Canada gained incidentally by the raids, because they convinced New Brunswick of the advantages of Confederation, and provided an excellent argument for an effective militia in connection with the new Dominion.

Bibliography: Macdonald, *Troublous Times in Canada*; Burpee, *Fenian and other Raids* (in *Canada in the Great World War*, vol. i.).

RED RIVER EXPEDITION, 1870

Map No. 40

THE outbreak among the half-breeds of Red River was mainly due to "obtuseness on the part of the Canadian Government and its officers." In 1869 the Canadian Government had come to an agreement with the Hudson's Bay Company for the transfer of Rupert's Land, but this agreement had not been officially confirmed by the Imperial Government. Neither the officers of the Company in the west nor the people of the Red River Settlement had been consulted, and to add to the confusion a Lieutenant-Governor had been sent out to organize the new territory, and surveyors to survey the country, before the transfer had been completed.

The ignorant half-breeds suspected that their lands were to be taken away from them, and under the fiery appeals of their leader, Louis Riel, broke out into open rebellion. The Lieutenant-Governor was not permitted to enter the country, and a Provisional Government set up with Riel as President. Donald A. Smith (afterwards Lord Strathcona) was sent out by the Canadian Government to endeavour to settle the difficulty, but his efforts toward a peaceful solution were brought to nought by the madness of Riel in executing a loyal settler named Thomas Scott.

When news of this cold-blooded murder reached the east a wave of indignation swept the country, and the Government immediately took steps to organize an expeditionary force. Under the command of Colonel (afterwards Viscount) Wolseley a mixed force of regulars and militia, about 1,100 men in all, left for the west in May 1870. They travelled by way of the Great Lakes to Prince Arthur's Landing (now Port Arthur), and from there by the old Kaministikwia route, through the very difficult country, much of it a wilderness of rock and muskeg, tangled forests and rock-strewn rivers, that lies between Lake Superior and Red River.

It would be hard to over-estimate the magnitude of the task of transporting a force of this size, with its guns, ammunition, stores, and provisions, through such a country. The route lay up the Kaministikwia River to Shebandowan at the height of land, then through a series of small lakes and streams to Rainy Lake, down Rainy River to the Lake of the Woods, down Winnipeg River with its numerous portages to Lake Winnipeg, and up Red River to Fort Garry.

The route can be readily traced on the map. Wolseley arrived on 24th August, but as the troops marched over the prairie to Fort Garry, Riel and his followers fled precipitately across the bridge over the Assiniboine and made their way south to the international boundary. The rebellion had come to an inglorious end.

While the main purpose of this map is to illustrate the route of Wolseley's expedition for the suppression of the Rebellion of 1869–70, it is also of interest from other points of view. Through this region between Lake Superior and the Red River runs the international boundary, following closely one of the old portage routes of the fur-traders to the Lake of the Woods. The watershed lies comparatively close to Lake Superior, and within a small area one finds the headwaters of three great water systems, streams taking their rise here whose waters discharge ultimately into the Gulf of St. Lawrence, the Gulf of Mexico, and Hudson Bay respectively.

Bibliography : Huyshe, *Red River Expedition ;* Burpee, *Red River Rebellion (Canada in the Great World War,* vol. i.) ; Willson, *Life of Lord Strathcona.*

NORTH SASKATCHEWAN REBELLION, 1885

Map No. 41

The causes of the rebellion that broke out in the valley of the Saskatchewan in the spring of 1885 were very similar to those that brought about the outbreak of 1869–70. The consequences were very different. The leader of the *Métis,* or half-breeds, in 1885 was the same Louis Riel who had been responsible for the rebellion of 1869–70, and who had subsequently been outlawed. He himself was no fighter, and his military lieutenant in 1869–70, Ambroise Lepine, was a mere bully devoid of military knowledge. In 1885, however, he had Gabriel Dumont, a " brave and resourceful leader, skilled in all the arts of Indian warfare, and with a good deal of natural talent for generalship." A very serious element in 1885 was the rising of the Indians under Poundmaker and Great Bear.

The first engagement between the rebels and organized authority was at Duck Lake, a small settlement near Fort Carlton, and about forty miles from Prince Albert. Dumont with a strong party of half-breeds met Major Crozier with a force of 100 mounted police, and compelled him to retire with the loss of 12 men and about 25 wounded. Fort Carlton was abandoned, and Crozier fell back on Prince Albert.

General Middleton, who had been sent out by tne Government, had just reached Winnipeg, and immediately mobilized all the troops there and telegraphed to Ottawa for reinforcements. With the 90th Rifles and a battery of nine-pounders he travelled by rail to Qu'Appelle, and there awaited the eastern troops. The building of the railway, then completed to the mountains, had greatly facilitated the movement of troops, guns, ammunition, and supplies from the east to the scene of operations.

Middleton decided to divide his men into three columns. The main force, under his own command, would march on Batoche, Riel's headquarters. The second, under Lieutenant-Colonel Otter, was to travel by way of Swift Current and the west side of the South Saskatchewan to Clark's Crossing, where it would form a junction with the main column. The third, under Major-General Strange, was to move north from Calgary to Edmonton. The first and second columns were to attack Riel at Batoche, and then proceed separately to Prince Albert and Battleford. They would then march west, join the third column, and dispose of the Indians. At the last moment the plans had to be changed, and Otter marched from Swift Current direct to Battleford.

The movements of the three columns can be conveniently studied with the aid of the map. Middleton himself marched from Qu'Appelle to Clark's Crossing. Here he divided his force of about 820 men, sending half across the South Saskatchewan, and advancing up both banks of the river. On the 24th of April Dumont attempted to ambush him at Fish Creek. The rebel leader had made rifle-pits in a deep ravine, where he also had the advantage of thick cover. The forces were about equal, the troops having the advantage of a couple of batteries, and Dumont of much superior marksmen. In the end Middleton drove most of the rebels out of the ravine, and they retreated to Batoche.

Meanwhile, Otter had advanced to Battleford, where he learned that Poundmaker with his braves was encamped at Cut Knife Hill, about thirty-eight miles from Battleford. Taking with him about 325 men, with two small guns and a Gatling, he managed to surprise Poundmaker at daybreak on May 2nd. The Indians, however, occupied a very strong position, and outnumbered the whites. After several hours' fighting, Otter managed to extricate his men from what had become a dangerous situation. Poundmaker failed to follow up his advantage, and was so discouraged by the daring of Otter's attack that the union of his force with that of Big Bear and their advance to join Riel were abandoned.

On April 20th Strange started for Edmonton. Early in the month Big Bear had attacked an isolated post of the Hudson's Bay Company at Frog Lake, massacred several men, and carried off the women. On the 15th of April he captured and looted Fort Pitt. Strange's task was to round up Big Bear and his war-party. This he did not succeed in doing, but so harried him from place to place that Big Bear had no further opportunity of doing harm.

To return to the main column, on the 9th of May Middleton reached Batoche. Riel's forces were well protected by natural cover and an ingenious system of rifle-pits and entrenchments. The next two days were spent in skirmishing. An attack on the enemy's position on the morning of the 12th failed through a misunderstanding. In the afternoon, however, the militia, grown tired of skirmishing, rushed the village. After a good deal of house-to-house fighting, the rebels were driven out and fled in disorder. Riel escaped, but was captured, and subsequently executed. Dumont fled to the United States. Poundmaker and Big Bear surrendered, were tried, and subsequently pardoned, and the rebellion came to an end.

Altogether some 5,885 men were engaged in the three columns against about the same number of rebels. The expedition cost Canada $5,000,000—the "price of procrastination." The half-breed grievances out of which the insurrection grew were trifling, and might and should have been remedied some time before.

Bibliography: Boulton, *Reminiscences of the North-West Rebellions*; Burpee, *The Saskatchewan Rebellion, 1885 (Canada in the Great War,* vol. i.); Denison, *Soldiering in Canada.*

IV.—POLITICAL DEVELOPMENT

THE series of maps that follow, Nos. 42–60, will be found interesting and instructive. They enable one to understand very clearly, at any rate from one angle, the story of Canada throughout the French and British regimes, the territorial changes brought about by discovery and exploration, and by the various wars between New England and New France, between England and France, and between British Canada and the United States. A factor of considerable importance, as will be seen in the maps from 1673 to Confederation, is the Hudson's Bay Company, with its immense and somewhat vague territory known as Rupert's Land granted to it under its charter. The region coloured red is that part of Rupert's Land acknowledged to be under the jurisdiction of the Company; the part shown in bars represents the additional territory claimed by the Company but not legally recognized.

NORTH AMERICAN COLONIES, 1643

MAP NO. 42

PORT ROYAL was taken by David Kirke in 1628, who also captured Quebec the following year. By the Treaty of St. Germain-en-Laye, 1632, which brought to an end what was known as King Charles's War, Great Britain restored to France the territory bordering on the St. Lawrence known as Canada, as well as Acadia and Cape Breton. Acadia included what are now the provinces of Nova Scotia and New Brunswick. The Penobscot was claimed as the western boundary of Acadia, dividing the English from the French settlements.

Canada at that time had no definite frontiers, but in a general way was bounded on the south by the British colonies; on the west or south-west by the immense region claimed by Spain; and on the north by the country about Hudson Bay, unexplored except along the borders of that great inland sea.

Lakes Huron and Ontario had now been discovered, and to some extent explored, and it is possible that before this date Lake Superior had also been discovered by Brûlé. Erie and Michigan had not been discovered, and nothing was known as to the extent of Superior. Beyond the Great Lakes all was unknown, but the Western Sea was supposed to lie somewhere beyond, though how far was purely a matter of conjecture.

Bibliography: Parkman, *Pioneers in the New World,* and *The Old Régime in Canada;* Dionne, *Champlain;* Colby, *The Founder of New France;* Hannay, *History of Acadia.*

NORTH AMERICAN COLONIES, 1655

MAP NO. 43

BETWEEN 1632 and 1655 Lakes Michigan and Erie had been discovered and partially explored by the French, missionary work had commenced on the south shore of Lake Superior, and a beginning had been made with the exploration of the vast region south and south-west of the Great Lakes. The discovery of the Mississippi was still in the future.

The principal change in territory during this period was in Acadia, where in 1654 the English, under Cromwell's orders, seized the country. For the next thirteen years, Acadia, including the mainland and the islands known to-day as Cape Breton and Prince Edward Island, was to remain under British rule, with Sir Thomas Temple as Governor.

Far to the south, France possessed a strip of coast on the Atlantic between Cape Fear and Spanish Florida, covered for the most part to-day by the States of South Carolina and Georgia. This region had been settled by French Huguenots as early as 1562. Before France could link this southern outlet to the Atlantic with her northern possessions in Canada by the exploration of the Mississippi, French Florida had become absorbed by the British colonies.

In the far north, England had established a claim by discovery to the lands immediately adjacent to Hudson Bay, but had as yet set up no formal claim to the interior. Nevertheless, in default of adverse occupation of any part of the Hudson Bay basin, she had a definite claim to that basin.

Newfoundland had been discovered by the British, and the first British colony dated from 1621. France disputed, and was to dispute for many years, Great Britain's claim to the island. Anticosti and the Magdalen Islands were included in New France.

On the Pacific coast the Spaniards had carried their explorations for some distance up what is now the coast of California.

Bibliography: Hannay, *History of Acadia;* Parkman, *The Old Régime in Canada.*

NORTH AMERICAN COLONIES, 1673

MAP NO. 44

UNDER the terms of the Treaty of Breda, 1667, Charles II. restored Acadia to France. On the other hand, as previously noted, the British colonies absorbed French Florida.

And in the far north England, through the Hudson's Bay Company, had begun to assert her claim to all territory draining into Hudson Bay.

In other respects the map of North America remained practically unchanged.

Bibliography: Hannay, *History of Acadia;* Parkman, *La Salle.*

NORTH AMERICAN COLONIES, 1697

MAP No. 45

BETWEEN 1667 and 1697 considerable territorial and political changes took place. Since the former year Canada had been nominally under the jurisdiction of the Governor of Quebec, but always with a local governor.

In the north, De Troyes, in 1686, captured the forts of the Hudson's Bay Company on the shores of the Bay. They were regained by the British, and in 1697 Iberville once more captured and destroyed the forts.

In the west, Radisson and Chouart, continuing their explorations, wintered among the Sioux in the country south-west of Lake Superior in 1661, and in the following year, it is believed, travelled around the western end of Lake Superior, and by way of Lake Nipigon reached the shores of James Bay. Perrot was on Lake Superior in 1670. Du Lhut also explored the country to the south and west of Lake Superior in 1678, and took possession of the land of the Sioux for France.

It is probable that in an earlier journey in 1658 Radisson reached the upper Mississippi. Ten years later Marquette started a mission on the south side of Lake Superior, and in 1673, with Jolliet, he reached the Mississippi and descended it to the mouth of the Arkansas. Two years earlier St. Lusson, at Sault Ste. Marie, had taken formal possession of the west for Louis XIV. In 1679 La Salle built Fort Crèvecœur on the Illinois River, and in 1692 descended the Mississippi to the Gulf of Mexico. He had been in the Ohio River country in 1669, but the Virginians had anticipated his visit by nearly twenty years.

France had now established a claim by discovery to much of the vast interior of the continent.

In 1689, when William III. became King of England, war broke out again with France and lasted for eight years. Frontenac was then Governor of Canada. In 1690 Sir William Phipps led an expedition from New England, seized and plundered Port Royal, then sailed around into the St. Lawrence, but failed to take Quebec.

The war was ended in 1697 by the Treaty of Ryswick, by which Port Royal and Acadia were restored to the French, and the posts on Hudson Bay restored to Great Britain.

France gained an outlet on the Gulf of Mexico at Mobile Bay and Biloxi, east of the Mississippi, and her claim to the valley of the Mississippi was not seriously disputed by Spain.

Bibliography: Parkman, *Frontenac*; Reed, *First Great Canadian*; Laut, *Pathfinders of the West*.

NORTH AMERICA—TREATY OF UTRECHT, 1713

MAP No. 46

WHAT was known as Queen Anne's War was terminated in 1713 by the Treaty of Utrecht between France and England.

By this treaty France renounced any claims she had to Rupert's Land; and also ceded Acadia to England, as well as what rights she had in Newfoundland, except certain fishing rights on the French shore; but retained Canada, Labrador, Anticosti, Cape Breton, and the Magdalen Islands. In 1710, Nicholson, with an expedition from Boston, had captured Port Royal, changed the name to Annapolis Royal, and taken possession of Acadia.

The boundaries between New France and the British possessions remained unsettled, and became a matter of dispute. France contended that Acadia as ceded to Great Britain was only the peninsula of Nova Scotia, while the latter claimed all the territory now included in Nova Scotia, New Brunswick. and the Gaspé peninsula.

In the interior of the continent French explorers had added the valley of the Mississippi to the territories of France, and the coast of the Gulf of Mexico from the Mississippi to and including Florida was also French. New Spain ran north to latitude 42° and south to the Isthmus of Panama, with the exception of British Honduras.

Bibliography: Parkman, *A Half Century of Conflict*, Fiske, *New England and New France*.

NORTH AMERICA—TREATY OF PARIS, 1763

MAP No. 47

AFTER 1713 France made a determined effort to secure a firm foothold on the vast interior of North America, and by a chain of forts from Louisbourg and Quebec, around by the Great Lakes, the Ohio, and the Mississippi, to New Orleans, endeavoured to confine the British colonies to the region between the Alleghanies and the Atlantic.

The settlement of Biloxi, on the Gulf of Mexico, was founded by Iberville in 1698. In 1711 Louisiana became an independent French colony, with New Orleans as its capital (1722). In 1731 it was created a Royal Province. In 1738 the Governor of New France was also Governor of Louisiana.

The War of the Austrian Succession (1741–48) renewed the struggle in America. Pepperell, with his New Englanders, captured Louisbourg in 1745. but by the Treaty of Aix-la-Chapelle three years later it was restored to France. Cornwallis built Halifax in 1749. The Seven Years' War (1756–63) brought the long struggle to an end.

This map shows the territorial changes in North America effected by the treaty of 1763. In the far north Rupert's Land remained as it was; the British claims to territory on the Arctic coast and in the Arctic archipelago had been considerably extended as the result of the discoveries of British Arctic explorers.

Britain gained the Spanish possessions east of the mouth of the Mississippi, including Florida, which was divided into East and West Florida.

At this date it is interesting to note that the entire eastern half of the continent, from the Gulf of Mexico to the Arctic, was British territory.

France having ceded Louisiana to Spain, the Spanish territories extended from the Mississippi to the Pacific, and, roughly speaking, from a line drawn from the source of the Mississippi to latitude 42° on the Pacific, south to the Isthmus of Panama, with the exception of British Honduras.

In the far north-west the map shows the discoveries of Bering about 1741, and the taking possession of what is now Alaska by Russia.

La Vérendrye and his sons between 1731 and 1744 explored the western country from Lake Superior to Lake Winnipeg, the Red and Assiniboine valleys, the Missouri and Yellowstone country, as well as the Saskatchewan in the north.

Bibliography: Burpee, *Pathfinders of the Great Plains*; Parkman, *Montcalm and Wolfe*.

BRITISH NORTH AMERICA, BY ROYAL PROCLAMATION, 1763

MAP No. 48

By the treaty of 1763, which brought to a conclusion the war between Great Britain and France, and by the Royal Proclamation of the same year, it was provided that the boundaries of Quebec should run from the head of the River St. John, which flows into the north shore of the Gulf of St. Lawrence about opposite the head of Anticosti, south-west to Lake St. John on the Saguenay and to Lake Nipissing, thence more or less parallel to the Ottawa River, and, crossing the St. Lawrence some distance above Montreal, to Lake Champlain, and along the height of land separating the St. Lawrence from the Atlantic, to the Baie des Chaleurs.

The map also shows what is called the "ancient boundary" between Nova Scotia and New England, as well as the more easterly boundary fixed by the treaty of 1763. The treaty of 1763 ceded to Great Britain not only Canada with all its dependencies, but also Nova Scotia or Acadia, Cape Breton, and the islands in the Gulf of St. Lawrence. There remained to France in the northern half of the continent nothing but the small islands of St. Pierre and Miquelon off the coast of Newfoundland.

Bibliography: Parkman, *Montcalm and Wolfe;* Wrong, *The Fall of Canada;* Wood, *The Father of British Canada.*

NORTH AMERICA—QUEBEC ACT, 1774

MAP No. 49

By the Quebec Act of 1774 the boundaries of that province, which had been created out of the old French colony of New France, were defined as extending north to the territories of the Hudson's Bay Company, south to the borders of New England and New York, and west to the Mississippi. The inclusion in Quebec of the area between the Ohio and the Mississippi aroused the indignation of the other British Colonies, as did also the granting of what they considered too generous concessions to the conquered French. This became one of the grievances that led to the American revolution.

Bibliography: Lucas, *History of Canada, 1763–1812;* Bradley, *Lord Dorchester;* Wood, *The Father of British Canada.*

NORTH AMERICA—TREATY OF VERSAILLES, 1783

MAP No. 50

By the Treaty of Versailles, 1783, the independence of the thirteen colonies forming the United States was acknowledged.

The boundary between the United States and the British colonies was to run from the Bay of Fundy up the St. Croix River to its source; then due north to the height of land between the St. Lawrence and the Atlantic; along the height of land to the Connecticut River; down that river to latitude 45°; thence west to the St. Lawrence, and through the Great Lakes and their connecting rivers to the west side of Lake Superior, and by a series of small lakes and rivers to the Lake of the Woods.

From the Lake of the Woods the boundary was to run due west to the Mississippi, which formed the western boundary of the United States down to the Spanish territories along the Gulf of Mexico. It was afterwards discovered that it was physically impossible to run a due west line to the Mississippi, the headwaters of which lay to the south of the Lake of the Woods.

Nova Scotia at this time included all of the mainland east of Chaleur Bay, and the island of Cape Breton, but not Prince Edward Island.

In 1783 the Bahamas Islands were finally conceded to Great Britain.

On the west coast, Captain Cook had made his momentous voyages of 1776–79, and explored the coast from 45° N. up to Icy Cape in Bering Strait.

Bibliography: Lucas, *History of Canada, 1763–1812;* Bradley, *Lord Dorchester;* Wood, *The Father of British Canada;* Laut, *Pioneers of the Pacific Coast.*

BRITISH NORTH AMERICA, 1791

MAP No. 51

The Constitutional Act of 1791 set forth the intention of the king to divide the province of Quebec into Upper and Lower Canada. This was done by Imperial Order in Council of August 24, 1791.

On the conclusion of peace in 1783 and the formal recognition of the United States, a large number of United Empire Loyalists left their old homes and emigrated north to the British colonies of Nova Scotia, New Brunswick, and Quebec. Many of these settled along the upper St. Lawrence and the shores of Lake Ontario and Lake Erie.

One of the principal objects of the Constitutional Act was to give these loyal settlers an opportunity to organize and develop the country west of the Ottawa River along their own lines.

Since 1783 the colony of Nova Scotia had been divided into two, that portion of it on the north side of the Bay of Fundy becoming New Brunswick. Cape Breton had also been made a separate colony in 1784, with Sydney, founded the following year, as its capital.

In the west and north no territorial changes had taken place.

Bibliography: Wallace, *The United Empire Loyalists;* Scott, *John Graves Simcoe;* Lucas, *History of Canada, 1763–1812.*

BRITISH NORTH AMERICA, 1818

MAP No. 52

During the French period a portion of the Labrador coast had formed part of New France. As then understood it extended into the Gulf of St. Lawrence, and was exploited by various proprietors and companies. By the Proclamation of 1763 the Labrador coast was annexed to Newfoundland. By the Quebec Act, 1774, it was reannexed to Quebec. In 1809, by the Labrador Act, the coast was once more annexed to Newfoundland.

Also by the Proclamation of 1763 Anticosti had been annexed to Newfoundland; transferred to Quebec in 1774; and back to Newfoundland in 1809. In 1825, to look forward, Anticosti was finally restored to Lower Canada, as well as that portion of the Labrador coast facing on the Gulf of St. Lawrence.

By the treaty of 1818 with the United States, it was agreed that the international boundary from the northwest angle of the Lake of the Woods should run due south to the 49th parallel, and along that parallel to the Rocky Mountains.

In 1811 the Hudson's Bay Company had granted to the Earl of Selkirk about 116,000 square miles of land in the Red River Valley, included partly in what is today the province of Manitoba and partly in the present states of North Dakota and Minnesota. In 1817 Selkirk made a treaty with the Indians of the Red River for possession of the territory. The following year his rights of course lapsed so far as that part of the country south of the international boundary was concerned. The first Selkirk settlers landed at York Factory and made their way inland to the Red River by way of the Hayes route and Lake Winnipeg. Other groups of settlers followed the same way in the succeeding years.

Since 1770 important explorations had been carried out in the interior of what is now western Canada as well as on the Pacific coast. Samuel Hearne in 1770–72 made a journey from Prince of Wales Fort on Hudson Bay to the mouth of the Coppermine, and back by way of Great Slave Lake. Alexander Mackenzie in 1789 explored the river that bears his name from Great Slave Lake to the Arctic, and in 1793 made his memorable journey overland to the Pacific.

Between 1785 and 1812 David Thompson explored and surveyed an enormous extent of territory between Hudson Bay and the Pacific, including the entire system of the Columbia and Kootenay Rivers. Vancouver, between 1792 and 1794, surveyed the Pacific coast from California to Alaska.

In 1808 Simon Fraser made his trip down the tumultuous Fraser River. Also in 1792 Robert Gray sailed into the mouth of the Columbia; and in 1804–5 Lewis and Clark travelled overland from the Mississippi to the mouth of the Columbia.

The vast territory west of the mountains, although it had been explored to some extent and the North West Company had built a number of trading posts in it, was still debatable land so far as national sovereignty was concerned. Nevertheless these explorations influenced to no small extent the political destiny of the region between the Great Lakes and the Pacific.

Bibliography : Gosling, *Labrador*; Martin, *Selkirk's Work in Canada*; Burpee, *Search for the Western Sea*; Bryce, *Mackenzie, Selkirk, Simpson*; White, *Boundary Disputes and Treaties* (Canada and its Provinces).

BRITISH NORTH AMERICA, 1825

MAP No. 53

IN 1821 the Hudson's Bay Company absorbed its old rival the North West Company, and obtained leases of the vast area extending from Rupert's Land to Russian America and the Pacific.

Although Cook, Vancouver, and other British explorers had covered the Pacific coast from the Columbia northwards, and also to a considerable extent southwards of the Columbia, the region between 42° and 54° 40′, known as the Oregon country, remained in dispute between Great Britain and the United States until the final settlement of the boundary west of the mountains in 1846.

By the treaty of 1825 between Great Britain and Russia the boundary of Alaska was settled. It was the interpretation of the boundary of the long coastal strip, commonly called the Panhandle, and differences of opinion as to the intentions of the treaty, that led to the long controversy between Canada and the United States, which was finally referred to an International Commission and decided in 1903.

Bibliography : Bryce, *The Remarkable History of the Hudson's Bay Company*; White, *Boundary Disputes and Treaties* (Canada and its Provinces).

BRITISH NORTH AMERICA, 1849

MAP No. 54

BY the treaty of 1842 the boundary was settled in the east between the United States and British territories; and by the treaty of 1846 the 49th parallel was agreed upon as the boundary from the Rocky Mountains to the Pacific.

The Hudson's Bay Company in 1838 obtained a further lease of the far western country for twenty-one years; and in view of the boundary having been settled at 49°, the western headquarters of the Hudson's Bay Company were moved from Fort Vancouver on the Columbia to Fort Victoria at the southern end of Vancouver Island.

In the east the old provinces of Upper and Lower Canada had been reunited by the Act of 1840 as the province of Canada.

Bibliography : White, *Boundary Disputes and Treaties* (Canada and its Provinces) ; Bryce, *The Remarkable History of the Hudson's Bay Company*; Shortt, *Lord Sydenham*; MacMechan, *Winning of Popular Government*.

BRITISH NORTH AMERICA, 1866

MAP No. 55

CANADA was now approaching that momentous step in her history, Confederation. What had formerly been Upper Canada had developed into a region of rapidly increasing importance, commercially and politically. The Red River Settlement was also growing apace, after a long period of discouraging conditions. In British Columbia, Vancouver Island had been made a separate colony in 1849, and in 1858, as a result of a gold rush, the mainland was erected into a colony, whose boundaries in that year were fixed in the north as the Skeena River and the Finlay, a branch of the Peace River. In 1866 the boundaries were extended to the 60th parallel.

Bibliography : Colquhoun, *Fathers of Confederation*; Bourinot, *Canada under British Rule*; Parkin, *Sir John Macdonald*; Grant, *History of Canada*.

DOMINION OF CANADA, 1873

MAP No. 56

CONFEDERATION had been in the air for many years as a more or less nebulous project, but in the 'sixties circumstances arose, particularly the American Civil War, which impressed upon the people of the British North American colonies the desirability and almost necessity of uniting for mutual protection. Transport and trade arguments were also driving home the practical advantages of confederation. At the same time the old provincial outlook and provincial prejudices died hard, and union would probably not have been brought about—at any rate not for many years—had it not been for the statesmanship and powers of leadership of such men as John A. Macdonald, Georges E. Cartier, Charles Tupper, and Alexander Galt.

The first definite step toward confederation was taken in 1864, when delegates from the Maritime Provinces met at Charlottetown to discuss the union of the three Maritime Provinces, and were persuaded by delegates from Canada to consider a larger union. They met the same year in Quebec, and drafted the terms of the British North America Act, which in 1867 was passed by the Imperial Parliament and proclaimed in Canada the same year.

It brought into the new Dominion of Canada the three provinces of Canada, Nova Scotia, and New Brunswick. Both Prince Edward Island and Newfoundland had been represented at Quebec, but their legislatures afterwards rejected the union proposals. Prince Edward Island came into the Confederation in 1873.

In the meantime the Dominion had acquired the rights of the Hudson's Bay Company in 1869, and transformed the western part of what had been known as Rupert's

Land, as well as the unorganized region beyond it as far as the Rocky Mountains, into the North-West Territories. In 1870 the old Red River Settlement came into the Dominion as the province of Manitoba; and the following year British Columbia joined the Union. Under the British North America Act what before 1840 had constituted the provinces of Upper Canada and Lower-Canada, and between 1840 and 1867 had been united as the province of Canada, was once more divided as the provinces of Ontario and Quebec.

Bibliography: Colquhoun, *Fathers of Confederation*; Parkin, *Sir John Macdonald*; Longley, *Sir Charles Tupper*; Pope, *Day of Sir John Macdonald*; Boyd, *Sir Georges Etienne Cartier*; Bourinot, *Canada under British Rule*; Grant, *History of Canada*; Skelton, *Sir Alexander Galt*.

DOMINION OF CANADA, 1882

Map No. 57

BETWEEN 1873 and 1882 a long and acrimonious dispute was carried on between Ontario and the Dominion, and more specifically between Sir John A. Macdonald and Sir Oliver Mowat, in regard to the western boundary of Ontario. The situation was complicated by a demand on the part of what was then called the "Postage Stamp" province of Manitoba for enlargement of its territory. The question was not finally settled until 1889, when an Imperial Order in Council was passed fixing the boundary between Ontario and Manitoba.

Meanwhile, in 1881, Manitoba had been considerably enlarged by an Act of the Dominion Parliament. In 1882 the districts of Saskatchewan, Assiniboia, Alberta, and Athabaska were created, occupying the region between Manitoba and British Columbia. The provisional district of Keewatin, with somewhat indefinite boundaries, had been established in 1876, and the remainder of the immense northern region, east and west of Hudson Bay, was known as the North-West Territories.

In 1880 an Imperial Order in Council was passed annexing to the Dominion all British territories in North America, together with the adjacent islands except Newfoundland. This brought into the Dominion the Arctic Islands, in so far as Great Britain could properly claim them.

Bibliography: Bourinot, *Canada under British Rule*; Grant, *History of Canada*; Biggar, *Sir Oliver Mowat*; Parkin, *Sir John Macdonald*; White, *Boundary Disputes and Treaties* (Canada and its Provinces).

DOMINION OF CANADA, 1898

Map No. 58

A COMPARISON of this map with map No. 57 shows substantial additions to the districts of Athabaska and Keewatin, and the carving out of the North-West Territories of the districts of Yukon, Mackenzie, Ungava, and Franklin. The unorganized territories of Canada had now all been transformed into districts. This demands a few words of explanation. The Order in Council of 1882 erected the four districts of Assiniboia, Saskatchewan, Alberta, and Athabaska. In 1895 an Order in Council was passed dividing the remainder of the North-West Territories into the districts of Ungava, Franklin, Mackenzie, and Yukon, and defining their boundaries; and adding about 143,500 square miles to the district of Athabaska. The same Order in Council recommended the addition by Act of Parliament of about 470,000 square miles to the district of Keewatin. The legislation in question was not introduced. In 1897 a further Order in Council was passed cancelling the Order in Council of 1895, as no steps had been taken to carry out its directions, and recommending that legislation should be introduced " to authorize the division of the portions of Canada not comprised within any province into nine provisional districts in accordance with the annexed description and map." That legislation was not introduced, and it would appear therefore that the districts, except in so far as they were authorized by the Order in Council of 1882, had no legal existence. Nevertheless in an Order in Council dated March 16, 1918, making certain changes in the boundaries of Mackenzie, Keewatin, and Franklin, the following language clearly indicates that in the opinion of the Dominion Government the Orders in Council of 1895 and 1897 had the effect of creating and defining the districts mentioned. "Whereas the provisional districts of Assiniboia, Saskatchewan, Alberta, and Athabaska were created by Order in Council of May 8, 1882, for the convenience of settlers and for postal purposes; the provisional districts of Ungava, Franklin, Mackenzie, and Yukon were created by Order in Council of October 2, 1895; and the boundaries of the said districts and of the provisional district of Keewatin were further defined by Order in Council of December 18, 1897." And the adoption of the Order in Council of 1918 indicates that the Dominion authorities were still of the opinion that districts could be created and defined by Order in Council. However this may be, legislation had been resorted to not only in 1905 to create the new provinces of Alberta and Saskatchewan, but also in 1906 to define the boundaries of Mackenzie, Franklin, Yukon, Keewatin, and Ungava.

Bibliography: Grant, *History of Canada*.

DOMINION OF CANADA, 1905

Map No. 59

IN 1898 the boundaries of Quebec were extended on the north to a line running from the Eastmain River to Hamilton Inlet and the Labrador boundary. In 1905 Keewatin was annexed to the North-West Territories. The same year Alberta and Saskatchewan became provinces of the Dominion, embracing territorially what had formerly been the four districts of Athabaska, Alberta, Saskatchewan, and Assiniboia.

Bibliography: Skelton, *Day of Sir Wilfrid Laurier*.

DOMINION OF CANADA, 1920-27

Map No. 60

SINCE 1905 several territorial changes have been made. In 1912 the boundaries of Manitoba were extended north to the sixtieth parallel and to the shores of Hudson Bay; Quebec had about 355,000 square miles added to its territory, including the whole of Ungava to Hudson Strait; and Ontario's boundaries were extended north to Hudson Bay, absorbing the southern portion of the old district of Keewatin.

By Order in Council in 1918, coming into force in January 1920, the three provisional districts of Mackenzie, Keewatin, and Franklin were defined respectively as: Mackenzie, bounded on the west by the Yukon Territory, on the south by the sixtieth parallel, on the east by the second meridian, and on the north by the Arctic Ocean; Keewatin, on the west by the second meridian, on the north by the Arctic coast excluding Boothia and Melville Peninsulas, on the east by the east coast of Hudson Bay, and on the south by the provinces of Ontario and Manitoba; and Franklin, embracing Boothia and Melville Peninsulas, with the Arctic archipelago. For the final settlement of the long-standing dispute over the Labrador boundary, see map and note No. 83.

Bibliography: *Canada Year Book*; *Canadian Annual Review*.

V.—INDUSTRIAL DEVELOPMENT

In the following group of maps, Nos. 61-68, 78 and 79, the industrial development of the country is illustrated; the first three showing the progress of settlement and the development of roads; No. 64 revealing the importance of Canada's extraordinary network of waterways, and at the same time illustrating the development of her earliest industry, the fur trade; Nos. 65-68 showing the growth of transportation facilities, roads, railways, and canals; No. 78 dealing with hydro-electric development, and No. 79 with mineral resources. The extent of Canada's timber resources and agricultural lands is suggested by Map No. 6.

EARLY SETTLEMENTS IN THE MARITIME PROVINCES

Map No. 61

The pioneers of settlement in the Maritime Provinces were the French, known in this part of New France as Acadians. Most of them came out from France between 1632 and 1658. A census taken in 1671 gave a total population of 392. In 1713, when Acadia was ceded to Great Britain by the Treaty of Utrecht, the population had increased to 2,500. Thereafter a number of Acadians, whose settlements had hitherto been confined to the mainland of what is now Nova Scotia, moved to Cape Breton, Prince Edward Island, and the valley of the St. John River. Settlements were also made on the Miramichi River and on Chaleur Bay. There are believed to have been at the time of the expulsion in 1755 about 16,000 Acadians in what are now the Maritime Provinces, of whom nearly 7,000 were deported. About a decade later they started drifting back to their old homes. The present Acadian population of the Maritime Provinces is over 150,000, descended from those who escaped deportation and those who returned from exile.

The earliest permanent British settlement was at Annapolis Royal (formerly Port Royal), captured from the French by Nicholson in 1710. Halifax dates from 1749. The town was founded by settlers brought out from England by Lord Cornwallis in that year. Lunenburg was founded by German settlers the following year. About 1755 emigration began from parts of New England to Nova Scotia. The movement of United Empire Loyalists to the Maritime Provinces started soon after the outbreak of the American Revolution, and reached its climax in 1783-84, after the signing of the Treaty of Versailles between Great Britain and the United States. The immigration of Scottish Highlanders to Cape Breton, Pictou, Miramichi, and Prince Edward Island began in 1767, and extended over the next quarter of a century. Irish immigration to New Brunswick followed the famine in the middle of the nineteenth century. The Irish settled mainly in the country west of the St. John River.

With the growth of settlement came the gradual development of a system of roads. By 1830, as shown on the map, main roads extended from Halifax to Windsor, Annapolis, Digby, and Yarmouth; down the outer coast of the peninsula to Lunenburg and Yarmouth; east to the straits of Canso and Cape Breton; through the isthmus to New Brunswick, and from there west to St. John and St. Andrews, up the St. John River, and up the gulf coast of the province to Campbellton. From these main thoroughfares branch roads crossed the provinces in various directions.

Bibliography: Hannay, *History of Acadia*; Richard, *Acadia*; Doughty, *The Acadian Exiles*; Murdoch, *History of Nova Scotia*; Haliburton, *Historical Account of Nova Scotia*; *Canada and its Provinces*, vol. xiii.; Rogers, *Historical Geography of Canada*, vol. iii.

EARLY SETTLEMENTS IN LOWER CANADA

Map No. 62

Settlements during the French régime in what is now the province of Quebec stuck pretty closely, as will be seen on the map, to the banks of the St. Lawrence and some of its principal tributaries, such as the Richelieu, Yamaska, and Chaudière. The earliest settlement, at Tadoussac, at the mouth of the Saguenay, dates from the beginning of the seventeenth century. In 1608 Champlain founded the city of Quebec; Three Rivers dates from 1634; and Montreal was established in 1642. Between that date and the end of the seventeenth century a number of other towns and settlements were founded, from below Quebec to Montreal, until there existed a fairly continuous line of population on the banks of the St. Lawrence, and spreading up the Richelieu and other rivers flowing into the main stream from the south.

Settlement on the northern tributaries of the St. Lawrence came at a much later date. British settlements in the old French province, after the conquest, were confined largely to what are known as the Eastern Townships, north of the Vermont border. This English-speaking population came partly from the old land and partly from New England, and of the latter some arrived shortly after the conquest and others came as United Empire Loyalists during and after the Revolution. In course of time English settlements gradually spread up the Quebec side of the Ottawa River to Hull, founded in 1800.

In the early days of the colony waterways furnished the only means of communication between the various settlements, and the St. Lawrence and its tributaries continued to be important thoroughfares. But gradually roads were built, and in 1734 a through road was completed between Quebec and Montreal, with a regular system of post-houses where conveyances were kept in readiness for travellers. There existed even during the French period something in the nature of a postal system between the two principal cities of Canada. After the cession of Canada to Great Britain, Benjamin Franklin, who had been deputy postmaster-general of the British colonies to the south for some years, came to Canada and established a post office at Quebec, with subordinate offices at Three Rivers and Montreal. Mail couriers maintained a monthly service between Montreal and New York, where the Canadian mails were forwarded to England by sailing packet.

Bibliography: Douglas, *Old France in the New World*; Parkman, *Old Régime in Canada*; Smith, *History of the Post Office in British North America*; *Canada and its Provinces*, vol. xv.; Rogers, *Historical Geography of Canada*, vol. iii.

EARLY SETTLEMENTS IN UPPER CANADA (TO 1840), AND ONTARIO

MAP No. 63

THE French at the time of the conquest had forts at Cataraqui (Kingston), Rouillé (Toronto), and Niagara, but the only real settlements were on the banks of the Detroit River.

As in the case of Quebec, early settlements in Upper Canada clung to the waterways—the upper St. Lawrence and the north shore of Lake Ontario, the Niagara and the north shore of Lake Erie. Gradually towns and settlements sprang up throughout the peninsula lying between Lakes Ontario, Erie, and Huron; spread north from Lake Ontario, and between the St. Lawrence and the Ottawa; and at a later date extended around the shores of Georgian Bay and up the Ottawa to North Bay and Sudbury. The earlier settlers were largely United Empire Loyalists, followed by Scottish, English, and Irish emigrants from the old land. The first Loyalist settlement was between the present sites of Brockville and Cornwall, and was composed largely of disbanded Highland soldiers and Scottish immigrants from western New York. It was quickly followed by the settlement of the Kingston to Bay of Quinte shore-line. An important part was taken by the Canada Company and its moving spirits John Galt and William Dunlop. Waterloo county, on the upper waters of the Grand River, was occupied by Pennsylvania Dutch.

As the first settlements were along the main waterways, so the early roads ran from Montreal up the St. Lawrence to Kingston and on to Toronto. From Toronto, Yonge Street was built north to Lake Simcoe, and Dundas Street from Lake Ontario to the site of London. Gradually the road system was extended to and along the Niagara frontier, from Toronto west to the Detroit River, north to Georgian Bay and west to Goderich on Lake Huron. A system of stages and mails was gradually established and extended throughout the province, to be followed some years later by railways.

Bibliography: Scott, *John Graves Simcoe*; Wallace, *The United Empire Loyalists*; Canniff, *Settlement of Upper Canada*; Scherk, *Pen Pictures of Early Pioneer Life in Upper Canada*; Rogers, *Historical Geography of Canada*, vol. iii.

WATERWAYS OF CANADA

MAP No. 64

IT would be difficult to over-estimate the importance of her waterways to Canada, particularly in her early history. If you will look at the map you will see that Nature has provided two immense water gateways on the east coast—the Gulf of St. Lawrence and Hudson Bay. As has already been noted, the routes of early explorers lay through one or other of these gateways. And as the story of Canada unfolds it will be seen that western discovery was carried out almost entirely by way of these water thoroughfares.

From the Gulf explorers gradually pushed their way westward up the St. Lawrence and the Ottawa to the Great Lakes, Huron, Ontario, Erie, Michigan, and Superior. From this main artery, the tide of discovery flowed on one side north by the Saguenay, St. Maurice, and other streams to rivers that interlocked at their headwaters and led down to James Bay; and on the other side by the Richelieu to Lake Champlain and the Hudson. All this of course was not accomplished in a day or a generation.

Farther west, portages led the adventurous traveller from Lake Ontario and Lake Erie to tributaries of the Ohio, from the foot of Lake Michigan to the Illinois, from Green Bay by way of the Fox River and Lake Winnibago to the Wisconsin, all these routes leading eventually to the Mississippi, and from the extreme end of Lake Superior, up the St. Louis and over to the upper waters of the Mississippi.

In course of time four distinct routes were found from Lake Superior to Lake Winnipeg: by way of the Kaministikwia River to Rainy Lake and thence down Rainy River to the Lake of the Woods and by way of Winnipeg River to Lake Winnipeg; by the Grand Portage route, following what is to-day the international boundary to the Lake of the Woods; from Fond du Lac, at the foot of Lake Superior, up St. Louis River, and by two alternative routes to Namakan Lake and to Rainy River, both on the international boundary; and finally, by way of Lake Nipigon through a series of rivers and lakes to English River, a tributary of Winnipeg River. The last-mentioned route was never used to any extent.

Through the northern gateway water routes led south and west to St. Lawrence waters and to the far west respectively, Rupert River, the Nottaway, Harricanaw, Moose, and Albany belonging to the former group, and the Churchill, Nelson, Hayes, and Severn to the latter. Although the other three rivers are much larger, the Hayes was the great thoroughfare between Hudson Bay and Lake Winnipeg for explorers and fur-traders.

From that great central reservoir, Lake Winnipeg, water routes led in every direction, not only to the Gulf of St. Lawrence and Hudson Bay, but to the Pacific, the Arctic, and the Gulf of Mexico.

The way to the Arctic followed the Saskatchewan, Cumberland Lake to the Churchill, up the Churchill to Methye Portage, down the Clearwater to the Athabaska, and by way of Athabaska Lake, Slave River, Great Slave Lake, and the Mackenzie to the sea; or from Great Slave Lake up the Yellowknife River to the Coppermine; or from the western end of Great Slave Lake to Backs River; or from Great Bear Lake over to the Coppermine; or again from the Mackenzie up the Liard and down the Pelly to the Yukon; or finally from the Mackenzie up Peel River and down the Porcupine to the Yukon.

The route to the south led up Red River, over to the Mississippi and down to the Gulf of Mexico; and that to the west by the Saskatchewan to Howse Pass and through the Rockies, or up the Athabaska to Athabaska Pass or Yellowhead Pass, and down the Columbia for the Fraser—the latter an extremely hazardous route—to the Pacific.

And these are by no means merely theoretical water routes. Explorers and fur-traders have travelled every one of them in boats or canoes. It is not only possible, but has been proved practicable time and again, for a man in a canoe to start from Lake Winnipeg, and, with nothing more than an occasional portage, reach the Atlantic or the Pacific, the Arctic, Hudson Bay, or the Gulf of Mexico.

Bibliography: Dawson, *St. Lawrence*; Burpee, *Search for the Western Sea*; Wood, *All Afloat*.

TRADING POSTS AND CANOE ROUTES

MAP No. 64

THIS map is designed to illustrate the development of the fur trade in Canada. The trading posts shown represent but a small proportion of the many posts which have been established from time to time by different companies, traders, and explorers, but they may serve to suggest the pivotal points in a long and involved and romantic story.

The fur trade in Canada divides itself into two main periods: the French régime and the British régime; and the latter covers the long rivalry and final merging of two powerful corporations, the Hudson's Bay Company and the North West Company.

During the French period, under one or other of the companies that attempted, not always very successfully, to combine settlement and the spread of Christianity with the fur trade, posts were built and operated along the shores of the St. Lawrence and the Gulf from Montreal to the Strait of Belle Isle, and on the various streams that flow into the St. Lawrence from the north.

Following these streams, men who were part trader, part explorer, and part military adventurer, made their way over the height of land and down to James Bay and Hudson Bay, where they came into conflict with the Hudson's Bay Company, captured some of their forts, and for a time maintained rival establishments.

Others, with whom trading was but a means to a noble end, carried the torch of discovery far into the west. The map will sufficiently reveal their course toward the setting sun. They sought an elusive Western Sea, and found a vast continent. The trading forts that were their stepping-stones to the discovery of the west stood at strategic points on the lakes and rivers that for the most part formed their thoroughfares.

Of the two British corporations, the Hudson's Bay Company dates back to the early period of French rule in Canada. Endowed by Charles II. in 1670 with an immense, and at that time extremely indefinite, territory, its jurisdiction was constantly disputed by New France. It was not, however, until after Canada had become British that the Hudson's Bay Company made any serious effort to extend its trade inland from Hudson Bay. It was then prodded into activity by the aggressive rivalry of the traders from Montreal who in 1795 had organized the North West Company.

For years the two trading bodies disputed the control of the rich fur country of the western plains, the rivalry becoming ever more bitter and determined until it finally ended in open strife and bloodshed. The leaders were finally brought to their senses, and in 1821 merged their interests in one company under the name of the older corporation.

Before the union, the North West Company had generally led the way in opening up new fields, and the great western explorers were for the most part Nor'-Westers. After the union, the rejuvenated Hudson's Bay Company pushed its operations into every remote corner of the continent, until its posts or its traders were to be found anywhere from Labrador to Vancouver Island, and from the Arctic coast to California. To-day the Company, still very much alive after more than two and a half centuries, while still maintaining its fur-trading posts, has adapted itself to modern conditions in Western Canada by establishing and maintaining a number of large and very efficient department stores.

This map also illustrates the important part played in the fur trade by portages and portage routes, the waterways of the country affording in most cases the only practicable means of transport. From the St. Lawrence, water routes led north to the height of land, and by portages to rivers flowing into James Bay. To the south, they led to Lake Champlain and the Hudson, and farther west, to the Ohio and the Mississippi. Many portages were involved in the Ottawa River route to Lake Huron. By the Great Lakes route, they were encountered only on the upper St. Lawrence and over the Niagara peninsula. West of the Great Lakes, portages had to be made in every direction: between Lake Superior and Lake Winnipeg; between that lake and Hudson Bay; on the Saskatchewan, the Churchill, the Athabaska, and the Peace; and west of the Rockies on the Fraser, Columbia, and other rivers.

The table on pages 42 and 43 gives the dates of founding of the principal posts.

On the fur trade in the French period, see Biggar's *Early Trading Companies of New France*, and the several volumes of Parkman's history. On the British fur trade, see Bryce's *The Remarkable History of the Hudson's Bay Company*, Willson's *The Great Company*, Davidson's *The North-West Company*, Cowie's *The Company of Adventurers*, Laut's *Conquest of the Great North-west*, Masson's *Bourgeois de la Compagnie du Nord-ouest*, and Mackenzie's *General History of the Fur Trade* in his *Voyages*.

EARLY COMMUNICATIONS—EASTERN CANADA

MAP No. 65

EARLY communications in what is now Canada were for many years almost entirely by water. Sailing ships connected Quebec, Halifax, Montreal, and St. John with the outer world. In the interior, travel in the early days was first by canoe, following two main thoroughfares from the St. Lawrence up the Ottawa to Lake Nipissing and Georgian Bay, and around by the Great Lakes, both routes leading from Lake Huron up St. Mary River to Lake Superior, and west to the Lake of the Woods and Lake Winnipeg.

In course of time sailing vessels, the earliest of which was La Salle's *Griffon*, launched in 1679 on the Niagara River, were built on the Great Lakes, in connection with the fur trade, and later to afford communication between the infant settlements along the lakes.

As early as 1788 there was a mail route, by courier, from Halifax to Quebec via Annapolis and St. John. The Annapolis-Halifax section was covered in three days in a one-horse carriage, and is described as "very rough." There were numerous other mail routes in the Maritime Provinces. Before 1840, four-horse stages ran from Halifax to Pictou, and from St. John to Fredericton, but at that time there seems to have been no stage north of the last-named point.

In 1809 the first Canadian steamboat, the *Accommodation*, made her initial trip from Montreal to Quebec. Seven years later the *Frontenac* was launched at Ernesttown on Lake Ontario.

In the great days of the sailing ship the builders of the Maritime Provinces won fame because of their beautiful and speedy clipper ships, which became known in all the great ports of the world.

In 1831 the *Royal William* was launched near Quebec, and two years later crossed the Atlantic to Gravesend—the first vessel to make the trip by steam power alone.

One of the shareholders of the *Royal William*, Samuel Cunard of Halifax, established the famous line of transatlantic steamships that still bears his name.

Transport by land for many years clung close to the waterways, roads being built from town to town —Quebec to Montreal, Kingston, and Toronto. Later these roads were extended into the interior.

Among the more famous of the early roads were Yonge Street, from Toronto to Lake Simcoe, and Dundas Street, from Lake Ontario to the site of London.

Similarly the early railroads stuck close to the pioneer lines of travel, the first Canadian railway, connecting the Richelieu with the St. Lawrence at Montreal, being built in 1835-36. At that time, and for some years afterwards, a traveller making his way, for instance, from Halifax to Quebec, would take a boat to Portland, Maine; thence travel by rail to Boston and inland to Lake Champlain; there he would take a boat to the foot of the lake; then continue his journey on the first Canadian railway, from St. Johns on the Richelieu to

Laprairie, opposite Montreal ; and finally travel from Montreal to Quebec by steamboat. To-day one travels to Europe or across the continent of America in less time.

Other railways were gradually constructed, which developed later into two big systems—the Grand Trunk in Quebec and Ontario, and the Intercolonial in the Maritime Provinces.

The first Canadian canals were built by the Royal Engineers round the Coteau and Cascades Rapids on the Upper St. Lawrence between 1779 and 1783. Five years later the North West Company built a small canal at Sault Ste. Marie.

In 1831 the Chambly Canal was built on the Richelieu River to afford communication between the St. Lawrence and Lake Champlain.

Between 1824 and 1829 the first Welland Canal was constructed between Lake Erie and Lake Ontario ; and between 1826 and 1832 the Rideau Canal connected Ottawa, on the Ottawa River, with Kingston on Lake Ontario.

Bibliography : Skelton, *The Railway Builders ;* Wood, *All Afloat ;* Burpee, *Pioneer Transportation in Canada* (Handbook of Canada for the British Association, 1924).

THE GREAT LAKES—SHIPPING AND CANALS

Map No. 66

This map, although confined to three out of the five Great Lakes, gives a pretty good idea of the possibilities, from the point of view of transport, of the adjacent inland seas. If, for instance, a steamer started from Fort William or Duluth, at the western end of Lake Superior, and wished to deliver its cargo at Liverpool, it would be to-day a practical possibility, if the draft of the vessel was not more than 14 feet.

Sailing east, it would first have to get through the St. Mary's River, connecting Lake Superior with Lake Huron. Round the rapids at Sault Ste. Marie in that river Canada has built a canal (opened 1895), and the United States has four locks (opened in 1881, 1896, 1914, and 1919 respectively). The five locks range in depth from 17 feet to 24½ feet.

Having passed through one of these locks, and steamed through the dredged channel below, the vessel would traverse Lake Huron, St. Clair River, Lake St. Clair, and Detroit River, the last three artificially deepened, and down Lake Erie to the Welland Canal at its eastern end.

Here three canals have been successively under construction. The original Welland Canal, only 8 feet deep, was opened in 1829 ; the second, with a depth of 14 feet, was completed in 1887 ; and the Canadian Government is now building a ship canal which will have a depth of 30 feet in the locks.

The Welland Canal brings the vessel into Lake Ontario, and from there it passes into the St. Lawrence, where it will have a succession of canals to go through— the Galops, Rapide Plat, and Farran's Point, collectively known as the Williamsburg Canals (opened in 1847), with 9 feet depth, and enlarged about thirty years later to 14 feet ; then the Cornwall Canal (completed 1843), with a depth of 9 feet, and subsequently enlarged to 14 feet ; the Soulanges Canal (opened 1899), also 14 feet, which took the place of the older Beauharnois Canal on the south side of the river (now used as a power canal), which in turn replaced the 6-feet canals built in 1783.

Finally, the vessel would pass through the Lachine Canal immediately above Montreal, first built in 1825, with a depth of 4½ feet, deepened to 14 feet in 1885. It has been proposed that all these canals between Lake Ontario and Montreal should be replaced by ship canals of the same depth as the new Welland.

From Montreal the vessel would sail down the St Lawrence through the ship channel between Montreal and Quebec, begun in 1844, with a depth of a little over 10 feet, and to-day almost completed to 35 feet.

Eventually, therefore, when the ship canals on the upper St. Lawrence have been built, it will be possible for a large ocean-going vessel to take on a cargo at Fort William or Duluth and deliver it at Liverpool or any other port of the world.

In addition to the canals mentioned, the Rideau Canal enables vessels of small draft to travel between Ottawa and Kingston ; and the Trent Navigation permits vessels of still smaller draft to cross the great peninsula from the Bay of Quinte on Lake Ontario to Georgian Bay. As a matter of fact the western end of the Trent Navigation has not yet been completed. Vessels are carried over two short stretches by marine railways. The route west of Lake Simcoe follows the Severn to Georgian Bay.

Also, on the United States side, the Erie Barge Canal and the Champlain Canal afford communication between the Hudson River at Albany and Lake Erie and the St. Lawrence respectively.

The potentialities of the Great Lakes as a transport route are suggested by the fact that during the limited period of navigation a much larger traffic passes up and down the Detroit River than through the Suez Canal.

As will be seen by the map, this part of Canada is now very well supplied with railway facilities. The main lines of traffic run from Montreal to Toronto and the frontier at Sarnia and Windsor, with two great transcontinental lines east and west between the Atlantic and the Pacific, and north and south branches connecting Toronto with North Bay, Sudbury, and Cochrane in the north, and with Buffalo in the south.

Generally speaking, this map shows in a comprehensive way the development of transportation facilities in and about the older part of Ontario, which is the most thickly settled part of the Dominion, and most highly developed from an industrial point of view.

Bibliography : *Canada Year Book ;* Wood, *All Afloat.*

RAILWAYS OF CANADA : ERA OF CONSTRUCTION, 1837-65

Map No. 67

In this map may be studied the development of railway construction from 1837 to the present time. The several periods of construction are shown on the map by separate symbols. It will be convenient to take up each period separately. In the first place we see the beginnings of railway transport in Canada, the initiation of that national railway policy that was to play a tremendously important part in the political, social, and economic development of the country.

The first railway in Canada, the Champlain and St. Lawrence Railway, was opened by Earl Gosford on July 23, 1836. It ran from Laprairie on the St. Lawrence, near Montreal, to St. Johns on the Richelieu River. The first train consisted of four cars drawn by horses. Locomotive power was applied in 1837. The length of the line was 16 miles. By the middle of the century there were 66 miles of railway in what is now Canada.

The era of railway development really began in 1851. In that year an Act was passed making provision for the construction of a main trunk line through what are now the provinces of Quebec and Ontario ; and delegates from the various provinces went to England to arrange for the construction of the Intercolonial Railway. The line from Halifax to Truro and Windsor was completed in 1858, and from St. John to Shediac in 1860. Four years later Sandford Fleming began work on the surveys of the main line from Rivière du Loup to connect with the railways already built in the Maritime Provinces.

NOTES ON THE MAPS

The Grand Trunk Railway dates from 1851, when the Act of incorporation was passed for a railway from Montreal to Toronto. That line was completed in 1856. An additional section had in the meantime been opened from Montreal to Portland, Maine, in 1853. The system was extended from Toronto to Sarnia in 1858, and from Richmond to Levis and Rivière du Loup in 1860. The Victoria bridge at Montreal had been opened the previous year. In 1865 there were over 2,000 miles of railway in what is now Canada.

As will be seen by a reference to the map, the foundation of the railway system of the new Dominion had been well laid before confederation. The Intercolonial was being surveyed and parts of it were completed. The Grand Trunk extended from Rivière du Loup to Sarnia. And far-sighted men already dared to dream of a transcontinental railway from ocean to ocean.

Bibliography : Skelton, *The Railway Builders ;* Fleming, *The Intercolonial.*

RAILWAYS OF CANADA : ERA OF CONSTRUCTION, 1865-86

Map No. 67

THE one event of overmastering importance in the era of railway building in Canada between 1865 and 1886 was the planning and completion of the first transcontinental railway, the Canadian Pacific. It was even more vital than the completion of the Intercolonial in 1876. The significance of this daring undertaking of a railway from ocean to ocean in welding together the weak and widely scattered provinces of the young Dominion can readily be understood. It was as supremely important to the effective union of the western and eastern parts of Canada as the Intercolonial was to the union of the Maritime Provinces and the old province of Canada, now Ontario and Quebec.

Even before 1865 plans had been put forward in speeches and pamphlets for the establishment of a transport route across the continent in British North America. Various routes were proposed, and different combinations of rail-and-water transport or all-rail. In 1862 Sandford Fleming had written that " A continuous line of railway, with electric telegraph, is best calculated to meet the permanent wants of this country, and serve the interests of the Colonial Empire, than any other means of communication between the two oceans." Nine years later he was appointed Engineer-in-Chief of Surveys for the Canadian Pacific Railway, and in 1885 he had the satisfaction of seeing the last spike driven by Donald A. Smith (afterwards Lord Strathcona) at Craigellachie, in the Gold Range.

It was a marvellous achievement, as daring in its conception as in its execution. Courage and imagination and faith were needed, both by statesmen and railway builders, to drive a line of steel across Canada from the Atlantic to the Pacific, through a country as yet sparsely populated in the east and with only a handful of people in the west. It was freely predicted, by otherwise well-informed men, that the railway would ruin the country, that it would never earn enough to pay for the grease on its axles. Men who had put all their fortunes into the undertaking had many desperately anxious moments ; but they lived to see Canada's first transcontinental railway an assured success, and to know that it had not only welded together the scattered provinces of the Dominion, but had become an important link in the chain of Empire. In 1886 the railway mileage of Canada had increased to over 11,000.

Bibliography : Skelton, *The Railway Builders ;* McLean, *National Railways Overland* (Canada and its Provinces, vol. x.).

RAILWAYS OF CANADA : ERA OF CONSTRUCTION, 1886-1900

Map No. 67

THIS may be regarded as an intermediate stage in the transportation history of the Dominion—between the building of the first transcontinental and the construction of the second and third transcontinentals.

From 1886 to 1900 the Canadian Pacific threw out branches in every direction, particularly in the western provinces. During this same period the courage and resourcefulness of two men, William Mackenzie and Donald Mann, made possible the building of a system of railways which became known as the Canadian Northern, and was afterwards to be developed into a second transcontinental line. The Grand Trunk, after a period of depression and stagnation, had, under the efficient management of Charles M. Hays, entered upon a new lease of life. It soon came to be realized, however, that success in any large sense depended upon the extension of the system into the west, where the Grand Trunk might share in the prosperity of the prairie provinces, particularly in carrying their ever-increasing grain harvests to the eastern markets. This western development was not to be realized for some years to come. In 1900 the railway mileage had grown to considerably over 17,000.

Bibliography : Skelton, *The Railway Builders.*

RAILWAY SYSTEMS, 1927

Map No. 68

IN the first quarter of the twentieth century Canada has witnessed an extraordinary expansion of her railways, from 17,000 miles to over 40,000. A second and a third transcontinental line have been completed from ocean to ocean—the Canadian Northern in 1915, and the Grand Trunk Pacific about the same time. The latter, or rather the eastern extension of it known as the National Transcontinental, built by the Dominion Government, boldly carried through the unoccupied clay belt of northern Ontario and Quebec.

Both the Canadian Northern and the Grand Trunk Pacific, after crossing the western prairies, pierced the Rockies by the Yellowhead Pass. The former then turned south-west to Vancouver, while the latter ran west to Prince Rupert. Of the extraordinary achievement of those who had projected and built the Canadian Northern, Dr. Skelton says : " In 1896 a railway 100 miles long, beginning and ending nowhere, operated by thirteen men and a boy ! In 1914 a great transcontinental system practically completed, over 10,000 miles in length, and covering seven of Canada's nine provinces ! The impossible had been achieved."

But both these transcontinental systems had been made possible only by heavy subsidies and guarantees both by the Dominion and Provincial Governments. Times grew hard, the railways got into difficulties, and leaned ever more heavily upon the country. Finally the Government, faced with the alternative of annually pulling the Canadian Northern and Grand Trunk out of their financial holes, or taking them over, reluctantly decided on the latter plan. As a consequence the Canadian Northern, the Grand Trunk Pacific, the National Transcontinental, and eventually the Grand Trunk, became merged with the old Intercolonial in a vast system known as the Canadian National Railways, with a total mileage of over 20,000. With a few minor

exceptions, the railways of Canada are to-day consolidated in two big systems—the Canadian Pacific and the Canadian National.
The most important of the lines outside these systems is the Timiskaming and Northern Ontario, commenced by the Ontario Government as a colonization road in 1902, and now extending north from North Bay through the famous silver and gold country of Cobalt, Gowganda, and Porcupine to Cochrane on the Canadian National. Another line, included in the national system, that has been the subject of bitter controversy, is the Hudson Bay Railway, designed some day to carry wheat from the Canadian prairies by way of Hudson Bay to the European markets.
Bibliography: Skelton, *The Railway Builders.*

HYDRO-ELECTRIC DEVELOPMENT

MAP No. 78

WITHOUT attempting to trace the development of water power in Canadian industry back to its early beginnings, when its use was confined to the immediate vicinity of the waterfall, it is sufficient to note that the modern water-power industry dates from the invention of the electric generator about 1895, and has grown steadily and rapidly since that year.

It is estimated that the total water-powers throughout the Dominion exceed 40,000,000 commercial horse-power at ordinary minimum flow. This total is distributed very unequally among the provinces, Quebec and Ontario having much the larger shares, then Manitoba and British Columbia, with only small quantities available in the other provinces.

It may be noted, however, that with the exception of British Columbia, which has both, the provinces possessing the larger water-powers have little or no coal, and vice versa.

Of the total water-powers available there are now actually developed or under construction (1926) nearly 4,000,000 horse-power, involving a capital investment of about $700,000,000.
Bibliography: *Canada Year Book.*

MINERALS DEVELOPED

MAP No. 79

A REFERENCE to the map and the accompanying tables makes it clear that minerals form one of the most important and widespread of the natural resources of Canada. The value of the annual mineral production reached a maximum in 1920 of nearly $228,000,000. Of the metals, gold has been found in commercial quantities in five of the nine provinces as well as in the Yukon, silver in two and the Yukon, copper in six and the Yukon, nickel in Ontario alone, zinc in three, lead in three and the Yukon, iron in five. Coal is found in five of the provinces as well as in the Yukon. The deposits in the Prairie Provinces, though of comparatively low grade, are of almost incalculable extent. It is also important to remember, as pointed out in the preceding note, that while those parts of the Dominion that are rich in coal are comparatively poor in water-powers, the provinces that lack coal—Ontario, Quebec, and Manitoba—are extraordinarily rich in water-powers. Prince Edward Island alone is lacking in both. Historically, the earliest working of mineral deposits in Canada was in connection with the St. Maurice Forges,

using bog iron in 1733. Although copper was not commercially worked until 1770, its discovery goes back to the days of the French régime, when it was found on the shores of Lake Superior. The first commercial development of lead, zinc, coal, and gypsum goes back to the eighteenth century. The other minerals all date from the nineteenth century.
Bibliography: Malcolm, *Mineral Industry of Canada;* Wilson, *Precious Metals in Canada* (Handbook of Canada for the British Association, 1924).

PRINCIPAL MINERALS OF CANADA, WITH DATES OF FIRST COMMERCIAL WORKING OF PRINCIPAL DEPOSITS

Cobalt . Ont. (1892), Sudbury District; (1904), Cobalt District.
Copper . Ont. (1770), Shore of Lake Superior; (1846), Lake Huron; (1864), Bruce Mines; (1889), Sudbury District.
Que. (1847), Eastern Townships; (1925), Rouyn.
N.S. (1882), Cheticamp Mines.
N.B. (1884), Dorchester; (1863), Adams and Simpson Islands.
B.C. (1894), Trail Creek and Toad Mountain.
Yukon (1906), Whitehorse.
Man. (1915), The Pas District—Discovery of " Mandy " and " Flin Flon " Mines.
Gold . . Que. (1847), Chaudière Valley; (1870), Beauce; (1925), Rouyn.
B.C. (1858), Caribou and Quesnel; (1874), Cassiar; (1890), Lode Gold at Rossland and Boundary; (1919), Premier.
N.S. (1860), Tangier.
Ont. (1866), Hastings Company; (1909), Porcupine; (1912), Kirkland Lake; (1925), Red Lake.
Yukon (1878), Forty Mile Creek; (1896), Klondyke.
Man. (1915), Rex Mine discovery; (1917), The Pas District.
Iron . . Que. (1733), St. Francis District; (1872), Bristol Mines.
Ont. (1800), Normandale; (1899), Helen Mine.
N.S. (1828), East River; (1849), Londonderry; (1889), Brookfield.
N.B. (1848), Woodstock; (1902), Bathurst.
B.C. (1872).
Lead . . Que. (1744), Lake Temiscaming, actively exploited between 1877 and 1903.
B.C. (app. 1817), " Blue Bell " discovered in 1825; (1887), Ainsworth Camp; (1892), Sandon Camp.
Ont. (1868), Frontenac lead mine.
Yukon (1909), " Silver King "; (1921), Keno Hill.
Nickel . Ont. (1889), Sudbury District; mining began 1886; First refining in Canada, 1918.
Silver . . B.C. (1858), with placer gold; (1887), silver-lead ores.
Ont. (1866), Thunder Bay District—Silver Islet; (1904), Cobalt.
Yukon (1899), with placer gold; (1909), " Silver King "; (1921), Keno Hill.
Zinc . . Que. (1744), Lake Temiscaming; (1910), Notre Dame des Anges; Calumet in

NOTES ON THE MAPS

Zinc . . the early nineties; (1910), Gaspé deposits discovered.
Ont. (1889), Rossport; discovered in 1881; (1902), Richardson Mine shipments begun.
B.C. (1899), "Lucky Jim"; Kootenay District.

Asbestos . Que. (1878-79), Thetford Mines; (1898), Black Lake.

Coal . . N.S. (1720), "Cow Bay"; (1784), North Sydney.
N.B. (1825), Grand Lake.
B.C. (1836), Vancouver Island; (1865), Queen Charlotte Group; (1897), Crow's Nest.
Alta. (1882), Lethbridge.
Sask. (1885), Souris Valley.
Yukon. Records from 1901 only.

Graphite . Que. (1847), near Grenville; (1866), Buckingham District.
N.B. (1853).
Ont. (1870), North Elmsley and Oliver's Ferry; (1896), "Black Donald" at Calabogie.

Gypsum . N.S. (1779).
Ont. (1822), Paris.
N.B. (previous to 1847; in 1854 The Albert Manufacturing Company of Hillsboro organized.)
Man. (1901), at Gypsumville.
B.C. (1911).

Natural Gas . . Ont. (1888).
Alta. (1891), Medicine Hat; (1912), Bow Island.
N.B. (1912).

Petroleum Ont. (1858), Lambton Company.
N.B. (1912).
Alta. (1913), Black Diamond.

Salt . . N.B. (1800), Sussex.
Man. (1820), Lake Winnipegosis.
Ont. (1865), South-Western Peninsula.
N.S. (1919), Malagash.

VI.—BOUNDARY DISPUTES AND SETTLEMENTS

This group of maps, which deals with the Oregon and San Juan, Maine–New Brunswick, Labrador, Alaska, and North-West Angle boundary disputes, should be studied in connection with those relating to Discovery and Exploration (Nos. 8–24. and 26) and the Political Development group (Nos. 42–60).
In particular, compare No. 80 with No. 23 and Nos. 52–55; No. 81 with Nos. 17 and 42–54; No. 82 with Nos. 42–60; No..83 with Nos. 23 and 47–59; and No. 84 with Nos. 26 and 47–54.

OREGON BOUNDARY, 1846

Map No. 80

To understand the meaning of the Oregon Boundary Question, it is necessary to run very briefly over the history of discovery and exploration on the north-west coast. In 1578 Drake, for England, took formal possession of " New Albion," near the site of San Francisco. In 1603 Vizcaino, for Spain, explored the coast up to lat. 42° N. In 1741 Bering and Chirikof, for Russia, explored the coast from the Aleutian Islands down to lat. 55° N. In 1774 Perez, for Spain, reached 54° N., and in 1775 Heceta, for Spain, discovered the mouth of the Columbia, which he named Rio de San Roque. In the same year Bodega y Cuadra and Maurelle, for Spain, took formal possession near lat. 57° N. and explored the coast to lat. 58° N., thus overlapping the Russian discoveries.
In 1777–78 Cook, for Great Britain, explored the coast from 44° N. to Icy Cape in the Arctic. Between 1791 and 1795 Vancouver, for Great Britain, made a detailed survey of the coast from lat. 38° N. to the peninsula of Alaska. In 1792 Grey, for the United States, entered and named the Columbia, and the same year Broughton, one of Vancouver's lieutenants, explored the river for one hundred miles.
Meanwhile Mackenzie in 1793, Fraser in 1808. and Thompson between 1807 and 1811, for Great Britain, and Lewis and Clark in 1805 for the United States, explored and surveyed the interior between the Rockies and the sea.
These varying claims, based upon discovery, together with the diplomatic negotiations between Great Britain and Russia and Great Britain and Spain, and the respective claims based upon occupation by the North West Company and the Hudson's Bay Company and United States settlers in the valley of the Columbia, produced a very involved situation. The treaty of 1818 had made the 49th parallel the international boundary as far west as the Rockies. There remained in dispute the immense area west of the mountains from 45° to 54° 40'. Negotiations were entered into at various times between Great Britain and the United States with a view to settling the boundary west of the mountains, but as no agreement could be reached the territory was jointly occupied by mutual consent until 1846, when the Oregon Treaty adopted the 49th parallel as the boundary from the Rockies to the Pacific.
The international boundary thus established still left undecided how and where it should run from the mainland out between Vancouver Island and the coast to the open sea. All that was in dispute here was the identity of the main channel. Great Britain contended that it was Rosario Strait; the United States claimed Haro Strait. Between these channels lay a group of islands of which San Juan was the most important. After years of dispute and negotiation the question was finally referred to an arbitrator, who in 1872 decided in favour of the United States contention.
Bibliography : White, *Boundary Disputes and Treaties* (Canada and its Provinces, vol. viii.).

EASTERN CANADA–UNITED STATES BOUNDARY

Map No. 81

The recognition of the St. Croix River as the boundary between New England and what was then Nova Scotia, but subsequently became New Brunswick, dates back to 1621, when James I. granted to Sir William Alexander the Lordship and Barony of Nova Scotia. In the proclamation of 1763 the southern boundary of Quebec is defined as following the 45th parallel " along the highest lands which divide the rivers that empty themselves into the said River St. Lawrence from those which fall into the sea."

In 1782 Strachey, one of the British negotiators of the Treaty of Versailles, was instructed to claim the Penobscot and its tributaries as the boundary between Nova Scotia and Maine, on the ground that the region between the Penobscot and the St. Croix had formerly been claimed as part of New France.

In the boundary negotiations the United States at first proposed the St. John River as the boundary, but finally agreed to accept the St. Croix. A dispute then arose as to the identity of the latter, the United States claiming that the stream now known as the Magaguadavic was meant, and Great Britain contending for the stream then known as the Schoodic and now as the St. Croix. In 1798 the Commissioners appointed under the Jay Treaty decided in favour of the Schoodic, but adopted the east branch to its source.

The next difficulty was as to where the international boundary should run from the source of the St. Croix. The matter remained in dispute for many years. Under the Treaty of Ghent, 1814, a Commission was appointed to ascertain and determine the ' north-west angle of Nova Scotia " and the north-westernmost head of the Connecticut River, and to survey the line between the source of the St. Croix and the St. Lawrence.

One of the principal difficulties was that by the treaty of 1783 the boundary was to follow the " highlands," which were assumed to be a range of mountains or hills, but the survey showed that there were no such mountains in the neighbourhood.

It also appeared that the northern boundary of New York was three-fourths of a mile north of the 45th parallel, which was to be the international boundary. The awkward situation arose that about half a mile south of the surveyed line the United States had built a fort at a cost of a million dollars, which, with another fort then under construction, would be on British territory.

The Commissioners failed to reach an agreement, disputes arose respecting land grants and the cutting of timber on the disputed territory, and in 1827 it was decided to submit the question to an arbitrator. The King of the Netherlands was agreed upon, and in 1831 he rendered an award which gave Great Britain 4,100 square miles, or approximately one-third of the area in dispute. He also decided that the United States should be left in possession of its forts at Rouses Point.

The United States refusing to accept the award, negotiations continued to be carried on between 1831 and 1842, and in the meantime the so-called Aroostook War broke out, which brought the two countries to the verge of hostilities. Finally, by the Ashburton Treaty, signed in 1842, the territory in dispute was divided, Great Britain received 5,000 square miles, or 900 more than the King of the Netherlands had awarded, and the United States 7,000 square miles. The United States got Rouses Point in exchange for a slight adjustment of the boundary between Lake Champlain and the St. Lawrence.

Bibliography: White, *Boundary Disputes and Treaties* (Canada and its Provinces, vol. viii.).

CANADA AND ALASKA BOUNDARY

Map No. 82

Vitus Bering was sent by Peter the Great in 1725 to explore the region east of Kamchatka, the north-easternmost point of Asia. It was not, however, until some years later that his explorations were carried out, resulting in the discovery of what is now known as Alaska. Thereafter the Russians engaged in the American fur trade, and in 1799 the Russian-American Company was granted exclusive trading privileges on the American coast north of the 65th parallel. As both British and United States traders were engaged on the north-west coast, the Russian Government in 1821 claimed exclusive sovereignty over the north-west coast from 51° up to Bering Straits.

Both Great Britain and the United States promptly protested, and as a result of negotiations between Great Britain and Russia a treaty was signed in 1825 by which the boundary between Russian and British territory ran from the sea up Portland Channel to 56° N. lat., and thence followed the summit of the mountains parallel to the coast to the intersection of 141° W. long., and followed that line to the Arctic. Prince of Wales Island and all the islands north of it became Russian territory.

In 1867 the United States purchased from Russia all its American territory. The interest of Great Britain in the territory north of British Columbia led to protracted negotiations with the United States, and the discovery of gold in the Yukon in 1897 emphasized the need of a clear definition of the Alaska boundary. In 1903 a treaty was signed between Great Britain and the United States submitting the question to a tribunal of six impartial jurors. On this tribunal British and Canadian interests were represented by Lord Alverstone, Sir Louis Jetté, and A. B. Aylesworth, and those of the United States by Elihu Root, Senator Lodge, and Senator Turner.

There were no differences of opinion as to the identity of Portland Canal, but there were as to where the channel should run from the sea and which islands should be assigned to each country. Two different contentions were also put forward as to the intention of the Convention of 1825 regarding the boundary line north of Portland Channel, and particularly as to that part of the Convention which provided " that whenever the summit of the mountains which extend in a direction parallel to the coast . . . shall prove to be at the distance of more than ten marine leagues from the ocean, the limit between the British possessions and the line of coast which is to belong to Russia . . . shall be formed by a line parallel to the windings of the coast, and which shall never exceed the distance of ten marine leagues therefrom."

As to this, the British contention in general terms was that the ten marine leagues were intended to be measured from the outer coast, the effect of which would be to carry the boundary line across various inlets; while the United States contention was that the ten marine leagues were to run from the head of these inlets. In their award the majority of the tribunal accepted in part the principle of the United States contention, though the line ran approximately midway between the British and United States contentions. As provided for in Article VI. of the treaty of 1825, Canada had the right to navigate all rivers leading through the Alaska strip into the interior.

Bibliography: White, *Boundary Disputes and Treaties* (Canada and its Provinces, vol. viii.).

CANADA-LABRADOR BOUNDARY

Map No. 83

As understood during the French régime, and throughout the early period of British rule, Labrador embraced the coast, and an indefinite area inland, from St. John River, opposite the upper end of Anticosti Island, to the Strait of Belle Isle, and north-west to Cape Chidley. Canada has always contended that Labrador was confined to a strip along the coast. Newfoundland, on the other hand, has argued that Labrador embraces the entire peninsula north of a line drawn from the Strait of Belle Isle to James Bay.

By the proclamation of 1763, following the treaty of peace, Labrador, which had hitherto formed part of New France, was transferred to Newfoundland, under whose jurisdiction it remained until 1774. By the Quebec Act of that year Labrador, together with Anticosti and the Magdalen Islands, were restored to Quebec. They remained part of that province until 1809, when by the Labrador Act both the coast and the islands were re-annexed to Newfoundland.

In 1825 that portion of the Labrador coast facing on the Gulf of St. Lawrence—that is, from the St. John River to Anse Sablon, near the Strait of Belle Isle—together with Anticosti and the Magdalen Islands, once more became Canadian territory, while the outer strip from the Strait of Belle Isle to Cape Chidley remained Newfoundland territory. The extent of Labrador inland from the coast, which had been the subject of dispute between Canada and Newfoundland, was referred to the Privy Council in London, whose decision (1927), based on the evidence submitted, fixed the boundary as shown on the map.

Bibliography: White, *Boundary Disputes and Treaties* (Canada and its Provinces, vol. viii.); *Labrador Boundary Case*, 1927.

LAKE OF THE WOODS BOUNDARY

Map No. 84

IN the Treaty of Paris, 1783, between Great Britain and the United States, it was provided that the international boundary, when it reached the Lake of the Woods, was to run " through the said lake to the most north-western point thereof, and from thence, on a due west course, to the River Mississippi." This " most north-western point " was subsequently known as the North-West Angle of the Lake of the Woods. The negotiators of the treaty relied on inaccurate maps, and it was not until 1797 that the fact was established by David Thompson that the proposed due west line from the North-West Angle to the Mississippi was a geographical impossibility, as the source of the Mississippi lay south of that line.

In subsequent negotiations various expedients were suggested by one side or the other for connecting the North-West Angle and the Mississippi by a boundary line. The Treaty of Ghent, 1814, definitely fixed the " most north-western point of the Lake of the Woods " as in lat. 49° 23′ 55″ N. and long. 95° 14′ 38″ W., but said nothing about the course the boundary was to take beyond that point.

The Treaty of London, 1818, provided that the boundary line should run due south from the North-West Angle " to its intersection with the 49th parallel of north latitude, and along that parallel to the Rocky Mountains."

A reference to the map will show that this peculiar decision in connection with the international boundary left an isolated bit of Minnesota quite apart from the rest of the United States—surrounded in fact by the Lake of the Woods and Canadian territory.

The North-West Angle is also of interest historically because on its southern shore the western explorer, La Vérendrye, built Fort St. Charles in 1732. Many years later one of the recognized routes of travel from the Lake of the Woods to Red River ran from the head of the North-West Angle.

Bibliography: White, *Boundary Disputes and Treaties* (Canada and its Provinces, vol. viii.).

VII.—POPULATION—DISTRIBUTION AND RACIAL ORIGIN

THIS group of maps, Nos. 69-77, studied with Nos. 67 and 68, presents a fairly complete picture of the origin and distribution of the people of Canada. Nos. 67 and 68 show the distribution of population in 1871 and 1921 respectively; the latter map gives the relative density, which could not be shown on the 1871 map as the data were not available; a comparison of the two maps brings out the extraordinary influence of the transcontinental railways on the shift of population from east to west; Nos. 69-76 give the Racial Origin of the Canadian people; and No. 77 pictures Canadian migration. These may be compared with Nos. 61-63, dealing with Early Settlements in the Maritime Provinces and in Upper and Lower Canada; and with the population figures on pages 33-34. Taken together we have the story of Canada's growth, at least from one angle: who they are, where they come from, where they first settled in Canada, their subsequent movements, and their numbers from time to time.

As to the Indian population, there is no evidence of decline, but on the other hand the probabilities point to a moderate but steady increase since Confederation. It should be pointed out that the figures in Table (5) on page 34 are for Indians only, and do not include Eskimos.

Bibliography: *Canada Year Book; Census of Indians and Eskimos in Canada*, 1924.

RACIAL ORIGINS

Maps Nos. 69-76

THESE eight maps are designed to indicate the distribution throughout Canada at the last census (1921) of people of the following origin: (1) French, (2) English, (3) Scottish, (4) Irish, (5) Austrian and German, (6) Dutch, (7) Russian and Ukranian, (8) Scandinavian. The maps are drawn on the dot system, each dot representing 500 persons, and in each province the number of dots computed on that scale indicates the total number of inhabitants of a race in that province. The dots are placed, as a rule, where groups of 500 or more occur, each additional dot indicating 500 or fraction thereof from one-third. In the absence of groups of 500, one dot indicates a unit of about 300 or more. The exact location of each dot on the map has been carefully ascertained from the returns of the census for municipalities, townships, and other subdivisions. It should be borne in mind when studying the maps that many small groups and isolated dwellers may be found all over the country between those centres indicated by dots.

In some instances a race may be located in very small units scattered over a large extent of territory, in which case, where possible, the largest group is indicated by the dot. Thus, in the district of Timiskaming, Ontario, the inhabited portion of which extends from Lake Timagami to Cochrane, an area of about 175 miles long by 70 miles wide (12,500 square miles), there are 832 Germans settled in more than seventy centres, the largest group of which numbers only 60. The total of 832 requires two dots on the map.

In certain densely populated centres, such as Montreal and Toronto, it is impossible to indicate the number of inhabitants by isolated dots, and here the density is shown by solid shading. The exact number is easily ascertained from the census tables.

Only those races which number at least 100,000 have been plotted, although sixty-eight distinct races are represented in Canada. There are two exceptions to this, namely, the Hebrews, numbering 126,196, and the Indians, numbering 110,596. No maps have been made for these races, as the former are universally congregated in cities and towns, while the latter are widely scattered over extensive areas and are somewhat nomadic and shifting.

While these maps are both interesting and valuable in the light they throw on the origin of the Canadian people, it is necessary to avoid drawing from them false conclusions as to racial characteristics in any particular part of Canada at the present time. In other words, the present characteristics of the Canadian people are traceable only to a limited degree to their racial origin as shown on these maps. For instance, certain sections of Ontario and Nova Scotia are given in the census as predominantly German in origin, whereas the original German settlers came to Canada over a century ago from the United States, not from Germany, have since intermarried with other races, and to-day, save only in names, bear no noticeable characteristics of German origin. The same process, in more or less degree, is going on all over Canada.

From Winnipeg to the Rockies this group of maps, especially Nos. 73 to 76 inclusive, gives a graphic impression of the results of the great immigration of 1900-14.

Compare with these maps the maps and notes relating to Early Settlements, Canadian Migration, and Railway Construction and Population.

CANADIAN MIGRATION

MAP No. 77

A CAREFUL study of this map will make fairly clear the spread of settlement throughout the Dominion. During the French period it was pretty well confined to the banks of the St. Lawrence and Acadia (Nova Scotia).

After the cession of Canada to Great Britain the first great migration was that of the United Empire Loyalists from the Thirteen Colonies to the Maritime Provinces and Upper and Lower Canada. Some slight English settlement had before this reached Halifax and Annapolis Royal in Nova Scotia.

The green lines represent Scottish migration to Pictou, Nova Scotia, and Prince Edward Island, as well as Selkirk's Red River Settlement, which came in by way of Hudson Bay.

The United Empire Loyalists had also been preceded by a comparatively thin stream of settlers from New England to Quebec.

Periods of depression accounted for the exodus of population from Canada to the United States about 1850 and again about 1890.

With the growth of the eastern provinces a slow but steady stream of British immigrants started about 1860; and with the building of the Canadian Pacific Railway began the movement of settlers to western Canada from eastern Canada, the United States, Great Britain, and continental Europe.

On the Pacific coast an earlier British migration started by sea about the middle of the nineteenth century, together with a spasmodic influx of miners from California and eastern Canada and the United States; and that vexed problem, the migration of Orientals to the Pacific coast.

The table on page 33 gives the actual figures by provinces for the racial origin of the people of Canada.

Bibliography: *Canada and its Provinces*, vols. xiii., xv., xvii., xix., xxi.

STATISTICS OF POPULATION

(1) POPULATION OF CANADA, 1620-1861

Date.	Region.	White Population.	
1620	Quebec	60	
1641	New France	240	
1663	,,	2,500	(Quebec, 800)
1665	,,	3,215	
1667	,,	3,918	
1672	,,	6,705	
1675	,,	7,832	
1679	,,	9,400	Acadia, 515
1683	,,	10,251	
1686	,,	12,373	,, 885
1692	,,	12,431	
1693			,, 1,009
1698	,,	15,355	
1706	,,	16,417	
1713	,,	18,119	
1720	,,	24,234	Isle St. Jean, 100
1727	,,	30,613	,, 330
1731			Acadia (northern part), 7,598
1739	,,	42,701	
1749			Halifax, 2,544, First (English) Settlers.
1752			Nova Scotia, 4,203 (British and German).
1754	,,	55,009	
1760		70,000	
1762			Nova Scotia, 8,104 (British).
1765	Province of Canada	69,810	
1784	,,	113,012	
1790	,,	161,311	(excluding Upper Canada)
1798			Prince Edward Island, 4,500

Date.	Assiniboia.	Upper Canada.	Lower Canada.	New Brunswick.	Prince Edward Island.	Nova Scotia.
1806	—	70,718	250,000	35,000	9,676	65,000 (est.)
1814	—	95,000	335,000	—	—	—
1817	—	—	—	—	—	81,351
1822	—	—	427,465	—	—	—
1824	—	150,066	—	74,176	—	—
1825	—	—	479,288	—	—	—
1827	—	—	—	—	—	123,630 (with C.B.)
1831	2,390	236,702	553,131	—	—	—
1834	3,356	321,145	—	—	119,457	—
1838	—	339,422	—	—	—	202,575
1841	—	455,688	—	—	47,042	—
1844	—	—	697,084	—	—	—
1849	5,391	—	—	—	—	—
1851	—	952,004	890,261	193,800	—	276,854
1856	6,691	—	—	—	—	—
1861		1,396,091	1,111,366	252,047	80,857	330,857

(2) RACIAL STATISTICS—1921 ; 1931

Census, 1921.	Prince Edward Island.	Nova Scotia.	New Brunswick.	Quebec.	Ontario.	Manitoba.	Saskatchewan.	Alberta.	British Columbia.	Total of Race in Nine Provinces.	Total in Canada, 1931.
English	23,313	202,106	131,664	196,082	1,211,660	170,286	206,472	180,478	221,145	2,544,106	2,741,419
Irish	18,743	55,712	68,670	94,947	590,493	71,414	84,786	68,246	54,298	1,107,309	1,230,808
Scottish	33,437	148,000	51,308	63,915	465,400	105,034	104,678	96,062	104,965	1,172,799	1,346,350
French	11,971	56,619	121,111	1,889,277	248,275	40,638	42,152	30,913	11,246	2,452,202	2,927,990
German	260	27,046	1,698	4,668	130,545	19,444	68,202	35,333	7,273	294,469	473,544
Austrian	2	682	80	1,901	11,792	31,035	39,738	19,430	2,993	107,651	48,639
Dutch	239	11,506	3,698	1,413	50,512	20,728	16,639	9,490	3,306	117,471	148,962
Scandinavian [1]	—	1,333	2,142	2,219	12,716	26,698	58,382	44,545	19,002	167,037	228,049
Russian	1	520	185	2,802	8,615	14,009	45,343	21,212	7,373	100,050	88,148
Ukrainian [2]	—	389	3	1,176	8,307	44,129	28,097	23,827	793	106,721	225,113
Totals	87,966	503,913	380,499	2,259,300	2,738,303	66,703	694,489	529,536	432,394	8,169,815	9,459,022
Other races	649	19,924	7,377	101,899	195,359	543,415	63,021	58,918	92,188	606,038	917,764
Grand Total	88,615	523,837	387,876	2,361,199	2,933,662	610,118	757,510	588,445	524,582	8,775,853	

[1] Includes Swedish, Norwegians, Danish, and Icelandic. Yukon, 4,157; N.-W. Territories, 7,988; Navy, 485 — 12,630
[2] Includes Bukovinian, Galician, Ruthenian, Ukrainian.
N.B. *1941 figures not available when revised edition went to press.* Total population of Canada . . . . . . 8,788,483 | 10,376,786

STATISTICS OF POPULATION

(3) POPULATION BY PROVINCES, 1871-1941

Province or Territory.	1871.	1881.	1891.	1901.	1911.	1921.	1931.	1941
Prince Edward Island	94,021	108,891	109,078	103,259	93,728	88,615	88,038	95,047
Nova Scotia	387,800	440,572	450,396	459,574	492,338	523,837	512,846	577,962
New Brunswick	285,594	321,233	321,263	331,120	351,889	387,876	408,219	457,401
Quebec	1,191,516	1,359,027	1,488,535	1,648,898	2,005,776	2,361,199	2,874,215	3,319,640
Ontario	1,620,851	1,926,922	2,114,321	2,182,947	2,527,292	2,933,662	3,431,683	3,787,655
Manitoba	25,228	62,260	152,506	255,211	461,394	610,118	700,139	729,744
Saskatchewan	—	—	—	91,279	492,432	757,510	921,785	887,747*
Alberta	—	—	—	73,022	374,295	588,454	731,605	796,169
British Columbia	36,247	49,459	98,173	178,657	392,480	524,582	694,263	809,203*
Yukon Territory	—	—	—	27,219	8,512	4,157	4,230	4,687*
N.-W. Territories	48,000	56,446	98,967	20,129	6,507	7,988	9,723	10,661*
Royal Canadian Navy	—	—	—	—	—	—	485	—
Total	3,689,257	4,324,810	4,833,239	5,371,315	7,206,643	8,788,483	10,376,786	11,475,916*

* Preliminary population figures.

(4) PERCENTAGE DISTRIBUTION OF POPULATION, 1871-1941

Province or Territory.	1871.	1881.	1891.	1901.	1911.	1921.	1931.	1941*
	Per cent.	Per cent.	Per cent.	Per cent.	Per cent.	Per cent.	Per cent.	Per cent.
Prince Edward Island	2.55	2.52	2.25	1.92	1.30	1.01	0.85	0.82
Nova Scotia	10.51	10.19	9.32	8.56	6.83	5.96	4.94	5.02
New Brunswick	7.74	7.43	6.65	6.16	4.88	4.41	3.94	3.97
Quebec	32.30	31.42	30.80	30.70	27.83	26.87	27.70	29.07
Ontario	43.94	44.56	43.74	40.64	35.07	33.38	33.07	32.89
Manitoba	0.68	1.44	3.16	4.75	6.40	6.94	6.75	6.33
Saskatchewan	—	—	—	1.70	6.84	8.62	8.88	7.77
Alberta	—	—	—	1.36	5.19	6.70	7.05	6.90
British Columbia	0.98	1.14	2.03	3.33	5.45	5.97	6.69	7.09
Yukon Territory	—	—	—	0.51	0.12	0.05	0.04	0.04
N.-W. Territories	1.30	1.30	2.05	0.37	0.09	0.09	0.09	0.10
Royal Canadian Navy	—	—	—	—	—	—	—	—
	100.00	100.00	100.00	100.00	100.00	100.00	100.00	100.00

* Preliminary figures.

(5) INDIAN POPULATION

Province or Territory.	1872.	1900.	1924.	1931.
Alberta	—	—	8,990	15,258
British Columbia	—	—	24,316	24,599
Manitoba	—	—	11,673	15,417
New Brunswick	—	—	1,606	1,685
North-West Territories	—	—	4,543	4,046
Nova Scotia	—	—	1,827	2,191
Ontario	—	—	26,706	30,368
Prince Edward Island	—	—	315	233
Quebec	—	—	13,191	12,312
Saskatchewan	—	—	10,271	15,268
Yukon	—	—	1,456	1,543
Canada	83,000	98,010	104,894	122,920

Eskimos in Northern Canada in 1924—6,703.
1941 figures not available for table (5) when book went to press.

CHRONOLOGICAL HISTORY OF CANADA

A.D.	
1000.	Norsemen discover America.
1492.	Columbus's first voyage to America.
1493.	Columbus's second voyage.
1497.	Voyage of John Cabot to east coast of North America.
1498.	Cabot discovers Hudson Strait and explores coast to the southward.
,,	Columbus's third voyage.
1500–2.	East coast of America from Greenland to Nova Scotia explored by Cortereal for Portugal.
1502.	Columbus's fourth voyage.
1513.	Balboa discovers the Pacific Ocean.
1520.	Fagundez explores coasts of Nova Scotia and Newfoundland for Spain.
1524.	Verrazano explores Nova Scotia coast for France.
1525.	Gomez explores from Florida to Cape Race for Spain.
1534.	Jacques Cartier's first voyage to Gulf of St. Lawrence.
1535.	Cartier, on his second voyage, ascends St. Lawrence to Stadacona (September 14) and Hochelaga (October 2).
1541.	Cartier's third voyage to the St. Lawrence.
1542–43.	Roberval winters at Cap Rouge and is rescued by Cartier on his fourth voyage.
1557.	Death of Cartier at St. Malo, France, September 1.
1558.	Diego Homem's map shows Bay of Fundy for first time.
1576.	Martin Frobisher reaches Baffin Land.
1585.	Davis explores Davis Strait to Baffin Bay.
1586–87.	Davis makes voyages to Arctic Canada.
1598.	De la Roche discovers Sable Island and tries to found a settlement for France.
1599.	St. Malo Company established.
1603.	Champlain lands on site of Quebec, June 22.
1604.	Champlain and De Monts sail to Acadia.
1608.	Champlain's second voyage.
1609.	Champlain discovers Lake Champlain and defeats the Iroquois near Crown Point.
,,	Henry Hudson discovers and explores Hudson River.
1610.	Hudson discovers Hudson Bay and winters in James Bay.
,,	Poutrincourt in Acadia.
1611.	Hudson turned adrift by mutineers in Hudson Bay.
,,	English from Virginia destroy French settlement at Port Royal.
1612.	Champlain made Lieutenant-General of New France.
,,	Button explores Hudson Bay.
1613.	Champlain ascends Ottawa River to Allumette Island.
,,	St. Sauveur and Port Royal destroyed by Argal.
1614.	Company of Rouen established.
1615.	Champlain explores Upper Ottawa River, Lake Nipissing, Lake Huron, and eastern end of Lake Ontario.
,,	Etienne Brûlé explores west end of Lake Ontario and country between Lake Ontario and Detroit River.
,,	Récollets arrive in Canada.
1616.	William Baffin explores Baffin Bay.
,,	First schools opened at Three Rivers and Tadousac.
,,	Bylot and Baffin reach Ellesmere Island.

A.D.	
1617.	First marriage in Canada—Etienne Jonquest and Anne Hébert.
1620.	Company of De Caën established.
,,	English settlement at Plymouth.
1621.	King James grants Nova Scotia to Sir William Alexander.
,,	Code of laws issued, and register of births, deaths, and marriages opened in Quebec.
1622.	Lake Superior possibly discovered by Etienne Brûlé.
1623.	First British settlement in Nova Scotia.
1625.	Jesuits arrive at Quebec.
1627.	Louis XIII. grants charter to Company of One Hundred Associates.
1628.	Sir David Kirke takes Port Royal and plants Scottish colony.
1629.	Quebec taken by Sir David Kirke, July 20.
,,	Acadia surrendered to English.
,,	Treaty of Susa.
1631.	Luke Foxe makes voyage to Hudson Bay and explores Fox Channel.
,,	Thomas James winters in James Bay.
1632.	Canada and Acadia restored to France by Treaty of St. Germain-en-Laye.
1633.	Champlain made first Governor of New France.
,,	William Alexander created Viscount Canada.
1634.	Lake Michigan discovered by Jean Nicolet.
,,	Founding of Three Rivers, July 4.
1635.	Death of Champlain at Quebec, December 25.
,,	Founding of Jesuits' College at Quebec.
1636.	De Montmagny sent out as Governor of New France.
1638.	First earthquake recorded in Canada.
1639.	Founding of Hôtel Dieu and Ursuline Convent at Quebec.
1640.	Discovery of Lake Erie by Chaumonot and Brébeuf.
1641.	Raimbault and Jogues reach Lake Superior.
1644.	Founding of Hôtel Dieu, Montreal, by Mademoiselle Mance.
,,	Maisonneuve defeats Iroquois at Montreal.
1645.	Fort La Tour (at mouth of St. John River) taken by Charnisay.
1646.	Exploration of the Saguenay by Dablon.
1647.	Lake St. John discovered by de Quen.
1648.	Council of New France created, March 5.
,,	D'Ailleboust de Coulonge appointed Governor.
1649.	Fathers Jean de Brébeuf and Gabriel Lalemant killed by Iroquois.
1651.	Jean de Lauzon made Governor.
1652.	Governor Duplessis killed by Iroquois at Three Rivers.
1654.	Port Royal taken by expedition from New England under Sedgewick.
1655.	Acadia restored to France by Treaty of Westminster.
1657.	Sulpicians arrive in Canada.
,,	Vicomte D'Argenson, Governor.
1658.	Radisson explores country south-west of Lake Superior and discovers the Mississippi.
1659.	François de Laval arrives in Canada as Vicar-Apostolic.
,,	Radisson and Chouart explore Lake Superior.
1660.	Dollard des Ormeaux and sixteen companions killed at the Long Sault, Ottawa River, May 21.
,,	Death of Governor D'Ailleboust de Coulonge.

CHRONOLOGICAL HISTORY OF CANADA

A.D.
- 1661. Baron D'Avagour appointed Governor.
- ,, Radisson explores country west and north of Lake Superior, winters among the Sioux, and apparently reaches James Bay.
- 1663. Company of One Hundred Associates dissolved.
- ,, Mézy appointed Governor.
- ,, Louis Robert becomes first Intendant of New France.
- 1665. Courcelles sent out as Governor.
- ,, Jean Talon appointed Intendant.
- ,, Population of New France, 3,215.
- ,, Carignan Regiment lands in Canada.
- 1667. Acadia restored to France by Treaty of Breda.
- 1668. Mission at Sault Ste. Marie founded by Marquette.
- 1669. Founding of Seminary of Quebec by Laval.
- 1670. Charles II. grants charter to Hudson's Bay Company.
- 1671. St. Lusson takes possession of Sault Ste. Marie country for French king.
- 1672. Comte de Frontenac arrives as Governor.
- ,, Albanel makes his way overland to Hudson Bay by way of Saguenay.
- 1673. Cataraqui (Kingston) founded.
- ,, Jolliet and Marquette reach the Mississippi.
- 1674. Laval becomes first Bishop of Quebec.
- 1675. Jacques Duchesneau appointed Intendant.
- 1678. Niagara Falls visited by Hennepin.
- 1682. Frontenac recalled.
- ,, La Barre sent out as Governor.
- ,, La Salle descends the Mississippi to the Gulf of Mexico.
- 1685. Marquis de Denonville becomes Governor.
- ,, Card money issued.
- 1686. De Troyes captures Hudson's Bay Company posts on James Bay.
- 1687. La Salle assassinated, March 18.
- ,, Denonville defeats Senecas, July.
- 1689. Frontenac reappointed Governor.
- ,, Massacre of whites by Indians at Lachine.
- ,, Beginning of French and Indian war.
- 1690. Sir William Phipps captures Port Royal, May 21, but is repulsed in his attack on Quebec, October 6-21.
- 1691. William and Mary grant Nova Scotia to Massachusetts Bay Company.
- ,, Henry Kellsey of the Hudson's Bay Company explores the western plains from Hudson Bay.
- 1692. Defence of Fort Verchères against the Iroquois by Madeleine de Verchères.
- 1694. Fort Nelson on Hudson Bay captured by Iberville. Subsequently restored.
- 1697. Iberville captures forts on Hudson Bay.
- ,, Treaty of Ryswick—places taken during the war are mutually restored.
- 1698. Death of Frontenac at Quebec, November 28.
- 1699. Louis de Callières appointed Governor.
- 1701. Boundary dispute between France and Hudson's Bay Company. Company offer to accept East Main River as southern boundary. Offer refused.
- 1703. Death of Governor De Callières at Quebec, May 26.
- ,, Marquis de Vaudreuil becomes Governor.
- 1709. Canada invaded by British.
- 1710. Port Royal taken by Nicholson.
- 1711. Part of Sir H. Walker's fleet proceeding against Quebec wrecked off Seven Islands.
- ,, Jacques Raudot appointed Intendant.
- ,, Louisiana made a colony.
- 1713. Treaty of Utrecht—Hudson Bay, Acadia, and Newfoundland ceded to Great Britain.

A.D.
- 1713. Louisbourg founded by French.
- 1719-37. Hudson's Bay Company sends various ships to search for North-West Passage.
- 1720. Governor and Council of Nova Scotia appointed, April 25.
- 1721. Burning of large part of Montreal, June 19.
- 1725. Death of the Marquis de Vaudreuil at Quebec, October 10.
- 1726. Marquis de Beauharnois appointed Governor.
- 1731. Gilles Hocquart becomes Intendant.
- ,, La Vérendrye begins his explorations of the west.
- ,, Louisiana becomes a Royal Province.
- 1732. La Vérendrye builds forts on Rainy Lake and Lake of the Woods.
- 1737. Iron first smelted at St. Maurice forges.
- 1738. Founding of Grey Nunnery at Montreal by Madame d'Youville.
- ,, La Vérendrye visits Mandan villages on the Missouri.
- 1739-40. Joseph la France explores country west of Lake Superior.
- 1742. Sons of La Vérendrye explore country far to the south-west.
- 1745. Taking of Louisbourg by Pepperell and Warren.
- 1747. Marquis de la Jonquière appointed Governor; captured at sea by the English; takes office, 1749
- 1748. Treaty of Aix-la-Chapelle.
- ,, Louisbourg restored to France in exchange for Madras.
- ,, François Bigot appointed Intendant.
- 1749. British immigrants brought to Nova Scotia by Governor Cornwallis, 2,544 persons.
- ,, La Galissonnière Governor.
- ,, Fort Rouillé (Toronto) built.
- ,, Death of La Vérendrye the elder.
- 1750. St. Paul's Church, Halifax, built, oldest Protestant (Anglican) church in Canada.
- 1752. Marquis Duquesne de Menneville, Governor of New France.
- ,, First issue of Halifax *Gazette*, first newspaper in what is now Canada, March 25.
- ,, Death of La Jonquière, May 17.
- 1754-55. Anthony Hendry explores inland from Hudson Bay to the upper Saskatchewan and winters among the Blackfeet.
- 1755. Marquis de Vaudreuil-Cavagnal governor.
- ,, Expulsion of the Acadians from Nova Scotia.
- 1756. Opening of the Seven Years' War between Great Britain and France.
- 1758. Final capture of Louisbourg by the British, July 26.
- ,, First meeting of the Legislature of Nova Scotia, October 7.
- ,, Montcalm wins at Ticonderoga.
- 1759. Taking of Fort Niagara by the British, July 25.
- ,, Beginning of the Siege of Quebec, July 26.
- ,, French victory at Beauport Flats, July 31.
- ,, Defeat of the French on the Plains of Abraham, September 13.
- ,, Death of Wolfe, September 13.
- ,, Death of Montcalm, September 14.
- ,, Surrender of Quebec, September 18.
- 1760. Victory of the French under Lévis at Ste. Foy, April 28.
- ,, Surrender of Montreal to the British, September 8.
- ,, British military rule set up in Canada.
- 1762. First British settlement in New Brunswick.
- 1763. Treaty of Paris, by which Canada and its dependencies ceded to Britain, February 10.
- ,, Rising of Indians under Pontiac, who take a number of forts and defeat the British at Bloody Run, July 31.

CHRONOLOGICAL HISTORY OF CANADA

A.D.
1763. Civil government proclaimed, October 7.
" Cape Breton and Isle St. Jean (Prince Edward Island) annexed to Nova Scotia; Labrador, Anticosti, and Magdalen Islands to Newfoundland.
" General James Murray appointed Governor-in-Chief.
1764. First issue of the Quebec Gazette, June 21.
" Civil government established in Canada, August 13.
1765. Publication of the first book printed in Canada, Catéchisme du Diccèse de Sens.
" Montreal fire-swept, May 18.
1766. Peace made with Pontiac at Oswego, July 24.
1768. Great fire at Montreal, April 11.
" Sir Guy Carleton (Lord Dorchester) Governor-in-Chief.
1769. Isle St. Jean (Prince Edward Island) separated from Nova Scotia and made a separate colony with a governor and council.
1770. Moravians found mission on Labrador coast among the Eskimo.
1770–72. Samuel Hearne's journey from Prince of Wales Fort to the mouth of the Coppermine River and back by way of Great Slave Lake.
1774. The Quebec Act passed, June 22.
1775. Quebec Act comes into force, May 1.
" Outbreak of American Revolution.
" Montgomery and Arnold invade Canada. Montgomery takes Montreal, November 12. Defeated and killed in attack on Quebec, December 31.
" Spanish reach lat. 61° on Pacific coast.
1776. United States troops defeated and driven from Canada by Carleton.
1777. General Frederick Haldimand, Governor-in-Chief.
1778. Captain James Cook sails the Pacific to Nootka Sound, Vancouver Island, and claims northwest coast of America for Great Britain.
" First issue of the Montreal Gazette, June 3.
1779. Quebec Library established.
1783. Organization of the North West Company af Montreal.
" Landing of United Empire Loyalists in Nova Scotia.
1784. New Brunswick (August 16) and Cape Breton (August 26) separated from Nova Scotia and made separate colonies.
1786. Dorchester again Governor-ln-Chief, April 22.
" Government of New Brunswick moved from St. John to Fredericton, October 23.
1787. Inglis appointed Anglican bishop of Nova Scotia —first Colonial bishopric in British Empire.
" Dixon and Duncan explore Pacific coast.
1788. King's College, Windsor, N.S., opened.
1789. Alexander Mackenzie descends to the Arctic by the river that bears his name.
1790–95. Spain relinquishes claim to north Pacific coast.
1791. Constitutional Act provides for division of the province of Quebec into Upper and Lower Canada, each with a lieutenant-governor and legislature.
" Colonel J. G. Simcoe appointed first lieutenant-governor of Upper Canada, September 12.
1792. First legislature of Upper Canada opens at Newark (Niagara), September 17.
" First legislature of Lower Canada opens at Quebec, December 17.
" Russian trading post established at Kodiak.
1792–94. George Vancouver in Discovery surveys Pacific coast of America from San Francisco to Bering Sea.

A.D.
1793. First issue of the Upper Canada Gazette, April 18.
" Importation of slaves into Upper Canada forbidden, July 9.
" Alexander Mackenzie makes overland journey by Peace Pass to the Pacific coast.
1794. Jay's Treaty, relating to commerce, navigation and boundaries between Canada and the United States.
1796. Seat of government of Upper Canada moved from Newark to York (Toronto).
1797. Russian-American Fur Company chartered.
1798. St. John's Island renamed Prince Edward Island.
1800. New Brunswick College founded (University, 1858).
" Jesuits' estates taken over by Government.
1803. Lord Selkirk sends settlers to Prince Edward Island.
1805. Paper made at St. Andrews, Lower Canada.
1806. First issue of Le Canadien, first Canadian newspaper printed wholly in French, November 22.
1807. David Thompson crosses Rocky Mountains by Howse Pass, and builds first trading post on Columbia.
1808. Simon Fraser explores the Fraser River to its mouth.
1809. Labrador Act annexes coast to Newfoundland.
1811. Lord Selkirk's Red River Settlement founded on land granted by Hudson's Bay Company.
" McGill University founded (Royal Charter, 1821).
" David Thompson completes survey of Columbia from source to mouth.
1812. Declaration of war by the United States, June 18.
" Americans under Hull cross the Detroit River, July 12.
" Detroit surrendered by Hull to Brock, August 16.
" Defeat of the United States forces at Queenston Heights and death of General Brock, October 13.
1813. British victory at Frenchtown, January 22.
" York (Toronto) taken and burned by the United States troops, April 27.
" British victory at Stoney Creek, June 5.
" British, warned by Laura Secord, capture a United States force at Beaver Dams, June 24.
" Commodore Parry destroys the British flotilla on Lake Erie, September 10.
" United States army under Harrison defeat the British at Moraviantown, October 5.
" Tecumseh killed, September 10.
" Victory of French-Canadian troops under de Salaberry at Chateauguay, October 26.
" Defeat of the United States forces at Crysler's Farm, November 11.
" British storm Fort Niagara and burn Buffalo, November 11.
1814. United States forces repulsed at La Colle, March 30.
" Capture of Oswego by the British, May 6.
" United States victory at Chippawa, July 5.
" British victory at Lundy's Lane, July 25.
" British from Nova Scotia invade and occupy northern Maine, July.
" British defeated at Plattsburg on Lake Champlain, September 11.
" Treaty of Ghent ends the war, December 24.
1815. Conflict between North West Company and Hudson's Bay Company.
" Red River Settlement destroyed but re-established by Governor Semple.

CHRONOLOGICAL HISTORY OF CANADA

A.D.
1816. Governor Semple killed at Seven Oaks, June 19.
,, Red River Settlement again dispersed.
1817. First treaty with North-West Indians, July 18.
,, Selkirk restores Red River Settlement.
,, Opening of Bank of Montreal; first note issued, October 1.
1818. Treaty of London relating to boundaries and fisheries.
,, Bank of Quebec founded.
,, Quebec Fire Insurance Company commences business.
1819. Halifax Fire Insurance Company incorporated.
,, Death of Duke of Richmond near village of Richmond.
1819–22. Franklin's overland expedition to the Arctic.
1820. Cape Breton reannexed to Nova Scotia.
1821. Union of Hudson's Bay Company and North West Company, March 26.
1824. Literary and Historical Society of Quebec founded.
1825. Labrador Act defines coast under jurisdiction of Newfoundland.
,, Great Miramichi fire, New Brunswick.
1826. Franklin and Richardson explore Arctic coast.
1827. Treaty relating to boundary west of the Rockies and between Maine and New Brunswick.
,, Coal mining at Stellarton, N.S., commenced.
1829. Upper Canada College founded.
,, John Ross discovers peninsula of Boothia on Arctic coast.
1831. North Magnetic Pole discovered by James Ross, June 1.
1832. Outbreak of cholera in Canada.
1833–34. George Back's overland expedition to Arctic by way of Great Fish River.
1834. Ninety-two Resolutions on Public Grievances passed by Assembly of Lower Canada, February 21.
,, Château St. Louis at Quebec destroyed by fire.
,, Selkirk grant reverts to Hudson's Bay Company.
1837. Report of the Canada Commissioners.
,, Rebellions in Upper Canada (William Lyon Mackenzie) and in Lower Canada (Louis Joseph Papineau).
,, Shops in Montreal first lighted by gas.
1838. Constitution of Lower Canada suspended and Special Council created, February 10.
,, Earl of Durham, Governor-in-Chief, March 30.
,, Martial law revoked, April 27.
,, Amnesty to political prisoners proclaimed, June 28.
,, Lord Durham, censured by British Parliament, resigns.
,, Dalhousie College, Halifax, founded.
1839. Lord Durham's Report submitted to Parliament, February 11.
1840. Act of Union, Upper and Lower Canada, passed, July 23.
,, Daguerreotypes taken in Quebec.
,, Exploration of Yukon River by Robert Campbell.
1841. Two provinces united as Canada, with Kingston as capital.
,, Meeting of first united Parliament, June 13.
,, Death of Lord Sydenham, September 19.
1842. Ashburton Treaty, August 9.
,, Baldwin-Lafontaine administration.
,, Queen's College, Kingston, founded.
1843. King's College, Toronto, founded; becomes University of Toronto, 1849.
,, Geological Survey of Canada established.
,, Death of Sir Charles Bagot, Kingston.
1844. Capital moved from Kingston to Montreal.

A.D.
1845. Sir John Franklin starts on his last Arctic Expedition.
1846. Oregon Boundary Treaty.
1847. Death of Sir John Franklin.
1848. Lafontaine-Baldwin administration in Canada.
,, Responsible government granted to Nova Scotia and New Brunswick.
1849. Rebellion Losses Bill passed and approved by Governor-General.
,, Rioting in Montreal and burning of Parliament buildings, April 25.
,, Capital removed to Toronto, November 14.
,, Vancouver Island placed under jurisdiction of Hudson's Bay Company.
,, Toronto *Globe* founded.
1849–54. Administration of Customs gradually transferred to Canada.
1850. Captain McClure discovers North-West Passage.
1851. Boundaries of New Brunswick settled.
,, Quebec becomes capital.
,, Hincks-Morin administration
1852. Fire at Montreal, July 8.
,, Laval University, Quebec, opened, December 8.
1853. Meteorological Bureau transferred to Canada.
1854. Reciprocity Treaty with the United States.
,, Seignorial tenure in Lower Canada abolished.
,, Secularization of Clergy Reserves.
,, Sugar refinery established in Montreal.
,, House of Parliament at Quebec burned.
1855. Government moved to Toronto, October 20.
,, Money orders introduced in Canada.
1856. Legislative Council of Canada made elective.
,, First meeting of Legislature of Vancouver Island.
,, Taché-Macdonald administration.
1857. Macdonald-Cartier administration.
,, Acadia College, Wolfville, founded.
1858. Introduction of Canadian decimal currency, July 1.
,, Brown-Dorion administration.
,, Cartier-Macdonald administration.
,, Colony of British Columbia established, August 20.
,, Control of Vancouver Island surrendered by Hudson's Bay Company.
,, Gold found in Tangier River, N.S.
,, 100th Regiment authorized.
1859. Canadian silver coinage issued.
1860. Government moved to Quebec.
,, Prince of Wales (King Edward VII.) arrives at Quebec and lays corner-stone of Parliament Buildings at Ottawa.
,, Prince of Wales College, Charlottetown, founded.
1862. Sandfield Macdonald-Sicotte administration.
1863. Sandfield Macdonald-Dorion administration.
1864. Taché-Macdonald administration.
,, Conferences on confederation of British North America: at Charlottetown, September 1; at Quebec, October 10 to 29.
,, Raid of United States Confederates from Canada on St. Albans, Vermont.
1865. Canadian legislature resolves on an address to the Queen praying for union of the provinces of British North America.
,, Belleau-Macdonald administration.
,, Proclamation fixing seat of government at Ottawa.
1866. Termination of the Reciprocity Treaty by the United States.
,, Raid of Fenians from the United States into Canada, May 31. They are defeated at Ridgeway, June 2, and retreat across the border, June 3.
,, First meeting at Ottawa of the Canadian Legislature, June 8.

CHRONOLOGICAL HISTORY OF CANADA

A.D.	
1866.	Proclamation of union of Vancouver Island to British Columbia.
,,	Quebec fire, October.
1867.	Royal assent given to the British North America Act, March 29. Act comes into force July 1.
,,	Union of the Provinces of Canada, Nova Scotia, and New Brunswick as the Dominion of Canada; old province of Canada divided into two and named Ontario and Quebec.
,,	Viscount Monck first Governor-General; Sir John A. Macdonald, Premier.
,,	Meeting of first Dominion Parliament, November 6.
1868.	Rupert's Land Act authorizes acquisition by the Dominion of the North-West Territories, July 31.
,,	Assassination of Thomas D'Arcy McGee at Ottawa, April 9.
1869.	Act providing for the government of the North-West Territories, June 22.
,,	Deed of surrender to the Crown of the Hudson's Bay Company's territorial rights in the North-West, November 19.
,,	Outbreak of the Red River Rebellion under Louis Riel.
1870.	Act to establish the province of Manitoba, May 12.
,,	North-West Territories transferred to the Dominion, and Manitoba admitted to confederation, July 15.
,,	General Wolseley's expedition reaches Fort Garry (Winnipeg), and Riel escapes to United States.
1871.	First Dominion census.
,,	Treaty of Washington, May 8, dealing with questions outstanding between Great Britain and the United States relating to Canada.
,,	British Columbia enters confederation, July 20.
,,	Last British troops leave Quebec.
1872.	Establishment of Public Archives of Canada.
1873.	Prince Edward Island enters confederation, July 1.
,,	Act establishing North-West Mounted Police.
,,	Alexander Mackenzie, Premier.
1874.	Ontario Agricultural College at Guelph opened.
1875.	North-West Territories Act, April 8, establishes a lieutenant-governor and council of the North-West Territories.
1876.	Manitoba abolishes Legislative Council.
,,	Supreme Court of Canada holds first session, June 5.
,,	District of Keewatin defined.
1877.	First exportation of wheat from Manitoba to the United Kingdom.
,,	University of Manitoba created.
,,	Great fire in St. John, N.B., June 20.
1878.	Sir John Macdonald, Premier.
,,	Boundaries of Ontario decided by arbitration.
1879.	Adoption by Parliament of a protective tariff (the "National Policy").
1880.	Royal Canadian Academy of Arts founded, March 6.
,,	Sir Alexander Galt appointed first High Commissioner for the Dominion of Canada in Great Britain, May 11.
,,	All British possessions in North America and adjacent islands north of the United States, except Newfoundland and its dependencies, annexed to Canada by Imperial Order in Council of July 31.
1881.	Boundaries of Manitoba enlarged.

A.D.	
1882.	Provisional districts of Assiniboia, Saskatchewan, Alberta, and Athabaska formed, May 8.
,,	Regina made seat of government of North-West Territories, August 23.
,,	First Agent-General sent to France.
,,	Royal Society of Canada founded.
1883.	Standard time adopted.
,,	Parliament Buildings in Quebec burned.
1884.	Sir Charles Tupper appointed High Commissioner in Great Britain.
,,	Order-in-Council settling boundaries of Ontario and Manitoba.
,,	Toronto Free Library established.
1885.	Outbreak of Riel's second rebellion in the north-west, March 26.
,,	Engagement at Fish Creek, April 24.
,,	Fight at Cut Knife, May 2.
,,	Capture of Batoche, May 12.
,,	Riel executed at Regina, November 16.
,,	Fraser Institute established at Montreal.
1888.	Fishery treaty between Canada and the United States.
1889.	Ontario boundary confirmed by Act of Parliament.
1890.	Manitoba School Act abolishes separate schools, March 31.
1891.	Death of Sir John Macdonald, June 6.
,,	Sir John Abbott, Premier, June 15.
1892.	Washington Treaty, providing for arbitration of the Bering seas seal fishery question, February 29.
,,	Boundary convention between Canada and the United States, July 22.
,,	Sir John Thompson, Premier, November 25.
1894.	Death of Sir John Thompson at Windsor Castle, England, December 12.
,,	Mackenzie Bowell, Premier, December 21.
1895.	Proclamation naming the Ungava, Franklin, Mackenzie, and Yukon Districts of the North-West Territories, October 2.
1896.	Sir Donald Smith (Lord Strathcona) appointed High Commissioner in Great Britain, April 24.
,,	Sir Charles Tupper, Premier, April 27.
,,	(Sir) Wilfrid Laurier, Premier, July 11.
1898.	Yukon District established as a separate territory, June 13.
,,	Preferential tariff in favour of Great Britain comes into force, August 1.
,,	Quebec boundaries enlarged.
1899.	Beginning of the South African War, October 11.
,,	First Canadian contingent leaves Quebec for South Africa, October 29.
1900.	Battle of Paardeburg.
"	Department of Labour of Dominion Government established.
,,	Death of Queen Victoria and accession of King Edward VII., January 22.
,,	Visit to Canada of Duke and Duchess of Cornwall and York (King George V. and Queen Mary).
1902.	End of South African War.
,,	Peace signed at Vereeniging, May 31.
1905.	Creation of the provinces of Alberta and Saskatchewan, September 1.
1906.	Roald Amundsen navigates North-West Passage.
"	Hydro-Electric Commission of Ontario established.

39

CHRONOLOGICAL HISTORY OF CANADA

A.D.
1908. Quebec tercentenary celebrations, July 20–31; visit to Quebec of Prince of Wales (George V.).
 " Rural mail delivery system inaugurated.
1909. Treaty with the United States relating to boundary waters and creating International Joint Commission.
1910. Death of King Edward VII. and succession of King George V., May 6.
 " Captain Bernier takes possession of Arctic Islands for Canada.
1911. (Sir) Robert L. Borden, Premier, October 10.
1912. Extension of the boundaries of Quebec, Ontario, and Manitoba.
1914. Death of Lord Strathcona and Mount Royal, aged ninety-four, January 21.
 " War with Germany, August 4; Austria-Hungary, August 12; with Turkey, November 5.
1915. First Canadian contingent lands in France and proceeds to Flanders, February.
 " Second Battle of Ypres, April 22.
 " Battle of St. Julien, April 24.
 " Battle of Festubert, May 20–26.
1916. Destruction of the Houses of Parliament at Ottawa by fire, February 3.
 " Battle of St. Eloi, April 3–20.
 " Battle of Sanctuary Wood, June 1–3.
 " Corner-stone of new Houses of Parliament laid by Duke of Connaught, September 1.
1917. Meetings in London of Imperial War Cabinet, March 20–May 2.
 " Imperial War Conference, March 21–April 27.
 " Capture of Vimy Ridge, April 9.
 " Appointment of Food Controller, June 21.
 " Battle of Loos, capture of Hill 70, August 15.
 " Passing of Military Service Act, August 29.
 " Parliamentary franchise extended to women, September 20.
 " Battle of Passchendaele, October 26–November 10.
 " General Election and Union Government sustained, December 17.
1918. Second Battle of the Somme, March–April.
 " Prime Minister and colleagues attend Imperial War Conference in London, June–July.
 " Battle of Amiens, August 12.
 " Breaking of Drocourt–Quéant line, September 2–4.
 " Capture of Bourlon Wood, September 27–29.
 " Bulgaria surrenders and signs Armistice, September 30.
 " Capture of Cambrai, October 1–9.
 " Capture of Valenciennes, October 25–November 2.
 " Turkey surrenders, October 31.
 " Austria-Hungary surrenders, November 4.
 " Germany surrenders, November 11.
1919. Death of Sir Wilfrid Laurier, February 17.
 " Signing of Peace Treaty at Versailles, June 28.
 " Arrival of H.R.H. the Prince of Wales for official tour in Canada, August 15.
 " Under Soldier Settlement Act, soldiers settlers granted loans and established on the land.
1920. Ratification of the Treaty of Versailles, January 10.
 " Sir Robert Borden is succeeded by Right Hon. Arthur Meighen as Premier, July 10.
 " First meeting of League of Nations Assembly begins at Geneva, Switzerland, November 15.
1921. Imperial Conference at which Canada is represented by Right Hon. Arthur Meighen, June 20–August 5.
 " Second meeting of Assembly of League of Nations at Geneva, September 5–October 5.

A.D.
 " New ministry (Liberal), with Right Hon. W. L. Mackenzie King as Premier, is sworn in, December 29.
 " Trade treaty with France.
1922. Hon. P. C. Larkin appointed High Commissioner in Great Britain, February 10.
 " Third Assembly of League of Nations opens at Geneva, September 4.
1923. National Defence Act of 1922 comes into effect, amalgamating Militia, Naval, and Air Force Departments, January 1.
 " Fourth session of League of Nations at Geneva, September 3.
 " Imperial Conference and Imperial Economic Conference in London, England.
 " Trade Agreement between Canada and Italy.
1924. Fifth session of League of Nations at Geneva.
 " Trade agreement between Canada and Belgium.
 " British Association for the Advancement of Science meets in Toronto, August.
1925. Australian trade treaty, 1925.
 " Canada–West Indies Conference and trade agreement.
 " General Election, October 29. The Conservatives carried the largest number of seats but had not a majority over all the other parties.
 " Sixth meeting of League of Nations.
1926. General Election results in the return of the Liberals under the leadership of Right Hon. W. L. Mackenzie King.
 " Viscount Willingdon succeeds Lord Byng as Governor-General.
1927. Labrador Boundary decided by the Privy Council, London, March 1.
 " Old Age Pensions Act passed.
1930. General Election results in the return of the Conservatives under the leadership of the Right Hon. R. B. Bennett.
1931. Right Hon. Earl of Bessborough succeeds Lord Willingdon as Governor-General.
 " First grain steamer sailed from Churchill.
 " Statute of Westminster passed by the British Parliament.
1932. Canadian Radio Broadcasting Act passed.
 " Imperial Economic Conference at Ottawa.
1933. Dominion-Provincial Conference at Ottawa.
1934. Bank of Canada incorporated. Commenced business, March, 1935.
1935. General election resulted in return to power of the Liberal Party under leadership of Rt. Hon. W. L. Mackenzie King.
 " Baron Tweedsmuir (John Buchan) succeeds Lord Bessborough as Governor-General of Canada.
1936. Death of King George V, and accession of H. M. King Edward VIII.
 " Hon. Vincent Massey appointed Canadian High Commissioner in Great Britain.
 " Abdication of King Edward VIII (Dec. 11), and accession of H. M. King George VI.
1937. Imperial Conference in London.
 " Old Age Pension Act amended to include pensions for blind persons.
1939. King George VI and Queen Elizabeth tour Canada.
 " Canada declared war against Germany, Sept. 10.
 " Order-in-Council establishing Wartime Prices and Trade Board.
1940. The Earl of Athlone appointed Governor-General of Canada, succeeding Lord Tweedsmuir who died in office.
 " Canada declared war on Italy, June 10.
 " Canadian Ministry of Defence for Air set up.
 " Department of National War Services established.
 " Unemployment Insurance Bill passed, July 29. In operation July 1, 1941.
 " National Registration in Canada.
1941. Canada declared war on Japan, Dec. 7.
 " Hon. Winston Churchill visits Canada.

CHRONOLOGY OF INTERCOMMUNICATION

1604. Road built by Champlain at Port Royal.
1606. First vessel built in what is now Canada at Port Royal.
1679. La Salle builds *Le Griffon* on Niagara River above the falls.
,, First sailing vessel on the upper lakes
1721. First post established between Montreal and Quebec.
1723. Five merchant ships and two men-of-war built on the St. Lawrence in Canada.
1733. First sailing vessel on Lake Superior.
1734. Road completed from Montreal to Quebec.
,, First lighthouse in Canada at Louisbourg.
1752. A 74-gun ship built at Quebec.
1761. Shipbuilding in Nova Scotia begun with building of schooner *James* at Yarmouth.
1763. First Canadian post offices established at Montreal, Quebec, and Three Rivers.
1781. First canals in Canada, to overcome the Cedar, Cascades, and Coteau rapids on the St. Lawrence.
1784. Mail route established between Halifax and Quebec.
1788. Sailing packet service established between Halifax and Great Britain.
1791. Post roads completed from Quebec to Kingston and in Maritime Provinces.
1793. Post roads in Upper Canada placed under overseers.
1794. Yonge Street built by Simcoe from Toronto north toward Lake Simcoe; and Dundas Street from Lake Ontario to the site of London.
1797. Canal and lock at Sault Ste. Marie built by North West Company.
1809. First Canadian steamer *Accommodation* runs from Montreal to Quebec.
1816. Stages started between Montreal and Kingston.
,, First steamer on St. John River, *General Smyth*, and on Lake Ontario, the *Frontenac*.
1817. Stages between Kingston and York (Toronto).
1825. Opening of Lachine Canal.
1826. *Columbus* launched at Isle of Orleans, 4,000 tons.
1829. First Welland Canal opened.
1832. Rideau Canal opened.
1833. Steamer *Royal William*, built at Quebec, leaves Pictou for England—first vessel to cross Atlantic entirely by steam.
1834. *Beaver* launched—first steamer on Pacific coast.
1835. First horse railway in Canada between Queenston and Chippawa.
1836. Opening of the first steam railway from Laprairie to St. Johns, Quebec.
1840. First ship of Cunard Line arrives at Halifax.
1842. Cornwall Canal opened.
,, Daily lines of stages established throughout what was then Canada.
1845. Beauharnois Canal opened.
1847. Montreal-Lachine Railway opened.
,, First electric telegraph service in Canada—Quebec to Toronto.
1850. Work begun upon St. Lawrence Ship Channel.
1851. Post Office transferred to Canadian control and first Canadian postage stamps issued.
,, First cable laid between New Brunswick and Prince Edward Island.
1852. Grand Trunk Railway chartered.
1853. Northern Railway opened—Toronto to Brantford.
1854. Allan Steamship Line established.
1855. Opening of Niagara Suspension Bridge.
1856. Grand Trunk line opened—Montreal to Toronto.
,, Cable laid between Cape Breton and Newfoundland.
1858. Completion of first Atlantic cable.
1860. Victoria Bridge at Montreal opened by Prince of Wales.
1861. First steamer on Red River, the *Pioneer*.
,, Street railways opened in Montreal and Toronto.
1865. Cariboo road completed.
1870. Dominion Steamship Line established.
1875. Prince Edward Island Railway opened.
,, First telephone line—Brantford to Paris.
1876. Opening of the Intercolonial Railway from Halifax to Quebec.
1878. Canada joins the Postal Union.
1881. First sod turned of Canadian Pacific Railway.
1883. First cantilever bridge in Canada over Niagara River.
1885. Last spike of Canadian Pacific Railway driven by Donald A. Smith (Lord Strathcona) at Craigellachie.
1886. First through train on Canadian Pacific Railway—Montreal to Vancouver.
,, First sod turned of Hudson Bay Railway.
1888. Parcel post established between Canada and the United States.
,, Work begun upon Chignecto Ship Railway.
1889. Canadian Pacific Steamship Line established.
1890. Cable laid from Canada to Bermuda.
1891. Grand Trunk Railway builds tunnel under Detroit River.
1895. Opening of Sault Ste. Marie Canal on Canadian side of river.
1896. Opening of the first link in what afterwards developed into the Canadian Northern Railway system.
1902. Grand Trunk Pacific Railway chartered.
,, First sod turned of Temiscaming and Northern Ontario Railway.
1903. National Transcontinental Railway begun—Moncton to Winnipeg.
,, Grand Trunk Pacific Railway begun.
1904. Dominion Railway Commission established.
1907. First message by wireless telegraphy between Canada and the United Kingdom.
1913. Work commenced on New Welland Canal.
1918. Organization of Canadian National Railways by Order-in-Council.
1919. Canada Highways Act passed.
,, Appointment of Government Receiver for the Grand Trunk Pacific Railway.
,, Formal opening of Quebec Bridge by Prince of Wales.
1920. Sale of Grand Trunk Railway to Canadian Government.
1922. Banff-Windermere highway opened through the Rockies.
1928. First Air Mail service in Canada.
1930. R-100, first trans-Atlantic air-liner to reach Canada.
1936. Department of Transport established.
1937. Trans-Canada Air Lines incorporated by Act of Parliament, April 10.
1938. Trans-Canada Highway nears completion.
1939. Commencement of daily flights from the Atlantic to the Pacific by the Trans-Canada Air Lines.
,, Canadian-British air mail service officially opened.
1940. Daily coast to coast air mail service provided.
1941. St. Lawrence Seaway Agreement between Canada and the United States signed at Ottawa, March 19.
,, Canadian Pacific Air Lines inaugurated.
1942. Trans-Canada Air Lines service extended to Newfoundland.
,, Alaska Highway opened.

CHRONOLOGY OF CANADIAN TOWNS

(Village, *v*; town, *t*; city, *c*.)

MARITIME PROVINCES

Name.	Founded.	Incorporated.
Amherst	1760	1889, *t*.
Annapolis[1]	1710	1893, *t*.
Campbellton	1776	1888, *t*.
Charlottetown[2]	1768	1855, *t*.
Chatham	1800	1896, *t*.
Dalhousie	1810	1837, *v*.
		1903, *t*.
Digby	1783	1890, *t*.
Dorchester	1787	1801, *v*.
		1911, *t*.
Fredericton	1785	1848, *c*.
Grand Pré	1675	—
Halifax	1749	1841, *c*.
Louisbourg	1713	—
Lunenburg	1753[3]	1888, *t*.
Moncton	1765	1875, *t*.
		1890, *c*.
Newcastle	1785	1899, *t*.
New Glasgow	1808	1875, *t*.
Pictou	1789	1873, *t*.
Richibucto	1787	1826, *v*.
		1915, *t*.
Sackville	1761	1903, *t*.
St. Andrews	1783	1903, *t*.
St. John[4]	1783	1785 *c*.
Shediac	1750	1827, *v*.
		1903, *t*.
Sydney	1783	1885, *t*.
		1904, *c*.
Truro	1761	1875, *t*.
Windsor	1710	1878, *t*.
Wolfville	1760	1893, *t*.
Yarmouth	1759	1890, *t*.

ONTARIO

Name.	Founded.	Incorporated.
Amherstburg	1796	1851, *v*.
		1878, *t*.
Belleville	1790	1834, *t*.
		1877, *c*.
Brantford	1830	1877, *c*.
Brockville	1785	1811, *v*.
		1832, *t*.
Chatham	1795	1855, *t*.
		1895, *c*.
Cobourg	1837	1850, *t*.
Collingwood	1848	1858, *t*.
Cornwall	1776	1834, *v*.
		1846, *t*.
Dundas	1801	1847, *v*.
Fort Erie	1857	1932, *t*.
Fort William[5]	1875	1892, *t*.
		1907, *c*.
Galt	1816	1857, *t*.
		1915, *c*.
Goderich	1828	1850, *t*.
Guelph	1827	1879, *c*.
Hamilton	1813	1846, *c*.
Kenora[1]	1879	1904, *t*.
Kingston[2]	1783	1838, *t*.
		1846, *c*.
Kitchener	1806	1871, *t*.
		1912, *c*.
London	1826	1840, *v*.
		1848, *t*.
		1854, *c*.
Niagara Falls	1850	1881, *t*.
		1904, *c*.
Niagara-on-the-Lake	1780	1845, *t*.
Ottawa	1827	1840, *t*.
		1854, *c*.
Owen Sound	1840	1857, *t*.
		1920, *c*.
Peterborough	1825	1850, *t*.
		1905, *c*.
Port Arthur	1866	1884, *t*.
		1906, *c*.
Prescott	1797	1860, *t*.
Richmond	1818	1850, *v*.
St. Catherines	1796	1845, *t*.
		1876, *c*.
St. Thomas	1810	1853, *v*.
		1881, *c*.
Sarnia	1833	1856, *t*.
		1914, *c*.
Sault Ste. Marie[3]	1887	1912, *t*.
		1922, *c*.
Stratford	1832	1853, *t*.
		1885, *c*.
Toronto	1793	1817, *t*.
		1834, *c*.
Welland	1830	1878, *t*.
		1917, *c*.
Windsor	1834	1858, *t*.
		1892, *c*.
Woodstock	1833	1851, *t*.
		1901, *c*.

QUEBEC

Name.	Founded.	Incorporated.
Asbestos	1899	1937, *t*.
Chicoutimi	1650	1879, *c*.
Drummondville	1874	1888, *t*.
		1936, *c*.
Hull	1800	1875, *c*.
Lachine	1675	1909, *c*.
Levis	1679	1861, *t*.
		1916, *c*.
Montreal	1642	1832, *c*.
Quebec	1608	1832, *c*.
St. Hyacinthe	1760	1850, *t*.
		1857, *c*.
St. John's	1666	1858, *t*.
		1917, *c*.
Sorel	1924	1937, *t*.
Sherbrooke	1800	1852, *t*.
Sorel	1672	1889, *c*.
Tadoussac	1600	—
Three Rivers	1634	1857, *t*.

[1] Port Royal founded 1605.
[2] Port la Joie founded about 1720.
[3] French village had existed there for many years before this date.
[4] Ouigoudi (Indian village); Fort la Tour, Fort Charnisay, French posts.
[5] Fort William, of North West Company, 1801.

[1] Rat Portage House, 1835.
[2] Cataraqui, 1673.
[3] First mission, 1641; permanent settlement by Marquette in 1668. Trading post both before and after cession of Canada to England.

CHRONOLOGY OF CANADIAN TOWNS

WESTERN PROVINCES

Name.	Founded.	Incorporated.
Battleford	1875	1904, t.
Brandon[1]	1879	1882, c.
Calgary	1875	1884, t.
Dawson	1896	1901, c.
Edmonton	1795	1904, c.
Lethbridge	1885	1890, t.
		1906, c.
Medicine Hat	1883	1899, t.
		1907, c.
Moose Jaw	1882	1884, t.
		1903, c.

[1] Brandon House (1704) stood about seventeen miles below present city of Brandon. At one time five rival fur-trading establishments stood at this point.

Name.	Founded.	Incorporated.
Nanaimo	1853	1874, t.
Nelson	1888	1897, t.
New Westminster	1853	1860, t.
Portage la Prairie[1]	1853	1907, c.
Prince Albert	1866	1885, t.
		1904, c.
Prince Rupert	1906	1910, t.
Qu'Appelle	1882	1904
Regina	1882	1903, c.
Saskatoon	1883	1903, t.
		1906, c
Vancouver	1881	1886, c.
Victoria	1843	1862, c.
Winnipeg	1860	1873, c.

[1] Fort la Reine, 1738.

CHANGES IN PLACE-NAMES OF CANADIAN HISTORY

MARITIME PROVINCES

Present Name and Date of Change.	Earlier Names and Date of Change.
Amherst, N.S. (1760).	Le Butte.
Annapolis Royal (1710).	Port Royal (1605).
Bay of Fundy.	Grand Baie.
Campbellton, N.B. (1776).	Martin's Point.
Cape Breton (1758).	Bacculau; Isle Royale (1712); Isle St. Lawrence.
Charlottetown (1768).	Port la Joie (1720).
Dochet Island (1797).	Isle Saincte Croix (1604); Bone Island.
Fredericton (1785).	St. Annes (1731); Osnaburg; Frederick Town.
Louisbourg (1713).	Havre l'Anglois; Port à l'Anglois.
Lunenburg, N.S. (1753).	Merliguish.
Miramichi River.	River of the Holy Cross.
New Brunswick and Nova Scotia (1784).	La Cadie (1603); Acadia; Nova Scotia (1621).
Prince Edward Island (1798).	Isle St. Jean (1600); St. John's Island (1763).
Richibucto, N.B. (1832).	Liverpool (1826).
Sable Island.	Santa Cruz; Isolla del Arena (1548).
St. John, N.B. (1785).	Town of Parr; Parrtown (1783); St. Johns (1785).
Shelburne, N.S. (1783).	Port Razoir; New Jerusalem (1775).
Sydney (1783).	Port Espagnol.
Windsor (1764).	Pisiquid (1710).
Wolfville, N.S. (1829).	Mud Creek (1760).

QUEBEC

Anticosti.	Isle de l'Assomption (1535).
Eastmain River.	Canute River.
Gaspé.	Honguedo (1535).
Gulf of St. Lawrence.	Golfo Quadrado; Grande Baie.
Hull, P.Q.	Wright Village (1800).
Joliette (1863).	Industrie (1823).
Labrador.	Terra Laboratoris (1520); Terre Neuve (1535).
Lake George.	Horicon; Lac St. Sacrament.
Lake of Two Mountains.	Lac de Soissons.
Magdalen Islands.	Les Araynes (1535); Isles Ramées (1590); Isles Madeleine (1632).
Montreal (1642).	Hochelaga; Ville Marie (1642).

Present Name and Date of Change.	Earlier Names and Date of Change.
Ottawa River.	La Grande Rivière; Rivière des Prairies (1650).
Quebec [city] (1608).	Stadacona.
Quebec [Province] (1867).	Canada (1535); Lower Canada (1791); Canada East (1840).
Quebec [part of] (1912).	Ungava (1895).
Rupert House.	Fort Charles (1668).
St. Johns (1835).	Dorchester (1815).
St. Lawrence River.	River of Canada; River of Hochelaga.
Sherbrooke (1818).	Lower Forks.
Sorel.	Fort Richelieu (1642); Fort William Henry (1787).

ONTARIO

Belleville (1816).	Meyer's Creek (1790).
Brockville (1811).	Elizabethtown.
Collingwood (1858).	Hurontario Mills (1848).
Cornwall (1834).	New Johnstown (1776).
Dundas.	Coote's Paradise (1801).
Fort Albany (1693).	Fort Albany (1670); Fort Ste. Anne (1686).
Fort Erie (1932)	Fort Erie Village annexed to Bridgeburg Town, and this latter name changed to Fort Erie (1932)
Fort Frances (1875).	Fort St. Pierre (1731), (La Vérendrye); Fort Frances (trading post).
Fort William (1875).	Fort Kaministiquia (1678); Fort William (1801), (trading post).
Galt (1827).	Shade's Mills (1816).
Isle Royale.	Isle Minong.
Kenora (1904).	Rat Portage House (1835); Rat Portage (1879).
Kingston (1783).	Cataraqui (1673); Fort Frontenac (1683).
Kitchener (1916).	Ebytown (1806); Berlin (1825).
Lake Ontario.	Lac Frontenac.
Lake of the Woods.	Lac des Isles; Lake of the Sandhills; Lac des Sioux.
Lake Simcoe.	Lac au Claies.
Lake Superior.	Lac Tracy.
Mackinaw (1796).	Michilimackinac (1668); Fort Mackinac (1760).
Moose Factory (1693).	Fort Moose (1671); Fort St. Louis (1686).

CHANGES IN PLACE-NAMES OF CANADIAN HISTORY

Present Name and Date of Change.	Earlier Names and Date of Change.
Niagara Falls (1881).	Elgin (1853); Clifton (1856); Suspension Bridge (1860).
Niagara-on-the-Lake.	West Niagara (1780); Newark (1792); Niagara (1798).
Ontario (1867).	Canada (1535); Upper Canada (1791); Canada West (1840).
Ontario and Manitoba (parts of).	Keewatin (1876); (still exists, but with different boundaries).
Ottawa (1854).	Bytown (1827).
Owen Sound (1856).	Sydenham (1840).
Peterborough (1827).	Scott's Plains (1825).
Port Arthur (1884).	Prince Arthur's Landing (1866).
Prescott (1860).	Johnstown (1797).
Rainy Lake.	Takamimouen; Lac la Pluie.
Sault Ste. Marie (part of).	Steelton.
Toronto (1834).	Fort Rouillé (1749); York (1793).
Welland (1858).	Merrittsville (1842).
Whitby (1854).	Windsor (1819).
Woodstock (1851).	Oxford (1833).
York Factory (1682).	Fort Bourbon (1694).

WESTERN CANADA

Present Name and Date of Change.	Earlier Names and Date of Change.
Bella Bella, B.C.	Fort M'Loughlin.
British Columbia (1858).	New Caledonia (1806).
British Columbia (part of, politically).	Vancouver and Quadra Island (1792); Vancouver Island.
Calgary (1884).	Fort Brisebois (1875), N.W.M.P.; Fort Calgary (1876), N.W.M.P.
Churchill.	Fort Churchill (1688); Prince of Wales Fort (1733).
Churchill River.	Missinipi River; English River.
Edmonton.	Fort Edmonton (1795).
Edmonton (part of).	Strathcona.
Esquimalt (1855).	Puerta de Cordova (1790).
Great Slave Lake.	Athapapuscow Lake.
Kamloops, B.C.	Fort Thompson (1810); Fort Kamloops.

Present Name and Date of Change.	Earlier Names and Date of Change.
Lake Winnipeg.	Lac des Christineaux; Lac Ouinipique.
Langley, B.C.	Fort Langley; New Langley; Derby.
Mackenzie River.	Great River; River Disappointment.
Manitoba (1870).	Selkirk Settlement; Red River Colony (1811); Assiniboia (1869).
Nanaimo (1852).	Colvilletown.
Nelson, B.C. (1897).	Salisbury (1888).
New Westminster (1860).	Queensborough (1853).
New Westminster (part of).	Sapperton (1859).
Peter Pond Lake.	Buffalo Lake.
Portage la Prairie.	Fort la Reine (1738).
Port Simpson.	Fort Nass (1831); Fort Simpson (1834), (site moved).
Saskatchewan and Alberta (1905).	Rupert's Land (1670); North-West Territories (1870); Assiniboia, Saskatchewan, Alberta, and Athabaska (1882).
The Pas, Man.	Port Pascoyac (1739); Pasquia.
Vancouver (1886).	Granville (1881).
Victoria, B.C. (1862).	Camosun; Fort Alberta (1843); Fort Victoria (1843).
Winnipeg (1862).	Fort Rouge (1736); Fort Gibraltar (1806); Fort Douglas (1815); Fort Garry (1821).
Yellowhead Pass.	Leather Pass.

UNITED STATES

Present Name and Date of Change.	Earlier Names and Date of Change.
Astoria.	Astoria (1811); Fort George (1813).
Detroit.	Fort Pontchartrin.
Pittsburgh.	Fort Pitt; Fort Duquesne.
Lake George.	Horicon; Lac St. Sacrament.
Mackinaw.	Michilimackinac.

A WORKING BIBLIOGRAPHY OF BOOKS RELATING TO CANADIAN HISTORY

REFERENCE WORKS

Encyclopædia of Canadian History. Lawrence J. Burpee. Toronto. (1926.)
Dictionary of Canadian Biography. W. S. Wallace. Toronto. (1926.)
Canadian Historical Dates and Events. Francis J. Audet. Ottawa. (1917.)
First Things in Canada. George Johnson. Ottawa. (1897.)
Handbook of Canadian Dates. F. A. McCord. Montreal. (1888.)
A Syllabus and Guide to Canadian History. R. G. Trotter. (1926.)
Atlas of Canada. J. E. Chalifour. Ottawa. (1915.)
The Canada Year Book. S. A. Cudmore. Ottawa. (*Annual.*)
Handbook of Indians of Canada. Ottawa. (1913.)
Literature of American History. J. N. Larned. Boston. (1902.)
Canada and Newfoundland. H. M. Ami. London. (1915.)
Canadian Economic Development. A. W. Currie. Toronto. (1942.)
History of the Canadian West. A. S. Morton. Edinburgh. (1939.)
Early Life in Upper Canada. E. C. Guillet. Toronto. (1932.)
History of Trade and Commerce. H. Heaton. Edinburgh. (1939.)

A general reference may be made here to the wealth of material relating to the history of Canada, in its broader aspects, in the Transactions and other publications of the Royal Society of Canada, the Canadian Historical Association, the Canadian Institute, the Ontario Historical Society, Nova Scotia Historical Society, Literary and Historical Society of Quebec, Public Archives of Canada, Ontario Archives, Quebec Archives, British Columbia Archives, and Nova Scotia Archives; also to the splendid series of publications of the Champlain Society of Toronto, and the series of reprints of the Radisson Society.

GENERAL HISTORIES

Canada and its Provinces. By various authorities. A. G. Doughty and Adam Shortt, general editors. 23 vols. Toronto. (1914.)
Chronicles of Canada. By various authorities, under the general editorship of George M. Wrong and H. H. Langton. 32 vols. Toronto. (1914–16.)
Canada: An Encyclopædia of the Country. Edited by J. C. Hopkins. 6 vols. Toronto. (1898–1900.)
History of Canada. William Kingsford. 10 vols. Toronto. (1887–98.)
Tercentenary History of Canada. F. B. Tracy. 3 vols. Toronto. (1908.)
The Story of Canada. Sir John Bourinot. London. (1896.)
Canada under British Rule. Sir John Bourinot. Toronto. (1901.)
A History of Canada. Charles G. D. Roberts. Boston. (1897.)
Short History of the Canadian People. George Bryce. New York. (1914.)
History of Canada. W. L. Grant. Toronto. (1922.)
Historical Geography of Canada. 3 vols. H. E. Egerton. Oxford. (1921.)
The Constitution of Canada. W. P. M. Kennedy. Toronto. (1922.)
Documents of the Canadian Constitution. W. P. M. Kennedy. Toronto. (1918.)
Cambridge History of the British Empire. Canada volume. (1927.)
History of Canada. James Bingay. Toronto. (1934.)

It has not been thought necessary, in a work of this kind, to include the histories of Canada in French, such as those of Garneau, Ferland, and Sulte. The same statement applies to the following sections.

SECTIONAL AND PROVINCIAL HISTORIES

France and England in North America. Francis Parkman. 11 vols. Boston. (1898.)
Precursors of Jacques Cartier. H. P. Biggar. Ottawa. (1911.)
Voyages of Jacques Cartier. H. P. Biggar. Ottawa. (1924.)
Cartier to Frontenac. Justin Winsor. Boston. (1894.)
Old France in the New World. James Douglas. Cleveland. (1905.)
New England and New France. James Douglas. New York. (1913.)
New France and New England. John Fiske. Boston. (1902.)
Cradle of New France. A. G. Doughty. (1909.)
Quebec of Yester-Year. A. G. Doughty. Toronto. (1932.)
Under Western Skies. A. S. Morton. Toronto. (1937.)
Lives and Times of the Patriots. E. C. Guillet. Toronto. (1938.)
Political Leaders of Upper Canada. William Smith. Toronto. (1931.)

BIBLIOGRAPHY

Jesuit Relations and Allied Documents. Edited by R. G. Thwaites. 73 vols. Cleveland. (1896-1901.)
Acadia. E. Richard. New York. (1895.)
Louisbourg. J. S. McLennan. London. (1918.)
French Régime in Prince Edward Island. D. C. Harvey. New Haven. (1926.)
History of Acadia. James Hannay. St. John. (1879.)
Cape Breton and its Memorials. Sir John Bourinot. Toronto. (1896.)
History of Brûlé's Discoveries and Explorations. C. W. Butterfield. Cleveland. (1898.)
History of the Discovery of the West by Jean Nicolet. C. W. Butterfield. Cincinnati. (1881.)
French Régime in Wisconsin. L. P. Kellogg. Madison. (1925.)
The Siege of Quebec. A. G. Doughty and G. W. Parmelee. 6 vols. Quebec. (1901.)
Fight with France for North America. A. G. Bradley. New York. (1901.)
The Fight for Canada. William Wood. London. (1905.)
The Fall of Canada, 1759-60. George M. Wrong. Oxford. (1914.)
A Canadian Manor and its Seigneurs. George M. Wrong. Toronto. (1926.)
Fall of New France. G. E. Hart. Montreal. (1888.)
A History of Canada, 1763-1812. Sir C. P. Lucas. Oxford. (1906.)
Arnold's Expedition to Quebec. John Codman. New York. (1901.)
Province of Quebec. Victor Coffin. Madison. (1896.)
The Last Forty Years. John C. Dent. Toronto. (1881.)
Loyalists of America. Egerton Ryerson. Toronto. (1880.)
Loyalists of the American Revolution. Lorenzo Sabine. Boston. (1864.)
The Canadian War of 1812. Sir C. P. Lucas. Oxford. (1906.)
The Making of Canada. A. G. Bradley. New York. (1908.)
Story of the Upper Canadian Rebellion. John C. Dent. Toronto. (1885.)
Canadian Rebellion of 1837. D. B. Read. Toronto. (1896.)
Humours of '37. Robina Lizars. Toronto. (No date.)
Country Life in Canada Fifty Years Ago. Canniff Haight. Toronto. (1885.)
In the Days of the Canada Company. Robina Lizars. Toronto. (1896.)
Roughing it in the Bush. Susanna Moodie. Toronto. (1923.)
Ten Years of Upper Canada. Thomas Ridout. London. (1891.)
Reminiscences. Sir Francis Hincks. Montreal. (1884.)
Story of Old Kingston. Agnes M. Machar. Toronto. (1908.)
Annals of Niagara. William Kirby. Welland. (1897.)
Confederation and its Leaders. W. O. Hammond. Toronto. (1917.)
Public Men and Public Life in Canada. James Young. Toronto. (1912.)
Reminiscences. Sir J. S. Willison. Toronto. (1919.)
History of Montreal. W. H. Atherton. Montreal. (1914.)
Toronto Past and Present. Henry Scadding. Toronto. (1884.)
Builders of Nova Scotia. Sir John Bourinot. Toronto. (1900.)
The St. Lawrence Basin. S. E. Dawson. London. (1905.)
The Search for the Western Sea. Lawrence J. Burpee. London. (1908.)
Early Trading Companies of New France. H. P. Biggar. (1901.)
The Remarkable History of the Hudson's Bay Company. George Bryce. Toronto. (1900.)
The North-West Company. G. C. Davidson. Berkeley. (1918.)
The Great Company. Beckles Willson. Toronto. (1899.)
The Conquest of the Great North-West. Agnes C. Laut. New York. (1908.)
Pathfinders of the West. Agnes C. Laut. New York. (1904.)
Vikings of the Pacific. Agnes C. Laut. New York. (1905.)
By Star and Compass. W. S. Wallace. Toronto. (1922.)
The Canadian North-West. G. M. Adam. Toronto. (1885.)
History of the North-West. Alexander Begg. Toronto. (1894.)
The Book of the West. H. A. Kennedy. Toronto. (1925.)
Manitoba. George Bryce. London. (1882.)
Alberta. Leo Thwaite. Chicago. (1912.)
The Women of Red River. W. J. Healey. Winnipeg. (1923.)
Reminiscences of the North-West Rebellion. C. A. Boulton. Toronto. (1886.)
Soldiering in Canada. G. T. Denison. Toronto. (1901.)
Policing the Plains. R. S. Macbeth. Toronto. (1921.)
History of British Columbia. Alexander Begg. Toronto. (1894.)
History of the Northern Interior of British Columbia. A. G. Morice. (1906.)
Forty Years in Canada. S. B. Steele. Toronto. (1915.)
Pioneers in Canada. Sir Harry Johnston. London. (1912.)
The Backwoodswoman. Isabel Skelton. Toronto. (1924.)
Quebec. Beckles Willson. Toronto. (1912.)
Labrador. W. G. Gosling. London. (1910.)

BIBLIOGRAPHY

Nova Scotia. Beckles Wilson. New York. (1911.)
History of Prince Edward Island. A. B. Warburton. St. John. (1923.)
The Intercolonial. Sandford Fleming. Montreal. (1876.)
The Making of a Great Railway. F. A. Talbot. London. (1912.)
History of the Canadian Pacific Railway. H. A. Innis. Toronto. (1923.)
The Canadian Provinces. John Nelson. Toronto. (1924.)
Wooden Ships and Iron Men. F. W. Wallace. London. (No date.)
Geography of the Dominion of Canada and Newfoundland. W. P. Greswell. Oxford. (1891.)
Canada in the Twentieth Century. A. G. Bradley. New York. (1908.)
Dominion of Canada. J. G. Colmer. London. (1884.)
The Great Dominion. G. R. Parkin. London. (1895.)
The British Empire at War. 5 vols. Sir C. P. Lucas. Toronto. (1921-23.)

HISTORICAL BIOGRAPHY

Makers of Canada Series. New Edition. By various authorities. W. L. Grant and George H. Locke, general editors. Toronto. (1926.)
Early Days in Upper Canada. W. A. Langton. Toronto. (1926.)
The Fighting Bishop. T. B. Roberton. Ottawa. (1926.)
Sir John Macdonald. Sir Joseph Pope. Ottawa. (1894.)
Life and Letters of Sir Wilfrid Laurier. O. D. Skelton. Toronto. (1921.)
Sir Alexander Galt. O. D. Skelton. Toronto. (1920.)
Sir Oliver Mowat. C. R. W. Biggar. Toronto. (1905.)
Life of Thomas D'Arcy McGee. Isabel Skelton. Gardenvale. (1925.)
Recollections of Sixty Years. Sir Charles Tupper. New York. (1914.)
Lord Minto. John Buchan. Toronto. (1924.)
Life and Letters of Lord Durham. Stuart Reid. London. (1906.)
Reminiscences. Sir Richard Cartwright. Toronto. (1912.)
Sir Georges Etienne Cartier. John Boyd. Toronto. (1914.)
Life of Lord Strathcona. Beckles Willson. London. (1915.)
The Earl of Elgin. George M. Wrong. Toronto. (1906.)
Life and Letters of Sir Charles Tupper. E. M. Saunders. London. (1916.)
The Scotsman in Canada. Campbell and Bryce. Toronto. (1911.)
The Irishman in Canada. N. F. Davin. London. (1877.)
Sandford Fleming: Empire Builder. Lawrence J. Burpee. London. (1915.)
General James Murray. R. H. Mahon. London. (1921.)
Pioneer Priests of North America. T. J. Campbell. 3 vols. New York. (1908-11.)
Life and Letters of James Wolfe. Beckles Willson. London. (1909.)
Lahontan. F. C. B. Crompton. Toronto. (1925.)
David Thompson. C. N. Cochrane. Toronto. (1924.)

BOOKS OF DESCRIPTION AND TRAVEL

New Voyages to North America. Baron de Lahontan. Edited by R. G. Thwaites. Chicago. (1905.)
A New Discovery of a Vast Country in America. Louis Hennepin. Edited by R. G. Thwaites. Chicago. (1903.)
Journals of La Vérendrye. Lawrence J. Burpee. Toronto. (1927.)
Jérémie's Narrative. M. Douglas and J. N. Wallace. Ottawa. (1926.)
Voyages through the Continent of North America. Alexander Mackenzie. New York. (1902.)
Journal of Voyages and Travels in North America. D. W. Harmon. New York. (1903.)
Travels and Adventures. Alexander Henry. Chicago. (1921.)
Adventures on the Oregon or Columbia. Alexander Ross. Chicago. (1923.)
New Light on the Early History of the Greater North-West. Journals of Alexander Henry and David Thompson. Edited by Elliot Coues. New York. (1897.)
Saskatchewan and the Rocky Mountains. Earl of Southesk. Edinburgh. (1875.)
Adventures on the Columbia River. Ross Cox. London. (1831.)
Narrative of a Voyage to the North-West Coast of America. Gabriel Franchère. Redfield. (1854.)
Wanderings of an Artist among the Indians of North America. Paul Kane. Toronto. (1925.)
The Great Lone Land. W. F. Butler. London. (1872.)
The Great Northland. W. F. Butler. London. (1873.)
Fur Traders of the Far West. Alexander Ross. London. (1855.)
North-West Passage by Land. Milton and Cheadle. London. (1865.)
Ocean to Ocean. George M. Grant. Toronto. (1926.)
Arctic Pilot. Shackleton and Gilbert. Toronto. (1942.)

BIBLIOGRAPHY

Indian Days in the Canadian Rockies. C. M. Barbeau. Toronto. (1923.)
The Lake Superior Country. T. M. Longstreth. Toronto. (1924.)
Labrador. W. T. Grenfell. Toronto. (1913.)
The Canadian Rockies. A. P. Coleman. Toronto. (1912.)
The Drama of the Forest. A. H. Heming. Toronto. (1925.)
The Friendly Arctic. V. Stefansson. Toronto. (1921.)
The Arctic Prairies. E. T. Seton. Toronto. (1911.)
The New North. Agnes D. Cameron. Toronto. (1910.)

See also publications of the Champlain Society and the Radisson Society, and the series *Early Western Travels*, edited by R. G. Thwaites.

PRINTED IN CANADA, 1942

ND - #0133 - 110825 - C0 - 229/152/5 - PB - 9781334216268 - Gloss Lamination